WOMEN,
CREATIVITY,
and the ARTS

Alice Barber Stephens, *The Women's Life Class* (ca. 1879: The Pennsylvania Academy of the Fine Arts, Philadelphia) Oil on cardboard (grisaille), 12" x 14". Courtesy of the Pennsylvania Academy of the Fine Arts, Philadelphia. Gift of the Artist. 1879. 2.

WOMEN, CREATIVITY, and the ARTS

Critical and Autobiographical Perspectives

EDITED BY

Diane Apostolos-Cappadona

and Lucinda Ebersole

CONTINUUM · NEW YORK

1995
The Continuum Publishing Company
370 Lexington Avenue
New York, New York 10017

Printed in the United States of America

Library of Congress Cataloging-in-Publication Data

Women, creativity, and the arts : critical and autobiographical perspectives /
edited by Diane Apostolos-Cappadona and Lucinda Ebersole.
p.   cm.
Includes bibliographical references and index.
ISBN 0-8264-0831-1
1. Women artists.   2. Creation (Literary, artistic, etc.)
I. Apostolos-Cappadona, Diane.   II. Ebersole, Lucinda.
NX164.W65W66 1995
700'.1'9—dc20   95-9109
                                                                    CIP

Acknowledgments will be found on pages 217–18,
which constitute an extension of this page.

*In memory of those who
have inspired us to raise questions
about women and creativity:*
Anna Brownell Murphy Jameson
George Sand
Isak Dinesen
and
Virginia Woolf

Contents

Editors' Acknowledgments

All books and their authors are indebted to friends and colleagues—volumes of collected essays and their editors even more so! We are grateful for the support of all those women whose essays are included herein as well as to those women artists, writers, and scholars who have inspired us to question the world as it appears to be. Like Anna Jameson, we have sought to maintain a balance between the feminist and the cultural; like George Sand, we have sought to pursue an individual sense of style; like Isak Dinesen, we have sought to affirm the centrality of memory in our work; and like Virginia Woolf, we have sought to locate "a room of one's own."

We are also pleased to acknowledge Werner Mark Linz, Continuum Publishing, for his initial encouragement and continuing support in the development of *Women, Creativity, and the Arts.* Also at Continuum Publishing, Cynthia Eller and Frank Oveis offered initial editorial counsel, while Evander Lomke and Ulla Schnell guided us through the production process. We are thankful for Richard Peabody's careful reading of and constructive comments on the drafts of this manuscript, and to Ann Burrola for her support during that critical time of editorial revision.

Diane Apostolos-Cappadona is grateful to those students enrolled in her spring 1995 Liberal Studies seminar, "Art, Creativity, and Gender," at Georgetown University for both their attention to and critique of the theories related to the issues of creativity and their relationships to gender identifications.

Diane Apostolos-Cappadona
Lucinda Ebersole
Washington, D.C.
April 1995

On the Creative Necessity
of Sacrifice

*There's only one thing in life for a woman; it's to
be a mother. . . . A woman artist must be . . . capable of
making the primary sacrifices.*
                    Mary Stevenson Cassatt to A. F. Jaccaci

Mythology is much abused. Once upon a time, western culture
depended upon mythology for the explication and nurture of public
and personal identities. Myths were true stories. In the modern world,
mythology has been deprecated and disabused of its authority. Mythology has become synonymous with fairy tales and the world of "make-
believe." This is a most unfortunate turn of events, because our under-
standings of gender identification, of art, and thereby of the artist were
grounded in the mythology of classical culture. As these myths are
now identified as part and parcel of the untruths of mythology, we
seek to find new ground upon which to establish gender, art, and
artist—and we have floundered.

The traditional mythology of the artist is pivotal to contemporary
interpretations of women and creativity. In medieval Christianity, the
artist was understood to be the vehicle through which God's creative
inspiration found form. Through his disciplined training and craftsmanship, the medieval Christian artist brought the implanted vision to
reality, cognizant that the inspiration and the artwork were gifts from
God, and that the artist was merely the vehicle for God's inspiration.
Therefore, the artist took no individual credit but rather identified
himself as a craftsman, not as originator or creator.

With the Renaissance and its cultural shift toward the human, the artist became an individual who originated and created new visions. The human was the measure of all things and his potential was unlimited. The ability to create works of art (literature, music, poetry, painting, sculpture) merely bolstered the renaissance artist's emerging sense of personal identity. At this same time, the public definition of genius also shifted from one favored by the gods to one of extraordinary creativity and originality. The genius brought forth masterpieces, new iconographies, and originated personal style.

In the 19th century, the romantic movement birthed a new and powerful definition of the artist as the rebel from society, the outcast who created out of a profound passion and who sacrificed everything— social status, monies, love, family—for this passion. As with the renaissance genius, the romantic artist was the fount of originality, but unlike the renaissance genius the romantic artist was critical of society and sought a better world. The development of "modern," or 20th-century, schools of art, and their ensuing definition of the artist, were indebted to the romantic myth of the artist.

For better or worse, the western mythology of the artist has been modeled upon and idealized in the *male* of the species. As lesser beings, women were not permitted the luxury of artistic training or the freedom to be creative. All of a woman's creative energy and power was to be concentrated upon the bearing and nurturing of children, with any residuals reserved for the maintenance of her home and husband. Clearly, motherhood required all of a woman's attention, energies, and commitment—any other activities or actions which limited her maternal duties were *verboten*. Curiously, one of the traditional theories about gender and creativity espoused the thesis that those men who became artists created works of art instead of children—what contemporary feminists might identify as a form of "womb envy." Thereby, those women who struggled to live a life of creative productivity were, most often, denied the privilege of marriage and family! If they married, it was usually a companionate marriage with either an older man who was mentor and/or patron of his wife's art. If they didn't marry, they were further exiled by a society that emphasized what it believed was woman's proper and God-given role. These independent, creative women were *different* from "normal" women—and no sound-thinking father would allow his daughters to learn about, let alone meet, such deviant beings.

Although the bibliography on the creative process is minimal, despite its centrality to the human condition and to human history, the texts that do exist support a multiplicity of theories about how the creative process operates. The classic characteristics of divine inspiration and disciplined skill combined with a profound passion pervade all the theoretical models. However, by its very nature it is impossible to delineate one singular mode for the creative process that "works" for *all* creative persons—gender, sexuality, race, class, artistic medium notwithstanding. In fact, the development of a singular model of creativity, like that of genius, is an impossibility. Similarly, there are probably some male artists who do create out of a desire to bear a child just as others create from a depth of inspiration and others still by a fascination with a problem of composition, iconography, or form. The concern here is not *how* or *why* human beings create but that they *do*.

All human beings are creative, expressing their creativity in differing ways, manners, amounts, and, at different times in their lives. Those who are creative artists—(painters, sculptors, poets, writers, dancers, composers)—are driven by a need to express an idea, a vision, and a moment of beauty through colors, shapes, words, sounds, gestures, the human body. The problem is the simple reality that the act of writing a poem or a novel, of painting a picture, of sculpting a form, of choreographing a dance, of composing an étude is not a simple or time-bounded activity. Rather, it requires a total commitment of energies and attention, and an ability to suspend time and space—eureka, the heart of the problem for creative women, whose total attention would be shifted away from their home and children to their art! Women can not merely produce both a child and a work of art *if* their commitment to themselves—to their art—dominates their lives.

When Sigmund Freud announced that the distinguishing factors of human identity were sexual and named the female as the lesser sex, he built upon centuries of patriarchal attitudes and cultural restrictions placed upon women, especially upon creative women. It is curious to note that Freud's theories on what he identified as "the woman problem" coincided with the burgeoning political and social activism of the initial modern women's movements. He struck a deep and still-felt blow to our cultural perceptions of sex, gender, and creativity when he named the male as active and dominant and the female as passive and submissive. Later, the psychologist Erik Erikson determined that men and women solve problems differently—the male being fundamentally oriented toward an exterior or outward solution and the female an inward or interior solution; thereby unconsciously paralleling their body parts to their activities and in some way affirming patriarchal culture's models of active men and passive women. Only with the advance of women psychologists, such as Karen Horney and M. Esther Harding, were voices raised in support of women's fundamental nature and powers as being other than *lesser than male* or suffering from *penis envy.*

In a fashion almost analogous to a belief in the psychological limitations of being female *and* creative were the social restrictions of education and class that combined with economic discrimination to confront women artists with an insurmountable authority. Those extraordinary women—like Artemisia Gentileschi or George Sand—who created despite these restrictions were forced to make other sacrifices, even to the extent of being *outcasts* from society. As the world moved into the 20th century, women began to surface more and more in the public domains. The women's movement has had a much longer history than the revolution birthed in the 1960s. Many of the contributors to this volume—Georgia O'Keeffe, Martha Graham, and Anaïs Nin, for example—were critical to our changed perspectives of the societal roles of women and of creative women.

The one constant factor among creative women is that each has found a way to create. By this I mean simply that each of these women, despite the restrictions of gender, sexuality, class, race, education, and economics, found "a room of one's own" and gave life to the creative urge. Some of the contributors to this collection have sacrificed the desire to have children or have had children only to find their creative energies frustrated. For example, Graham and O'Keeffe remained childless while Louise Nevelson, under financial distress, was forced to send her son to be raised by her parents. More recently, buttressed by both the feminist mythology of the superwoman and changing family patterns, women artists are having children *without* sacrificing their urge to create. For some their creative nature is even increased by the experience of motherhood, while others choose to raise their children and take a hiatus from work. A more curious, but perhaps natural, phenomenon is that the earlier model of women artists being the *daughters of artist fathers* is being overturned so that we now find women artists among the *daughters of artist mothers*. With the advances in health care for women and a societal reevaluation of menopause (and the menopausal woman), we find more and more truth to Margaret Mead's often paraphrased statement that no one is more creative than a menopausal woman. *Women, Creativity, and the Arts* stands as a preliminary witness to our changing cultural and social perceptions of women, and of creative women.

This volume has been designed to foster the study of women and creativity. To this end, we have sought to bring together classic and ground-breaking texts in which the authors have voiced fundamental and critical questions about cultural perceptions of women, gender, sexuality, and creativity. Most of the contributors write with a personal voice shaped by individual experiences of the creative process or by a fascination with creativity. Some authors offer the reader a methodology for analyzing the creative process in women, while others provide the foundational questions for further inquiries. All of these authors share the common bonds of being female and of having triumphed personally over the cultural limitations placed by Freud, Erikson, and the other formulators of western culture's definition of *Woman*.

Part I of *Women, Creativity, and the Arts* brings together a series of nine essays by psychologists, art historians and critics, literary critics, and sociologists who have sought in their varied methods and languages to pursue the role(s) of creative women. In this search, they have raised serious questions about the creative process, the definition of genius, cultural and social categorizations of "woman," and, in most cases, a prejudicial dearth of evidence.

Iris Bünsch's essay exploring western culture's normative roles for woman as saint, mother, or whore sounds the clarion call of one of the foundational themes in all the contributions to this collection—that a woman's search for reality is simultaneously a quest for true identity and results in a critique of the social constructs of western culture. For Bünsch, it is the varied "masks" which must be worn by a woman throughout her life that restrict the experience of reality and the recognition of individuality. Those women who reject their "masks" find themselves outside of "the system"—outcasts, if you will, from the society they wish to both transform and be a member of. Bünsch offers the model of the female athlete, a retrieval of the legendary Amazon, as a new role model for woman's search for identity and for the transformation of western cultural norms.

Jean Baker Miller identifies the commonalities in a woman's struggle for identity with the growth of personal creativity. She identifies personal creativity as a changing vision of oneself and finds this aspect of the creative process as fundamental to being female. The problem of the cultural construction of a social identity prevails, Miller suggests, as the impediment for women's inability, generally, to experience personal creativity. She calls for a redefinition, if not total reconstruction, of cultural constructions and social identities.

Christine Battersby raises, and then surveys, the question of the relationship between gender and creativity. Her essay provides both a personal and a historical foundation for new inquiries into both the creative process and cultural attitudes toward "gendered creativity." In her analysis of western cultural attitudes toward the genius, Battersby finds, not surprisingly, that the male genius has been both model and ideal. Ironically, she has personally experienced professional and intellectual prejudices against even the possibility of a *scholarly* investigation of the relationship between women and creativity, let alone women and genius.

Linda Nochlin's ground-breaking, and now classic, essay moves the reader into the realm of art history, specifically into feminist art history. Nochlin voices the realities of a male-dominated field—in both the practice of creating art and of writing/teaching art history. She argues persuasively that the biases and inadequacies of this male domination can be overturned with positive results for both the world of art and the world of art history, if not also for the larger realms of education and scholarly inquiry, by careful attention to the queries and critiques of the marginalized. The questions and method of her own inquiry into "why there have been no great women artists" offers a model for continuing examination of gender and culture in relation to art and art history.

Joelynn Snyder-Ott moves us to the personal world of the artist as she seeks to analyze the reality behind the category of women's art. Her examination of the distinctions between the *female experience* and the *male experience* take the reader beyond Erikson's initial comparison. Following Nochlin, Snyder-Ott also calls for the recognition of women's history as an essential element to education. She sees education as the fundamental destroyer of stereotypes and a vehicle for cultural transformation of social definitions of gender and identity.

bell hooks affirms the centrality of the aesthetic—as a way of seeing, of inhabiting space, and of becoming oneself—in a text that is both shaped and informed by autobiographical reflection. She moves beyond the personal into the communal when she establishes the contemporary reality among African-Americans who have had their fundamental aesthetic "yearn-for-beauty" replaced by the cultural imposition of consumerism (which then makes them acceptable to and assimilated into the predominant white-male culture). The retrieval of the fundamental aesthetic "yearn-for-beauty," hooks asserts, is at the heart of the African-American community's search for identification through both its African heritage, including dance, art, and narrative, and its transformation of those traditions through the American experience—resulting for example, in the Harlem Renaissance. hooks sees art and the aesthetic as integral to the struggle against racism and for authenticity. She calls for an aesthetic of blackness not as an alternative to, but as an essential element of, the generic cultural aesthetic.

Monique Wittig seeks in her questioning of the linguistic reality of the term *feminine* writing to break the boundaries not simply of language, linguistic and gender categories, and literary preconceptions about authorship but also of the political power of words. She calls for a realization that a great work of literature, usually defined as a classic, goes beyond the limitations and restrictions of historical periods, social attitudes, and individual authority to speak with a universal power and passion to *all* readers. Thus, Wittig calls for a recognition of both the foundational and the political in literature in which the author extends herself beyond the minority, the unique, and the singular to be universal and individual.

Patricia Meyer Spacks describes the relationship between the equations *woman as artist* and *woman as woman* in her analysis of such women writers as Dora Carrington, Margaret Anderson, Mary MacLane, and Mary McCarthy. The structural limitations of being female and being writer are contrasted to traditional stereotypes. Through careful exegeses, Spacks argues for a revision of these categories. Her comparison between the adolescent and the artist raises the central issues of emotional maturity and personal stability as central to energy and commitment. The woman artist, for Spacks, is immersed in, energized by, and revelatory of passion. The questioning of sexual identity and of unresolved sexuality signify the social constructs that curtail the development of women artists. Although only insinuated in her discussion of Isadora Duncan, Spacks' critical analysis of the woman as artist argues for the relationship between art and motherhood as interconnected expressions of female power.

Michele Wallace turns the reader's attention to the issues of women and creativity, especially in terms of marginalized women—blacks, Hispanics, and Asians. She calls for a recognition of the continuing dominance of white males as the arbiters of culture and of cultural values, and suggests the intrinsic threat of such a structure on *all* women. For Wallace, black feminist creativity is a substitute for economic and political power. The most difficult arena for creative black feminists is the world of the written word; after all, words *are* power. She surveys the 20th-century world of black women writers from Zora Neale Hurston to Alice Walker, and distinguishes between those who unconsciously support the system of cultural dominance and those who consciously argue for a redefinition of cultural, societal, and gender roles.

Part II of *Women, Creativity, and the Arts* is a collection of autobiographical reflections on being creative and female in the 20th century. The voices raised here indicate the gamut of the arts from painting to dance to sculpture to poetry to fiction to prose while simultaneously revealing the transformation of cultural attitudes toward creative women. The reader journies from several of the early-20th-century women who struggled against societal restrictions and cultural discriminations to be free *to be an artist* to those more contemporary women who continue to break new ground in the continuing limitations for creative women.

Each of these artistic personalities has struggled against the social and cultural constructions of what it means to be female—the denying of independence, individuality, activity, and the drive to create, and the advocating of dependence, silence, passivity, and motherhood. Some of these artists sacrificed their personal selves (denying themselves the right and the privilege to be wife *and* mother *and* artist), others reshaped their lives after their children had grown to young adulthood, still others tried to be wife, mother, and artist *simultaneously*, and some even dared to be different—in terms of race, class, or sexual orientation. The common denominator is that each of these women challenged society to live on the edge of cultural boundaries and to forge a sense of the aesthetic self driven by the passion to create.

Georgia O'Keeffe's autobiographical reflections offer an extraordinary view into the personal world of one of the 20th century's most private of artists. Committed to the reality that she did not want to be defined, characterized, or listed as *a woman artist* but as *an artist*, O'Keeffe's comments reveal a sense of total commitment to the intuition of an aesthetic vocation even before she was intellectually prepared to define what it meant to be an artist. Her empathetic language and strong visual memories of color, shape, and light affirm her basic aesthetic orientation to the world and were the foundation of her personal way of seeing.

Martha Graham's sense of vocation and commitment to the dance were no less profound than O'Keeffe's to painting. Graham believed she was born to be a dancer and had no choice in the matter—the choice was merely in the timing of when she became one. She passionately describes the power of the dance, of the discipline required of the dancer, and of the vocation of this "venture into the unknown." The unique ability of her body to express ideas, concepts, emotions, and feelings through movement separated Graham from her colleagues and contemporaries, and symbolized her way of seeing or being in the world.

Louise Nevelson's description of "tapping the real fibers of what life is about" in the making of a work of art eloquently attests to the passion of the creative artist. In her reflections on being most alive when she is engaged in the creative process, Nevelson affirms the reality of the suspension of time and space, and the exaltation of joy, at the moment of creation. Her description of the factor of the physical tiring before the creative in an artist offers room for further speculation on the creative process. Her analysis of her own requirements of empty space and alternate mundane activities between creative moments suggest that Nevelson's female artistic experience parallels that of other artists—male *and* female.

Anaïs Nin proposes that there is a "mutual benefit" for men and women in women's quest for identity. Seeking to redefine, if not reconstruct, the meaning of feminist and feminism, Nin finds that the social, cultural, and religious restrictions placed upon a woman, any woman, are definitional but not insurmountable. "Creativity," she emphasizes, "is an all-encompassing word . . ." She identifies creative women as those most trapped in the dialectical tension identified by Otto Rank as that dialectic between creative guilt and the guilt for not creating. Out of this tension, one might conclude, taking Nin's reading of Rank to a natural conclusion, comes some of the universal artistic works of women.

Muriel Rukeyser turns the reader's attention to the realm of the poetic and the dynamic encounter between poet, poem, and reader. For her, the poem is process, and thereby a continuing exchange of energy. Her eloquent description of how a poem comes to be provides a case study of the creative process with particular attention given over to the triadic relationship between "poet, poem, and witness." Echoing the attitudes of earlier artists, Rukeyser affirms the foundation of the creative personality as the recognition that "our art has life in time."

Ursula K. Le Guin empathetically analyzes the meaning and the symbolism of *being* a woman writer. In her carefully detailed description, Le Guin raises questions about the stereotypic nature of the woman author and critiques the cultural and societal foundations of such an image. As an alternative, she offers the recognition of reality in her piercing question, "What does a woman writing look like?" She surveys some works written by women for descriptive textual examples and in offering them to her readers attests to the power of the woman writer through her universalizing of the personal to elicit the dynamism of visual memory.

Alice McDermott confronts the traditional mythology of books versus babies, and discovers that her 1970s graduate student aversion to motherhood is distinctly out of kilter with the reality of her life as wife, mother, *and* writer. For her, the more intriguing question is the seldom if ever asked one: Why don't women writers who are mothers write about the extraordinary satisfaction of being mother and writer? Her conclusion is fear—not of being castigated by her younger or more liberated sisters—but fear that, once revealed for all to see, the truth of her happy life will be jinxed, destroyed, and gone forever in one swift keystroke of the computer.

Annie Leibowitz advocates the centrality of "listening to your own voice" in the formation of one's individual aesthetic and of one's individual persona. Once she permitted herself the trust her inner voice deserved, Leibovitz found that her aesthetic sense of beauty evolved in tandem with her personal and professional identity. The process of photography became an encounter with the surprise and the power of images that permitted her "to get at some essence of a person or an idea."

Audre Lorde's quest to say what "must be said" is established upon a recognition of the power of fear—fear of silence, of the unsaid, of the undone, of human limitations, of death. Authorship or the act of writing, for Lorde, goes beyond the simple narration of a story. It is a moment of empowerment when the personal becomes universal and triumphs over the situation of mortality. This black lesbian poet underwent a testing, an initiation if you will, when her experience of breast surgery forced a confrontation with time. Angry, fearful, stunned, depressed, relieved, and cognizant of human finitude, Lorde incorporated the gamut of human emotions into her understanding of language and found a renewed sense of her mission to create.

Without doubt, autobiographical reflection is a luxury and, for an artist, to reflect on the meaning of personal being and creativity is a primal experience of confession and expression. For most artists, and especially for women artists, time is the greatest enemy: to deviate time *and* energy from one's "work" to the writing of a reflective text is an insurmountable burden. For women artists such a burden becomes almost unthinkable. In the search for texts for this section of *Women, Creativity, and the Arts*, the unsaid intuition became reality when we were unable to locate substantial autobiographical reflections by women artists of color. Perhaps it will be a sign of how far women— most especially creative women—have come when readers can find readily accessible autobiographical texts by *all* women artists.

As with all attempts at interdisciplinary study, this collection contains a breadth of postures, methodologies, and tenors of interpretation. All the contributors have approached their individual topics with the passion and commitment that characterizes creative women. As editors of this volume, it has been our intention, if not our duty, to provide a forum for the many different voices without the establishment of any "critical" or identifiable line. This project was begun in order to debate the traditional litany as well as to foster further investigations. To these purposes, the volume concludes with a series of Special Topic Bibliographies which serve as introductions of classic and recent texts in the study of women and creativity—and which offer a supportive paraphrase of Virginia Woolf's dictum to encourage young women for they seem to be so fearfully angry.

Diane Apostolos-Cappadona
Georgetown University
Washington, D.C.
April 1995

·I·

ON
WOMEN
AND
CREATIVITY

The Reality of Woman

IRIS BÜNSCH

Women seem to have lived in their own kind of reality for centuries. Traditional history acknowledges only a few women who were either connected with eminent men or who somehow sneaked through the system and played important roles in political or cultural affairs, and recently even in scientific fields. It must be presumed that woman's masochistic self-abasement, her ability to endure schizophrenia, or to think simultaneously on different levels or in categories of relativity rendered considerable stability to the prevailing system of the respective times. A common trait of all recorded social systems was to neutralize women's creativity in every respect except the biological one. Women lived in a world where men defined the what, how, who, and why they were. A little girl learned early on that what she discovered by herself about herself, and the persons and things around her, was of little importance, but rather that she had to learn a role. This role was rigidly constructed, and not only prescribed a desirable behavior, but designed a costume, required a certain shape of body, a mask instead of a face—according to the taste of the times—and presupposed infinite acting skills. Girls, in other words, had to realize that reality was fictional, that life was a stage on which they were limited to playing only a suitable set of supporting parts. Of course, they were not typecast. On the contrary, they had to become "the type" to be cast at all, that is, to have the opportunity to obtain at least a small portion of social relevance as wife and mother. If a woman failed, she had to be content with a shadowy existence backstage or, worse, if she denied her prescribed role, she would have the short and fatal appearance at a metaphorical or actual stake. Given the choice between backstage and the stake, only the very courageous or stubborn ones risked the stake. No wonder that they were then associated with evil or unholy magic. In any case, Christian, and before that Jewish, thinking linked woman with the devil, eternally endangering man's holier aspirations. If you read the creation myth of the Old Testament closely, the message becomes rather startling. It clearly is Eve whose thirst for knowledge brings about the expulsion from Paradise. But her intellectual curiosity introduced the dialectical process of discriminating between right and wrong, good and evil, thus freedom of decision and independence of thought. However, exactly these intellectual faculties have always been described as typically male prerogatives. On principle, this was really a paradoxical situation that had to be resolved before it could become dangerous to stability.

Since woman was so interested in finding out about categories of thinking, and ultimately about reality, that she was willing to give up Paradise, that reality had to be withdrawn from her. Thus, male imagination put her on a fictional level and invented a code of behavior that made woman and her intellectual and spiritual curiosity as harmless as possible. At first, she was denied any form of intellectual activity, and attention was directed to her overwhelming sexuality. That, however, was also recognized as a real danger to mankind. Women were told that their only purpose in life was to love—men, of course. Again, a paradoxical situation arose: female sexuality was defined as a threat; on the other hand, the one and only goal of woman was to be love and the production of children. So love and sexuality had to be separated, without letting love acquire too many intellectual connotations. Love should be very practical and highly time-consuming, and—in order to avoid the consequences of Christ's irritating acknowledgment of the spiritual potential of women in the New Testament—should preferably be understood as a self-denying, pain-loving feeling.

Eventually, women were ordained to three major roles in history: the saint, the mother, and the whore. The saint was conceded a certain amount of spirituality, but she was very soon catapulted into a sphere that did not have much to do with this world. Hence, she could be neutralized into an object of adoration and admiration. But, being an object, she would remain passive and manageable. This, for instance, was the process that again undid another explosive myth of Christianity: the Holy Virgin. The idea of God needing a woman to make His son a human being in order to fulfill His plan of salvation contained a huge revolutionary potential. On the one hand, it seemed to confirm that God, who had no other human quality except His gender, stuck to the principle of male superiority, represented by a male God in a monotheistic religion. On the other hand, He who had created the world alone, had chosen a woman who had become the necessary helpmate to save His creation. And salvation was needed since God's work had become hybrid and man had proved unfit to properly use the intellectual insight and power Eve had obtained for them. But this was incomprehensible for the male societies in the Old World and the problem was solved in the "normal" way: Mary became a saint and was honorably banished from this world. Furthermore, she could be used in a very practical way for the elaboration on another role. Thus, she was constructed into the model of motherhood, grounded on self-denial and suffering. Not that the pattern was followed strictly in the ensuing centuries, but it was a wonderfully prophylactic means. This picture of the self-effacing mother built a wall against the most dangerous role for a woman, the biological one, because with its help she could acquire power. No male system could either adopt or eliminate this faculty if procreation was to keep going on. The mother had at first a mere physical function, but she also had a potential of spiritual influence on her children as well. Accordingly, she would have the most active role that could be ascribed to a woman. Now, the problem arose of how to construct her into a passive object in order to make her ineffective on a larger scale. This could not merely be done by eliminating her family name by marriage. Especially in classes where bodily work would not exhaust all her energy, a mother-role had to be invented that would neutralize her spiritual powers and prevent any attempt at intellectual independence. The mother had to be bound as firmly as possible into the social system, since it was she who was ultimately entrusted with the maintenance of its stability. It was her duty to pass on traditional role models to her children. Consequently, she had to think of herself as the soil in which her offspring grew and prospered, a function which had to be a fulfillment in itself. If she accepted this kind of secondhand life, she was promised the status of a saint. Thus, the biological function of motherhood was translated into a moral one. If she did not behave in the prescribed way, guilt would become a regulating force. The failing mother was considered a monster, worse than Herod, the baby-slaying tyrant. But when she enacted her role in the conditioned manner she would always procure the same kind of human material: she would prepare her children, especially the female ones, for the same kind of society in which she herself was brought up. In this way, the mother role is essentially conservative, and it is quite understandable why conservative regimes untiringly exult and propagate this interpretation. To have children who function adroitly in a given social system was the only success a woman could achieve; and if her children behaved differently, their mother would be the first one to be held responsible. Paradoxically, the passivity of the mother role made it the most forceful agent in holding up the norms of society and forfeiting the law of relativity. If her children failed, her life would prove a failure, too. Thus, as if it were meant as a kind of revenge for immobilizing the most creative power of woman by reducing it to giving birth to other humans who were to be normed, this suffocating mechanical circle found its most forceful expression in a phenomenon the Americans call "Momism." It described the secret but forceful reaction of women to powerlessness. Momism is the collective term for women who have gained enough influence over their husbands and/or sons to make them execute their more or less open wishes or orders. It is quite significant that the reversal of the "normal" situation characterizes the Mom as a fearsome and destructive force in social life or changes her into a grotesque caricature. On the other hand, this concept of a harmful mother figure reveals the hidden fears of male society combined with a telling lack of any self-recognition in the aspect of how men wield their power. Furthermore, it does acknowledge the essential influence education has on everybody and simultaneously the distorting mirror of Momism unveils the artificiality of the traditional mother image. Equally, a basic error of the conventional concept of the interrelationship between the ideal—from a male point of view—mother and her educational results becomes evident. Behind the whole structure, there lurks the expectation that the normative training will produce an outstanding normal creature—which is an irony in itself. The third role provided for women was that of the seductress, courtesan, or whore. After the phenomenon of the priestesses had died out, the courtesan's activity was the only professional one sanctioned by the hypocritical male society. To allow this kind of participation in the economic process was not difficult since it led in the same direction as male interests lay and, moreover, it could be kept under control by official moral condemnation. In ancient times or in other cultural spheres, the courtesan was even encouraged to be learned, since this added to the pleasure of her clients, who would consider themselves too cultivated to just satisfy their carnal desires. Furthermore, it was an exciting change from their wives, who either were duly illiterate or too exhausted by their daily chores to discuss Plato while in bed. Even the most accomplished courtesan was no threat to society, since her status was unimportant enough to be without influence. If ever she had the opportunity to pour her ideas in the ear of a man of power, she would still never rule in her own right. So the show could go on. The seductress, however, had to be taken seriously. She could emerge in any situation, was not to be recognized at first sight, was not restricted by a professional code, and could even overtly follow her own aims. She was the truly dangerous woman who sometimes even achieved influence. But then, of course, these women, such as Helen of Troy or Delilah, were always distasteful to mankind. But even if their victims were not whole armies, women like Carmen or, to give a historical example, Mata Hari, would dabble with higher values, for example man's self-respect.

Whole libraries have been filled with stories about the seductress/ courtesan myth. The existence of women like those created a problem that had to be solved over and over again. This was a drastic change from the other two female roles, since these could be defined and fixed once and for all. But also in this case, man would solve the problem, mostly in fiction and normally with a vengeance, even if the doubtful heroine might be given some notable traits. If she had led her male victims off the right path, she either died under pleasantly tragic circumstances, preferably of consumption, or by suicide. Or, in a more humane procedure, she would convert under pangs of remorse and succumb to the norms of society and lead a chaste and withdrawn life.

All these role images brought about the fact that women could be put into socially useful, and, in the long run, ineffective corners. The saint, the mother, and even the whore could all be employed in different ways to check unruly behavior. Thus, women have always had a social purpose, prescribed by others, but very seldom the chance to develop a sense of their own will or individuality. It can scarcely be imagined, however, that women could really have lived without any notion of their own personality. But it would always lead them into conflict with the concept of expected behavior. The result would have been a precarious and overtly consequential decision to deal with reality. But if she wanted to live on in peace she had to decide: either she accepted the constrictions made by others, or she would consciously play a role, acknowledging the relativity of reality or the fictional character of her reality. In the latter case, she just had to learn the text expected of her, wear the suitable costume, get her body in the shape that was considered pleasant, and find a mask that would not show too much of her individuality. She could do all that for the outside spectator but then she had to keep herself as distant from herself as possible and thus became a spectator of herself, constantly judging and adjusting her own performance. No wonder women have become addicted to mirrors.

If a woman was able to achieve this kind of split consciousness and to live with it, she might find out about her own reality, or her true identity. Those who were kept suspended in the middle, finding their own personality without learning the appropriate text for society became socially deviant. They could only go on living honorably by withdrawing into a ghetto such as a nunnery, or fatal reactions would prevent their living on at all. They would either be regarded as witches, or insane, and in consequence, they very often actually became mentally disturbed. Few women in history could consciously combine the destructive influence of norms with the possibly self-destructive recognition of being deviant by reacting aggressively themselves, or by sublimating their aggression into creative activities. They would invent a reality they could keep under control, which means a consciously subjective reality: they became artists. That is, they either made up their own world by painting or writing, or they made acting their profession: they all made use of fiction in order to create life.

It is true, the impact of female artists on cultural history has been slight if one only acknowledges the known quantity of published works, or rendered records of histrionic deeds. Only recently has the awareness been sharpened that there had been many more female authors, painters, and even composers than the selection by those in power to publish their efforts has hitherto admitted. Comparably little is known of the history of women on the stage, due to the morally doubtful associations connected with their professional endeavors. But the shortest is the span of time since women have been allowed to participate in activities in the field of sports. That is not astonishing, sports always used to mimic the male dominated sphere of war. Apart from legendary Amazons—who were as much discussed as they were feared—women were excluded from the serious play for power. There have always been attempts to endow war with a seemingly civilized face by inventing rules for the butchery, or by translating the fight into a ritualistic exchange of male strength and skill. Unconvincing as these cosmetic attempts may be to more humanistic minds, they have always been a great success with the masses. In sports the fictionalizing of an otherwise deadly combat has a similar effect as Aristotle's definition of the catharsis in Greek tragedy implies. The spectator can live through the development and all stages of a crisis without being actually involved in the goings-on.

The strange combination of a serious fight with theatrical aspects enhanced the surrogate crisis the spectator could experience. In recent times, sports still transport the sensational effect, but on the other hand, the conscious awareness of its fictional level has obviously been weakened. This becomes not only noticeable in the disastrous brutality of some soccer fans, but also, to a less dangerous degree, in the evaluation of certain sports heroes who became associated with national pride and identity. Perhaps it will become the responsibility of female athletes to save the more civilized aspects of sports, and sever them from their roots as "war without shooting," as Orwell defined them. On the whole, female athletes represent the more artistic feats in sports: entertainment and aestheticism. But again, as women, they are trained to acknowledge fictionality in reality, and so they can stick more easily to the metaphorical meaning of combat and competition. And if they play their game well, why should they not be allowed to enter the ranks of the great actresses of the century? Furthermore, being so new on the great stage of public appearance, the really outstanding female athletes had to find out how to do it their own way. Just imitating men would not help them and so they had to find their personal creative impulses that would enable them to rise up to higher ranks.

It is significant that, especially in this century, the discrepancy between the life of great women artists, athletes, or scientists, and the social norms they were brought up in, furthered creative impulses. Whatever the psychological motives for innovations may have been, vulnerability and the ensuing realization that accepting norms was as suffocating as the danger of breaking them was threatening were at least the most substantial causes. It was exactly that vulnerability that led to the bitter awareness of being prevented from doing the important, possible, and valuable things by the more than less manipulated and man-made circumstances that constitute reality. This does not mean that male artists lack sensitivity, but their kind of awareness is certainly of another quality. Male innovators, however great the obstacles they might encounter, can always look back to a tradition and a long series of role models even for the most enterprising and rebellious spirits. Women are denied this comforting cushion of confirmation and, by looking back to their tradition, will be actively discouraged, since they must find out that their aspirations are definitely wrong in every respect. If they are not already utterly discouraged by this, they will have to begin by reinventing the whole world from the beginning. They will have to create something completely new, a system of new values and concepts. And they have to do that by violating norms, role models, and seemingly eternal natural or moral laws. If they are artists, they can do so comparatively unmolested, as long as they do not claim any important social influence, or as long as they do not rise noticeably above mediocrity or "normality." In any case, such mental or spiritual independence is dangerous. Quite a few female writers who discovered the relativity of reality, for example Virginia Woolf, risked their sanity. Others, such as Christa Wolf, who wrote about the relativity of ideology in favor of humanism, risked their artistic integrity or political safety. These artists were obliged to operate in a landscape for which there existed no map at all, or where there were still huge white spots. So they had to draw other maps all by themselves, inventing a new, entirely personal and subjective identity as a basis for their messages. Fundamentally this meant a change from a negative point of view, from an essential distrust in norms and consequently their denial, to a positive one: the new conscious conception and affirmation of a system of humanistic and practical values, which is a lonely way indeed. Hence the emphasis on a personal and subjective point of view as an outcome of individual experiences in their narration. Reality was no longer an immobile network of normative rules, but it had to be questioned, explored, discovered, and, in the end, defined anew.

One of the most amazing ancestresses as a discoverer of a female worldview was the much discussed and much disputed revolutionary, Joan of Arc. She intruded into an area exclusively reserved to men, by achieving military success. And she did it by using an absolutely subjective explanation for her actions: her voices. When she referred to those, she made use of a sphere that was at first apparently safe, but on the other hand petrified by the traditional predominance and rigidly observed rituals of the Church. By personal charisma and with the help of her military successes, she was able to convince her countrymen for a time of the righteousness of her unheard-of doings. But then the political interest of the Church was violated to an unbearable extent: her voices and her individual behavior endangered the rigid system of the institution. Her condemnation and execution as a witch could not extinguish the revolutionary potential of her historical impact. Thus, several hundred years later, she was made into a saint, which safely installed her into the system by neutralizing her into social or political ineffectuality.

The inherent irony of her historical reception and evaluation is heightened by the fact that she made subtle use of traditional and generally acknowledged items, by justifying her actions with religious arguments. On the other hand, she appeared in men's clothes while she was doing a man's job, which was sensible as well as practical, but raised malevolent feelings on the side of the guardians of tradition and morality. Thus, she tried to keep the balance between her extravagant appearance and her basic faith in the principles of the Church. She could go on doing this quite safely until her success provoked resistance from those who rightly feared a growing instability within the establishment. The lever used to unhinge her popularity and to undo her achievements was a very simple argument. They condemned her violation of the true designation and natural position of a woman. There would have been no problem if she had either been a man, who could be identified with political and military success, or if she had failed in her aspirations. In the latter case, she could have been put aside as merely a crazy woman. In the end, she had done the right thing, she had changed the political situation of her country, and that means she had influenced reality. But as a woman she played the wrong role, had worn the wrong costume, and she had meddled with the reality of men. Thus, her success cost her her life.

Creativity with a Place to Go

JEAN BAKER MILLER

Personal creativity is a factor of supreme importance, which we have probably barely begun to appreciate. One exciting aspect of the current ferment by women is the fact that as they struggle for authenticity, they simultaneously illuminate their personal creativity. In so doing they elucidate the creativity that struggles in a more hidden way in all people at all times.

Personal creativity is a continuous process of bringing forth a changing vision of oneself, and of oneself in relation to the world. Out of this creation each person determines her/his next step and is motivated to take that next step. This vision must undergo repeated change and re-creation. Through childhood and adulthood, too, there are inevitable physical changes as one grows and then ages. These demand a change in one's relation to the world. Further, there are the continuous psychological changes that lead to more experience, more perceptions, more emotions, and more thought. It is necessary to integrate all these into a coherent and constantly enlarging conception of one's life.

Each person repeatedly puts together a conceptualization that has never been put together before—that is, one constantly creates a personal vision. Despite all our commonality, each of us, each day, creates our own particular attempt to put the picture together, as it were. It is never exactly the same as anyone else's, and it is never the same as the one we made yesterday. That is, we each repeatedly re-confront the necessity to "break up the gestalt," as Max Wertheimer has described it.[1] At best, our conceptions will be an accurate reflection of what we have experienced and how we feel and think about the experience. The closer we can come to this ideal of authenticity, the better off we are. And the more we can act in terms of our own conceptions, the more whole and authentic we feel. Having acted, we can go back and "correct" our conceptions about the world, about ourselves, about what we want.

It is true that the very ways we find to conceptualize experience are in large measure given to us by the culture in which we learn "how to think and feel," or even learn what thinking and feeling are. But people are also continually straining against the boundaries of their culture— against the limiting categories given by that culture—and seeking the means to understand and to express the many experiences for which it does not suffice. This is true for all people. For women today it is a preeminent factor. As we have seen, there are fundamental reasons why women do not easily find the means at hand to express and conceptualize their experience. But they are struggling to develop these means. In this way, too, women's current endeavor can more clearly illuminate the hidden mental events that go on in all people.

It is certainly true that throughout history economic conditions have forced (and continue to force) most people into a life of drudgery, with little opportunity to think beyond the immediate task of sustaining life. It is also true that even in this situation the human mind is constantly at work, giving meanings to it all, trying to make it understandable. The mind does not seem to be, in today's parlance, "a closed system" but rather a system capable of infinite enlargement. The closer the mind can connect with what one is actually experiencing the better its inherent creativity can flourish. The more opportunity we have to put our mental creations into action, the more comprehensively we can, in turn, feel and think. One builds on the other.

The exciting and enlightening impact of the women's experiences we have discussed can be appreciated when we realize that they are on the cutting edge of a new and larger vision. Their personal creativity is an absolute necessity in the attempt to find a way to live *now*. The women, who are finding a way to deal with their own intensely felt experience, are at the same time creating a more general new vision of womanhood. For this vision to flourish, they and other women will have to create new social institutions to support and enlarge it. It is precisely at such points that one sees that the real motivation for a new form of living arises today in women out of intensely felt personal needs. The ways of achieving this new form of living will likewise have to be women's ways; to achieve ways of living that will attend to all women's needs, the forms inevitably will have to include more mutuality, cooperation, and affiliation, on both a personal and a larger social scale.

We have not dealt here with women who are particularly advanced in their sense of who they are and what they want. In fact, there are women today who are outstanding in their ability to act on the basis of their own perceptions and evaluations, who are already far along the road to creating a new way of living. Such women have a strong conviction of their own worth and of their own right to self-development and authenticity. Some have a background of high accomplishment; others have a strong sense of fighting for a valuable cause. The attempt here has been to get at the underlying forces affecting all women as a group, the nodal points from which forward movement can spring. The events in the lives of specific women are examples in the attempt to talk about these forces. Part of the reasons for doing so, however, is the hope of demonstrating that the *now* for authenticity and creativity do not belong only to the advanced, the educated, or the elite. These forces are played out in different forms for women in differing circumstances, but they are necessities for all of us.

In our time we have heard a great deal about people's lack of authenticity. What we cannot hear so clearly is that, for half of the population, the attempt at authenticity requires a clear and direct risk. For women to act and react out of their own being is to fly in the face of their appointed definition and their prescribed way of living. To move toward authenticity, then, also involves creation, in an immediate and pressing personal way. The whole fabric of one's life begins to change, and one sees it in a new light. As one woman put it, "I keep seeing everything with a different meaning now. Most days I feel as if I'm ad-libbing my way through. I don't follow the script I used to know." For this new and much more intense personal creating there are no certain guideposts. There are often anguish and anxiety, but there are also clear satisfactions and joys along the way, even long before there is anything like a sense of completion.

NOTES

1. Max Wertheimer, *Productive Thinking* (Harper, 1959).

Amongst the Ghosts

CHRISTINE BATTERSBY

Over Christmas 1986 the BBC broadcast a radio series called *Wives of the Great Composers*. The assumption underlying these supposedly humorous talks was that the great composers had lives that mattered, and wives (and mistresses) who also mattered—but only to the extent that they helped the great geniuses of music father their timeless progeny. Clara Schumann featured; but it was her husband's music that was played, not her own. George Sand appeared as an adjunct to Chopin; but she was barely recognizable as a great and influential novelist. Instead she wore the conventional 19th-century disguise of a "masculine" woman. And the treatment of Cosima Wagner made it puzzling that either Richard Wagner or Nietzsche should have found this termagant so compelling. The eccentricities of the male geniuses were excused; but not those of their partners. The latter were treated favorably only insofar as they fitted comfortably into a narrow range of sexual roles: as love objects, muses, scribes, or housekeepers to the class of great musicians. One woman was particularly inspiring. Her composer-husband, Carlo Gesualdo (c. 1560–1615), murdered her and re-lived that act again and again in strange and original melodies which were ahead of his time.

As I listened to these programs (turning off from time to time in real anger and impatience), I thought about the ghosts that Virginia Woolf writes about, the ones that disturb all creative women:

> Outwardly, what is simpler than to write books? Outwardly, what obstacles are there for a woman rather than for a man?

> Inwardly, I think, the case is very different; she has still many
> ghosts to fight, many prejudices to overcome.[1]

I kept seeing myself, aged sixteen, reading in the library at grammar
school. Whenever I could find the time I would gravitate toward two
shelves by the window, one above the other. On the upper shelf were
books of biographies of great artists—mostly composers, but including
painters, and some men of letters. I can remember no books about
women on this shelf. On the lower shelf was a curious selection of
books (some very old) on rules of conduct for women. Some of these
books were lavishly illustrated with pictures of stays and other even
more extraordinary contraptions. Amongst these books I can remember no books of critical commentary; nothing ironic; nothing that
distanced itself from the conventional etiquette described. When I
should have been doing other things, I enjoyed getting out these books
and having a good laugh over them. The lives of women then seemed
so distant from my own life, I found it hard even to imagine the
connections.

Of the two sets of books the ones I read most obsessively were the
artistic biographies. The ones on the lives of the great composers were,
I think, my favorite. It was these that I supplemented with similar
books from the public library, and which I devoured along with survey
books on music and modern art. I can now barely reconstruct what I
thought of these texts. But I know they were important to me. My
most secret fantasy was to be a singer, but since I knew I would be
useless at it I never even tried. Being a composer would have been
much more realistic. (I learned poems and quotations for A level by
making up tunes. I think I set the whole of *King Lear* to music.) But
this was not a career that ever occurred to me. Just as there was nothing
in the ladies' etiquette books that seemed to impinge on my own life,
so there was nothing in the books of biographies of composers. At
least some singers were women! It was only later I discovered the
blues, and the way women blues singers combined performance and
invention. But it wouldn't have helped much. I was the wrong color.
And by that time the fantasies about what I could do had turned into
a tendency to fall in love with certain kinds of creative men.

The ghosts from my past that confronted me as I listened to *Wives
of the Great Composers* were ones that came to me from my school-
days. Long before I decided to study the Romantics as a graduate
student, I had acquired their admiration for "originality" and "creativ-

ity." Romanticism valued artists for their capacity to express their own feelings and imaginings in their works. Authenticity and sincerity became the most important kinds of truth: more important by far than faithfully mirroring Nature, Beauty, or Goodness. The originality of the artwork was not seen as a reflection of the external world, but of the mind and the personality that brought that work into existence. Consequently, the uniqueness and individuality of the artist's own character also became aesthetically significant. From Byron and William Blake to Nietzsche and Van Gogh, the typical genius was atypical: in one way or another, an Outsider, misunderstood by society and at odds with it. The history of art was represented as the history of the achievements of isolated individuals at war with the Establishment. But Romanticism always represented that extreme form of individualism in terms of male social roles and male power.

In *On Heroes and Hero-Worship* (1840) Thomas Carlyle made sincerity, originality, and inspiration necessary characteristics of "'genius,' the heroic quality we have no good name for."[2]

> The most precious gift that Heaven can give to the Earth; a man of "genius" as we call it; the Soul of a Man actually sent down from the skies, with a God's-message to us. . . .
>
> . . . A messenger he, sent from the Infinite Unknown with tidings to us. We may call him Poet, Prophet, God;—in one way or other, we all feel that the words he utters are as no other man's words. Direct from the Inner Fact of things;— he lives, and has to live, in daily communion with that.[3]

The genius is born, not made. He is inspired by God and is, in fact, a kind of god himself, with Protean powers to take on different forms and roles in the various ages and stages of historical development:

> [T]he Hero can be Poet, Prophet, King, Priest or what you will, according to the kind of world he finds himself born into. I confess, I have no notion of a truly great man that could not be *all* sorts of men. The Poet who could merely sit on a chair, and compose stanzas, would never make a stanza worth much. He could not sing the Heroic warrior, unless he himself were at least a Heroic warrior too. I fancy there is in him the Politician, the Thinker, Legislator, Phi-

losopher;—in one or the other degree, he could have been, he is all these.[4]

The genius can be *all* sorts of men; but he is always a "Hero," and never a heroine. He cannot be a woman. Nor are his social duties consistent with those of fulfilling mundane domestic and reproductive tasks, nor of living a life of enforced, upper-class ease. The genius is male (however capable of empathizing with, or even impersonating, female psychology). Carlyle's pseudo-religious language makes clear the pretensions of the genius theory: the genius's power is modeled on that of God the Father: the king and patriarchal ruler of the Christian universe. God the Father is the "Author of Nature"; human authors, artists, and composers mimic divine creativity. The artist constructs a mini-world by imposing meaning and significance on formless matter; what his work means is a function of what he intended it to mean, and of the strength of his will in bending words, images, and sounds to his design. Like God, the author possesses authority. Power, energy, and divine inspiration are revealed in all facets of the artist's production. The better the artist, the more nearly he approaches omnipotence: his hand is omnipresent in the work of art, and detectable in even the most insignificant details.

But the artist, unlike the Christian God, is supposed neither omniscient, nor necessarily good. The work of art is created by the self, but in the dark part of the mind—amongst the emotional intensities of the male unconscious. The artist's self is divided; the universe of art that he creates is Manichean. In the theology of art criticism the devil has creative powers as well as God. And the devil is generally located amongst the driving forces of male lust. The sexual antics of the male genius are thought of as causally related to his art. They are also, therefore, redeemed by that art. Whether the great artist visits brothels, is homosexual, murders his wife, or is simply promiscuous, he can still be celebrated as a great and god-like human being. Much contemporary biography of geniuses reads like hagiography: these are the new saints (devil-driven saints), whose sayings and sufferings must be recorded. The genius is unconventional, bohemian, unique—often, like Byron himself, "mad, bad and dangerous to know." This caricature of genius has even spilled over from the arts onto the figure of the "Mad but Brilliant Scientist" . . . another variation on the theme of male genius.[5]

Programs like *Wives of the Great Composers* implicitly gender the notion of artistic greatness in the same ways that I did while still at school. I couldn't be a Real Artist (I supposed), because the kind of authentic, self-centered, and bohemian life that an Artist lived was not (remotely) like my own. Nor could this be a realistic ideal for a young girl growing up in the suburbs—however much she hated them. But without that kind of life and personality, I considered it impossible to be interesting enough to have a fully developed self worth expressing. I'm not complaining about the upbringing that produced these misconceptions. I feel sufficiently remote from my teenage self not to feel angry on my own account. But I still do feel rage as I listen to programs of this type. I also feel sad when year after year I see eighteen-year-old students entering university with the same preconceptions about creative gender roles that I had. I offered a paper on "Women and Genius" to a student society. After the posters had gone up I received reports of male students in the Philosophy common room discussing the advertised topic with genuine puzzlement. "What could the argument be? After all, not all geniuses had wives or girlfriends!" The posters themselves were also covered with revealing graffiti, some of which suggested that I would only be able to talk for ten minutes on such a subject. None of my other posters have ever attracted graffiti.

Professional art critics and academics like to pretend that Romanticism is a disease that has been cured by the hygiene of history. Not for the 1980s the mythology of artist as hero, creating in a state of ecstasy that often crosses the boundaries into clinical madness. Poststructuralists assure us that the author is dead, adding their voices to previous generations of Marxist critics who have undermined the authority and isolation of the lone author. But in popular culture we find the old vocabulary, and the figure of the artist as hero, as alive and well as ever. Which pictures are bought, which books are read, which plays performed, which films are shown in art centers is largely a product of an aesthetic that assumes the centrality of the author to the work of art. Indeed, it is because of this that a feminist aesthetic cannot simply join the post-structuralists and their allies in deploring the individualism and the elitism of an aesthetic that builds on individually great artists. The concept of genius is too deeply embedded in our conceptual scheme for us to solve our aesthetic problems by simply amputating all talk of genius, or by refusing to evaluate individual authors and artists. Before we can fundamentally revalue the old aesthetic values, the concept of genius has to be appropriated by feminists, and made to work for us.

The new formalist aesthetics of post-structuralism would like to replace the author with the text; the painter with the canvas; the composer with the score, or even the musical performance. But this new aesthetic is self-defeating. Given the nature of modern art, there seems no way to define a work of art except in terms of that which is produced by an artist. But who is "the artist"? How can he be distinguished from the man in the street, or from the bohemians and poseurs who aspire to this title? Because the new aestheticians don't try to re-describe the figure of the artist, but instead set out to deprive him of all authority, they actually help the old Romantic aesthetics to thrive in the world outside specialist journals and outside university walls.

An extramural course on Michelangelo and Van Gogh offered by my university to the inhabitants of a local town advertises itself with the following two-sentence summary: "Illustrated comparison of two artists of genius who suffered greatly. Their lives, words and works will be contrasted." Thus, precisely at the boundary that separates specialist academics from those with a general interest in the arts, we still find courses structured around the old Romantic concept of the genius. Indeed, once one starts listening and watching out for the word "genius," it is soon noticeable how much work this word still does in the description and evaluation of cultural achievement. Even those academics who have given up using the word often still cling to the old assumptions about genius in the way that they talk, write, and think about human creativity. This was proved to me in 1987 by a conference on "Genius: The History of an Idea" that was organized by one of the interdisciplinary groupings within my home university.

The setting up of the conference had been nothing to do with me. In fact, I had been startled to read the circular that came around about it over twelve months before. The organizers were no doubt equally surprised (and, I suspect, rather embarrassed) when they discovered that they had picked a topic which coincided with the book I had already started to write. When the overlap was pointed out, I was asked if I would be willing to give a paper to the conference on the topic of "Women and Genius." I agreed, of course, and began to put together fifty minutes of thoughts on the gendered origins of the modern concept of genius in the 18th century. Some time later it was my turn to be embarrassed. Talking to one of the representatives of a publishing company, I gathered he expected my paper to be included in the book of conference papers that his firm would issue. I was puzzled, and mumbled some excuse about my material perhaps being published elsewhere. Nobody had said anything to me about publishing my piece.

I waited for some time to see if I would receive an invitation to publish from the editors of the volume. Nothing happened. So eventually, with some awkwardness, I telephoned to try and find out what was proposed. I was told that the idea was to publish only some of the papers, to invite some extra papers from academics unable to attend, and that my paper was not deemed relevant to the overall enterprise, which was centered round the "classical" concept and tradition of genius. This rationale seemed to me to be mildly eccentric, but not altogether implausible. The conference had already been advertised, and I did not wish to be rude or pushy, so I made no fuss about it. It was only when I got to the conference and heard the other papers, and also realized that (as far as I could tell) I was the only speaker being excluded from the proposed volume, that I began to feel angry.

Practically every speaker used William Duff—but none apparently knew of the existence of his book on women. The comments of other authors, such as Coleridge, were treated as if they applied equally to all human beings, regardless of sex. For the two days that the conference lasted I felt as if I were stuck in a kind of time-warp. Here I was back in exactly the same scholarly world that I had abandoned nearly fifteen years before. I had expected to detect heavily ironic quotation marks around the word *genius*. But they were not much in evidence. I found myself listening to quite lengthy (and solemn) discussions about whether or not there has ever been a genius who was sane. As Newton's biography was inspected for the signs of insanity that are associated with genius, it was I who felt mad. Despite the (very occasional) use of the pronouns *she* and *her*, gender was not an issue. One man asked why I so obsessively focussed my questions on this topic.

Footnotes were being added to the traditions of scholarship with which I was familiar; but the framework of assumptions was undisturbed. The only thing that was different this time around was that the first paper of the conference went out of its way to stress that the history of the concept *genius* and the history of the word "genius" were unconnected. This, I supposed, was a response to the attack that I, as a feminist, was expected to mount. But this new defensiveness indicated no real change in attitude. In the time-honored way, the terms *man* and *male* were muddled by the speaker. My own paper was positioned right at the end of the proceedings. That, and my exclusion from the volume, made it feel as if the issue of gender was only a footnote to "real" academic scholarship on the question of genius, instead of being positioned (as it should be) at its heart.

Feminist academics will know exactly how I felt. They are all too used to being pushed to the margins of an academic enterprise, or hearing their arguments speedily dismissed by too quick an appeal to "authorities" and "traditional" scholarship. Because sympathetic criticism is so rare, and because ideological objections nearly always masquerade as purely "objective" criticisms, we never know where we are, which voices are sincere and which are dishonest. We are always made to feel that our words are being left unpublished because we are mediocre bores with bees in our bonnets. Others might squirm as our bees enter their bonnets and sting . . . but they rarely let on. Feminist academics waste a lot of time speculating about the underlying reasons for some particular response. Perhaps there was an entirely innocent explanation? . . . How can we be sure? We anxiously (or angrily) inspect the words used, looking for clues in the language.

A senior colleague came into my office to complain (in the mid-1980s!) that I had listed "Philosophy of Women" amongst my research interests. "There's no such subject," he said. "Yes," he agreed, "'Philosophy of Man' is a subject. No," he insisted, "'Philosophy of Woman' is not. You might as well say you're interested in 'Philosophy of Dog,' or 'Philosophy of Doorknob.'" Similes are often the only clue. But it is not often that language is as blatant as this. Sometimes I feel a kind of nostalgia for the (relatively) honest misogyny of prefeminist days. Cultural prejudice against women has, to some extent, gone underground. These days it is the fake friends of feminism who are our more dangerous enemies. This is not because their arguments are any more valid, but because time has to be wasted exposing the inner pig before they can be refuted. It is also, of course, because somebody who deceives himself about his motives for objecting will never back down. An alternative specious objection will simply be adopted.

When tackled about their attitudes to the creative capacity of women, most modern males would deny that they retain elements of misogyny. But the long list of responses that I collected to early (spoken or written) versions of my book, *Gender and Genius: Towards a Feminist Aesthetics*, suggest that many have fooled themselves by the false teeth that smile out of their mirrors. The first phrase was usually something like, "I agree with every word you say." Then comes a "BUT," and a rider. Some of the more startling of these were:

> I'm not convinced that women are capable of great achievement in . . . [a variety of subject areas, most commonly mathematics, music, metaphysics, and other disciplines described as "abstract"].

> Great female artists are virile, or . . . have masculine sexual energy.

> Women don't suffer the kinds of psychological disorder conducive to genius.

> It is a proved psychological fact that all really creative men [he means "males"] are feminine.

> All great painters have produced pornographic drawings, and have a strong male sex drive.

Really, I prefer the response of the colleague who said, "What you are doing is exciting and very important. But I do wish you'd take the feminism out!" The others missed the point of my arguments in as radical a way. At least with this last reply I knew exactly where I stood.

All these responses involve preconceptions about creative gender roles that have been conditioned by the way genius has been portrayed during the past two hundred years. All take maleness as the norm for artistic or creative achievement, however "feminine" that male might be. Great artists and scientists have *male* sexual drives, whether or not they are biologically female. Males can *transcend* their sexuality; females are *limited* by theirs—or, if not, must themselves have *male* sexual energy. These comments from "sophisticated" academics reveal a kind of tunnel vision that makes female creativity a puzzling exception to the norm of male capacities.

The way that creativity is still gendered today reveals itself in a variety of hidden (and not so hidden) ways. Cultural misogynists have learnt to disguise themselves, and hide their sexual prejudices behind innuendo, omissions, or even behind claims that they are really women's allies. In "Grunts from a Sexist Pig," for example, Anthony Burgess pretends ignorance of the reasons that have in the past led to his award of a pink marzipan pig from the Female Publishers of Great Britain.[6] He presents himself as fair and open-minded: "I believe that the sex of an author is irrelevant, because any good writer contains both sexes."[7] He listens to, and agrees with, feminists, using the musicians Thea Musgrave and Ethel Smyth—"a great feminist herself"—to dismiss as "nonsense" the claims of other feminists that there will be one day a great woman composer "when women have learned to create like *women* composers, a thing men have prevented their doing in the past."[8]

Burgess must suppose all women to be simple-minded if he expects us to believe that the humorous title he gives his piece does not describe it exactly. Feminists have become used to reading articles like his backwards, and watching for the mess around the beast's rear end. And there it is, sure enough: "I believe that artistic creativity is a male surrogate for biological creativity. . . . "[9] Well, fancy that! How then are we to explain all those great women writers? Mr. Burgess has thought of an answer to this, too:" . . . if women do so well in literature it may be that literature is, as Mary McCarthy said, closer to gossip than to art." Did McCarthy really say this? I haven't the patience to find out. In any case, quoting what somebody else says does not make that statement true. This type of pseudo-logical reasoning is called an "argument from authority," and is one of the oldest tricks in the textbooks of rhetoric.

"But no one will be happier than I to see women produce the greatest art of all time, so long as women themselves recognize that the art is more important than the artist."[10] If only this were the case, and creative women did not have to continually fight to be recognized by those who demand male lusts of artists. Burgess pretends not to see how such practices discriminate against female artists: "Take music, for instance. Women have never been denied professional musical instruction—indeed, they used to be encouraged to have it—but they have not yet produced a Mozart or a Beethoven."[11] This from a man who claims knowledge of the writings of Ethel Smyth! In *Female Pipings from Eden* (1933), this British composer charted in detail the reasons why

> . . . to-day it is absolutely impossible in this country for a woman composer to get and to keep her head above water; to go from strength to strength, and develop such powers as she may possess.[12]

Is it good news or bad news for women that Burgess's type of concealed misogyny is now more common than the open variety amongst writers on culture? I suppose we should be relieved that we now have to hunt (though not very hard) for the likes of Paul Ableman. In *The Doomed Rebellion* (1983), he argues in a much more frank way than Burgess that the male's sexual drive ensures that the arts "were originally, and remain essentially, expressions of male consciousness."[13] Ableman refuses to allow that the differential success of male and female creators has been produced by social pressures—or by the type of sexual stereotyping that he himself indulges in. It is much "more likely that the host of relatively minor female writers and thinkers had, in fact, reached the limits of their capacity"—a capacity determined by biological difference.[14] Because a man cannot be "biologically creative" (i.e., become pregnant), he is

> . . . driven to fulfill his creativity "out there". . . . A woman may go "out there" but part of her is always tempted back towards her womb and the future, and the divided impulse, which blunts her culturally creative drive, is undoubtedly the reason why so few women ever produce major cultural contributions.[15]

Ableman had previously explained this notion of the "out there": "A man's empire begins at the tip of his penis. . . . A woman's empire is within."[16] It is her womb . . . and its physical container her body.

Ableman argues for this thesis by setting up a contrast between male sexuality—"a surface phenomenon," given that "the male penis and testicles are both on the surface, or beyond the surface, of his body"—and the "incomparably richer" female sexuality. Since the womb is located deep within the body, it is argued that a reproductive drive is "integral" to female consciousness.[17] That a male has hormonal urges is not seen as a limiting factor on his autonomy or rationality: they are "marginal" to his mind . . . and "male sexuality can almost be considered ancillary to his masculinity."[18] But woman is Other: she is not-fully-individual and not-fully-human. Designed by Nature solely for the purpose of perpetuating the species, women's "biological, and hence psychological, mission remains child-bearing and home-building and, sooner or later, it will assert itself."[19] Like a fish or a bird, a woman is genetically programmed into obeying the demands of instinct . . . into becoming pregnant, "a bulky egg on legs"![20]

Via such simple-minded dichotomies—and a series of apparently willful self-deceptions—Ableman rehearses the kinds of arguments that have been commonly employed to represent female genius as somehow "against nature." Although, in excusing rape, men have been anxious to excuse their acts by reference to their overwhelming sexual urges, when it comes to cultural creation the rhetoric is different. Males, it seems, can transcend their animal nature to produce culture; females cannot. The openness of Ableman's cultural misogyny is now unusual. Some of the underlying sentiments, I fear, are not. Old prejudices resurface as established truths. According to these stale preconceptions, a woman can't participate in the creative process without becoming unsexed. As Andrew Germant explains in *The Nature of Genius* (1961),

> . . . nearly always highly gifted women, approaching in some degree the nature of a genius, are masculine. In certain instances we have proof of that masculinity, as in George Sand. Eminent women scientists are nearly always plain or have definitely masculine features. They are actually half men, physically and mentally, their primary sexual organs happening to be female.[21]

This same author (a scientist) earnestly explains why men are more likely to be creative when in love and before "intimacy":

> With the chemistry of the matter partly well established, there is every evidence for a hormonal activity of the testes, a positive activation of the brain. This influence is general, found in every individual; in a genius, it is of greater importance, since the activity it promotes is at an incomparably higher level than in others.[22]

What is supposed to be common to all men and all "individuals" turns out to apply only to males. Women, obviously, can't be fully individual. Furthermore, women who approach genius also approach maleness. For Germant, George Sand typifies the great female writers (and scientists). She *almost* has genius; she *does* have male sex hormones—all she lacks is balls!

Mental energy is secreted by male glands. Consequently, Germant treats the sexuality of great male and female achievers in quite different ways. Although he describes intellectually talented women as "mascu-line," what he really means is that they are "pseudo-males": "Nature is playing here on borderline fields, producing unusual types, unusual in two ways."[23] Thus, it is an "abnormality" of *brain* and *body chemistry* that turns a woman into a great—probably homosexual—artist or scientist. By contrast, male homosexuality (usually so despised in our culture) is not viewed as "a pathological sex deviation"—and is even condoned—in the case of equivalent males:

> For a man of exceptional mental powers it may be that women are not adequate spiritual company. . . . [A] true genius may find it difficult to exchange his ideas with a woman and to receive the expected impetus for further work from a conver-sation with her. . . .

> There may be other causes. The Greek sculptors maintained that the male body was superior in beauty to the female. No wonder then that a genius in whom the mental concept of beauty dominates over the natural instincts is led to choose a partner of ideal beauty in preference to one of second rate.[24]

Germant's book—dedicated to his wife—was still in print as I started to write *Gender and Genius: Towards a Feminist Aesthetics*! In it we find many of the clichés of the most debased forms of Romanti-cism. "Hermaphrodite": a being with the sexual organs of *both* sexes. "Androgyne": a being with clearly defined sexual organs, but with *psychic* bisexuality. These two categories have been applied differently to women and men ever since the Romantics re-valued "feminine" characteristics of mind . . . and housed them in the bodies of *male* geniuses. Although a Renaissance woman was credited with a too way-ward and too fanciful imagination, it is Germant's *woman* who is un-able to cope with "anything fantastic and imaginary."[25] Germant's idealized woman—an "eminently practical" housewife and mother—contrasts markedly with the passive and narcissistic creature described by Ableman, but the rationale for excluding women from culture is exactly the same. Women, it seems, are involved in a primary way in the processes of reproduction; while the males' role is merely "second-ary." Women's "chief destination" is the "perpetuation of the human species," and that is why they have evolved as down-to-earth creatures with minds that tend "to the concrete, the easily visualizable."[26] "[T]he genius's pursuit is essentially 'idle,' hence the true woman, the true mother has a mentality incompatible with such kind of creative activity."[27]

Germant's use of George Sand to epitomize the problem of female genius—and to prove all talented women unnatural freaks—could (apart from the scientific jargon) have been written over a century before. As one of the critics writing in the *London Review* of 1864 put it:

> The greatest female author living is certainly George Sand. How much has George Sand given up to gain her literary crown. She has simply abandoned distinctive characteristics, not to say the distinctive mission, of her sex. She has gratified her genius by immolating to it her instincts and her nature.[28]

The more Sand's genius and art were admired, the more *male* she became:

> She is boyish, an artist, she is great-hearted, generous, devout, and *chaste;* she has the main characteristics of a man; *ergo* she is not a woman.[29]

Balzac's emphasis on Sand's chastity in this last sentence is unusual. In general, commentators magnified her one (unsubstantiated) lesbian relationship. They even used her sexual relationships with younger men to prove her own *male* lusts. For it was not just her sexual habits— not even her mannish garb—that proved her a man. It was her "genius." It was obviously this kind of logic that led Elizabeth Barrett Browning to write her sonnet "To George Sand: A Recognition" (1844). It opens with the words *"True genius, but true woman,"* and goes on to stress Sand's "woman's hair," which *"all unshorn/Floats back dishevelled strength in large flame."* Although Sand *"burnest in a poet-fire,"* her *"woman-heart beat evermore / Through the large flame."* Sand might have cut off her hair, and worn men's clothes. She might also (possibly) have been bisexual. But, as her English contemporary indicates, she is still a *woman* with *female* passions and sexual energies. To pretend otherwise is, as we will see, to recycle the mythology that was used to confine females within the domestic and reproductive space that men had marked out for them.

NOTES

1. Virginia Woolf, "Professions for Women," in *Women and Writing* (The Women's Press, 1979), 62.
2. Thomas Carlyle, *On Heroes and Hero-Worship* (The World Library, n.d. [1840]), 209.
3. Ibid., 58, 62.
4. Ibid., 106.
5. The description of Lord Byron is provided by Lady Caroline Lamb, the most notorious of his many mistresses. Byron (bisexual, promiscuous, and rich in vice) is the archetypal Romantic literary genius. But the archetype for the sciences is provided by the fictional Dr. Frankenstein. It is surely no accident that *Frankenstein* (1818) was dreamed up by Mary Shelley during months spent in Switzerland in 1816 with Byron, Claire Clairmont and Percy Bysshe Shelley—Mary Wolstonecraft Godwin's husband-to-be.
6. Anthony Burgess, "Grunts from a Sexist Pig," in *Homage to Quert Yuiop: Selected Journalism 1978–1985* (Abacus, Sphere 1987 [1986]), 1.
7. Ibid., 3.
8. Ibid., 7.
9. Ibid., 4.
10. Ibid., 4.
11. Ibid., 3–4.
12. As quoted in Carol Neuls-Bates, ed., *Women in Music: An Anthology of Source Readings from the Middle Ages to the Present* (Harper and Row, 1982), 280.
13. Paul Ableman, *The Doomed Rebellion* (Zomba, Bee in Bonnet Book, 1983), 61.
14. Ibid., 59.
15. Ibid., 59–60.
16. Ibid., 42.
17. Ibid., 19.
18. Ibid., 23, 19.
19. Ibid., 31.
20. Ibid., 21.
21. Andrew Germant, *The Nature of Genius* (Charles C. Thomas, 1961), 114–15.
22. Ibid., 87.
23. Ibid., 115.
24. Ibid., 90–91.
25. Ibid., 113.
26. Ibid., 113.
27. Ibid., 113–14.
28. Elizaberg K. Helsinger with R. L. Sheets and W. Veeder, eds., *The Woman Question: Literary Issues*, Volume III of *The Woman Question: Society and Literature in Britain and America* (Manchester University Press, 1983), 21.
29. Honoré de Balzac as quoted in Joseph Barry, ed., *George Sand in Her Own Words* (Anchor, 1979), xv.

Why Have There Been No Great Women Artists?

LINDA NOCHLIN

While the recent upsurge of feminist activity in this country has indeed been a liberating one, its force has been chiefly emotional—personal, psychological, and subjective—centered, like the other radical movements to which it is related, on the present and its immediate needs, rather than on historical analysis of the basic intellectual issues which the feminist attack on the status quo automatically raises.[1]

Like any revolution, however, the feminist one ultimately must come to grips with the intellectual and ideological basis of the various intellectual or scholarly disciplines—history, philosophy, sociology, psychology, etc.—in the same way that it questions the ideologies of present social institutions. If, as John Stuart Mill suggested, we tend to accept whatever *is* as natural, this is just as true in the realm of academic investigation as it is in our social arrangements. In the former, too, "natural" assumptions must be questioned and the mythic basis of much so-called fact brought to light. And it is here that the very position of woman as an acknowledged outsider, the maverick "she" instead of the presumably neutral "one"—in reality the white-male-position-accepted-as-natural, or the hidden "he" as the subject of all scholarly predicates—is a decided advantage, rather than merely a hindrance or a subjective distortion.

In the field of art history, the white Western male viewpoint, unconsciously accepted as *the* viewpoint of the art historian, may—and does—prove to be inadequate not merely on moral and ethical grounds, or because it is elitist, but on purely intellectual ones. In revealing the failure of much academic art history, and a great deal of history in general, to take account of the unacknowledged value system, the very *presence* of an intruding subject in historical investigation, the feminist critique at the same time lays bare its conceptual smugness, its meta-historical naïveté. At a moment when all disciplines are becoming more self-conscious, more aware of the nature of their presuppositions as exhibited in the very languages and structures of the various fields of scholarship, such uncritical acceptance of "what is" as "natural" may be intellectually fatal. Just as Mill saw male domination as one of a long series of social injustices that had to be overcome if a truly just social order were to be created, so we may see the unstated domination of white male subjectivity as one in a series of intellectual distortions which must be corrected in order to achieve a more adequate and accurate view of historical situations.

It is the engaged feminist intellect (like John Stuart Mill's) that can pierce through the cultural-ideological limitations of the time and its specific "professionalism" to reveal biases and inadequacies not merely in dealing with the question of women, but in the very way of formulating the crucial questions of the discipline as a whole. Thus, the so-called woman question, far from being a minor, peripheral, and laughably provincial sub-issue grafted on to a serious, established discipline, can become a catalyst, an intellectual instrument, probing basic and "natural" assumptions, providing a paradigm for other kinds of internal questioning, and in turn providing links with paradigms established by radical approaches in other fields. Even a simple question like "Why have there been no great women artists?" can, if answered adequately, create a sort of chain reaction, expanding not merely to encompass the accepted assumptions of the single field, but outward to embrace history and the social sciences, or even psychology and literature, and thereby, from the outset, can challenge the assumption that the traditional divisions of intellectual inquiry are still adequate to deal with the meaningful questions of our time, rather than the merely convenient or self-generated ones.

Let us, for example, examine the implications of that perennial question (one can, of course, substitute almost any field of human endeavor, with appropriate changes in phrasing): "Well, if women really *are* equal to men, why have there never been any great women artists (or composers, or mathematicians, or philosophers, or so few of the same)?"

"Why have there been no great women artists?" The question tolls reproachfully in the background of most discussions of the so-called woman problem. But like so many other so-called questions involved in the feminist "controversy," it falsifies the nature of the issue at the same time that it insidiously supplies its own answer: "There have no great women artists because women are incapable of greatness."

The assumptions behind such a question are varied in range and sophistication, running anywhere from "scientifically proven" demonstrations of the inability of human beings with wombs rather than penises to create anything significant, to relatively open-minded wonderment that women, despite so many years of near-equality—and after all, a lot of men have had their disadvantages too—have still not achieved anything of exceptional significance in the visual arts.

The feminist's first reaction is to swallow the bait, hook, line and sinker, and to attempt to answer the question as it is put: that is, to dig up examples of worthy or insufficiently appreciated women artists throughout history; to rehabilitate rather modest, if interesting and productive careers; to "rediscover" forgotten flower painters or David followers and make out a case for them; to demonstrate that Berthe Morisot was really less dependent upon Manet than one had been led to think—in other words, to engage in the normal activity of the specialist scholar who makes a case for the importance of his very own neglected or minor master. Such attempts, whether undertaken from a feminist point of view, like the ambitious article on women artists which appeared in the 1858 *Westminster Review*,[2] or more recent scholarly studies on such artists as Angelica Kauffmann and Artemisia Gentileschi,[3] are certainly worth the effort, both in adding to our knowledge of women's achievement and of art history generally. But they do nothing to question the assumptions lying behind the question "Why have there been no great women artists?" On the contrary, by attempting to answer it, they tacitly reinforce its negative implications.

Another attempt to answer the question involves shifting the ground slightly and asserting, as some contemporary feminists do, that there is a different kind of "greatness" for women's art than for men's, thereby postulating the existence of a distinctive and recognizable feminine style, different both in its formal and its expressive qualities and based on the special character of women's situation and experience.

This, on the surface of it, seems reasonable enough: in general, women's experience and situation in society, and hence as artists, is different from men's, and certainly the art produced by a group of consciously united and purposefully articulate women intent on bodying forth a group consciousness of feminine experience might indeed be stylistically identifiable as feminist, if not feminine, art. Unfortunately, though this remains within the realm of possibility it has so far not occurred. While the members of the Danube School, the followers of Caravaggio, the painters gathered around Gauguin at Pont-Aven, the Blue Rider, or the Cubists may be recognized by certain clearly defined stylistic or expressive qualities, no such common qualities of "femininity" would seem to link the styles of women artists generally, any more than such qualities can be said to link women writers, a case brilliantly argued, against the most devastating, and mutually contradictory, masculine critical clichés, by Mary Ellmann in her *Thinking About Women*.[4] No subtle essence of femininity would seem to link the work of Artemisia Gentileschi, Mme. Vigée-Lebrun, Angelica Kauffmann, Rosa Bonheur, Berthe Morisot, Suzanne Valadon, Käthe Kollwitz, Barbara Hepworth, Georgia O'Keeffe, Sophie Taeuber-Arp, Helen Frankenthaler, Bridget Riley, Lee Bontecou, or Louise Nevelson, any more than that of Sappho, Marie de France, Jane Austen, Emily Brontë, George Sand, George Eliot, Virginia Woolf, Gertrude Stein, Anaïs Nin, Emily Dickinson, Sylvia Plath, and Susan Sontag. In every instance, women artists and writers would seem to be closer to other artists and writers of their own period and outlook than they are to each other.

Women artists are more inward-looking, more delicate and nuanced in their treatment of their medium, it may be asserted. But which of the women artists cited above is more inward-turning then Redon, more subtle and nuanced in the handling of pigment than Corot? Is Fragonard more or less feminine than Mme. Vigée-Lebrun? Or is it not more a question of the whole Rococo style of eighteenth-century France being "feminine," if judged in terms of a binary scale of "masculinity" versus "femininity"? Certainly, if daintiness, delicacy, and preciousness are to be counted as earmarks of a feminine style, there is nothing fragile about Rosa Bonheur's *Horse Fair*, nor dainty and introverted about Helen Frankenthaler's giant canvases. If women have turned to scenes of domestic life, or of children, so did Jan Steen, Chardin, and the Impressionists—Renoir and Monet as well as Morisot and Cassatt. In any case, the mere choice of a certain realm of subject matter, or the restriction to certain subjects, is not to be equated with a style, much less with some sort of quintessentially feminine style.

The problem lies not so much with some feminists' concept of what femininity is, but rather with their misconception—shared with the public at large—of what art is: with the naive idea that art is direct, personal expression of individual emotional experience, a translation of personal life into visual terms. Art is almost never that, great art never is. The making of art involves a self-consistent language of form, more or less dependent upon, or free from, given temporally defined conventions, schemata, or systems of notation, which have to be learned or worked out, either through teaching, apprenticeship, or a long period of individual experimentation. The language of art is, more materially, embodied in paint and line on canvas or paper, in stone or clay or plastic or metal—it is neither a sob story nor a confidential whisper.

The fact of the matter is that there have been no supremely great women artists, as far as we know, although there have been many interesting and very good ones, who remain insufficiently investigated or appreciated; nor have there been any great Lithuanian jazz pianists, nor Eskimo tennis players, no matter how much we might wish there had been. That this should be the case is regrettable, but no amount of manipulating the historical or critical evidence will alter the situation; nor will accusations of male-chauvinist distortion of history. There *are* no women equivalents for Michelangelo or Rembrandt, Delacroix or Cézanne, Picasso or Matisse, or even, in very recent times, for de Kooning or Warhol, any more than there are black American equivalents for the same. If there actually were large numbers of "hidden" great women artists, or if there really should be different standards for women's art as opposed to men's—and one can't have it both ways—then what are feminists fighting for? If women have in fact achieved the same status as men in the arts, then the status quo is fine as it is.

But in actuality, as we all know, things as they are and as they have been, in the arts as in a hundred other areas, are stultifying, oppressive, and discouraging to all those, women among them, who did not have the good fortune to be born white, preferably middle class and, above all, male. The fault lies not in our stars, our hormones, our menstrual cycles, or our empty internal spaces, but in our institutions and our education—education understood to include everything that happens to us from the moment we enter this world of meaningful symbols, signs, and signals. The miracle is, in fact, that given the overwhelming odds against women, or blacks, that so many of both have managed to achieve so much sheer excellence, in those bailiwicks of white masculine prerogative like science, politics, or the arts.

It is when one really starts thinking about the implications of "Why have there been no great women artists?" that one begins to realize to what extent our consciousness of how things are in the world has been conditioned—and often falsified—by the way the most important questions are posed. We tend to take it for granted that there really is an East Asian Problem, a Poverty Problem, a Black Problem—and a Woman Problem. But first we must ask ourselves who is formulating these "questions," and then, what purposes such formulations may serve. (We may, of course, refresh our memories with the connotations of the Nazis' "Jewish Problem.") Indeed, in our time of instant communication, "problems" are rapidly formulated to rationalize the bad conscience of those with power: thus, the problem posed by Americans in Vietnam and Cambodia is referred to by Americans as the "East Asian Problem," whereas East Asians may view it, more realistically, as the "American Problem"; the so-called Poverty Problem might more directly be viewed as the "Wealth Problem" by denizens of urban ghettos or rural wastelands; the same irony twists the White Problem into its opposite, a Black Problem; and the same inverse logic turns up in the formulation of our present state of affairs as the "Woman Problem."

Now, the "Woman Problem," like all human problems, so-called (and the very idea of calling anything to do with human beings a "problem" is, of course, a fairly recent one), is not amenable to "solution" at all, since what human problems involve is reinterpretation of the nature of the situation, or a radical alteration of stance or program *on the part of the "problems" themselves.* Thus, women and their situation in the arts, as in other realms of endeavor, are not a "problem" to be viewed through the eyes of the dominant male power elite. Instead, *women* must conceive of themselves as potentially, if not actually, equal subjects, and must be willing to look the facts of their situation full in the face, without self-pity, or cop-outs; at the same time they must view their situation with that high degree of emotional and intellectual commitment necessary to create a world in which equal achievement will be not only made possible but actively encouraged by social institutions.

It is certainly not realistic to hope that a majority of men, in the arts or in any other field, will soon see the light and find that it is in their own self-interest to grant complete equality to women, as some feminists optimistically assert, or to maintain that men themselves will soon realize that they are diminished by denying themselves access to traditionally "feminine" realms and emotional reactions. After all, there are few areas that are really "denied" to men, if the level of operations demanded be transcendent, responsible, or rewarding enough: men who have a need for "feminine" involvement with babies or children gain status as pediatricians or child psychologists, with a nurse (female) to do the more routine work; those who feel the urge for kitchen creativity may gain fame as master chefs; and of course, men who yearn to fulfill themselves through what are often termed "feminine" artistic interests can find themselves as painters or sculptors, rather than as volunteer museum aides or part-time ceramists, as their female counterparts so often end up doing; as far as scholarship is concerned, how many men would be willing to change their jobs as teachers and researchers for those of unpaid, part-time research assistants and typists as well as full-time nannies and domestic workers?

Those who have privileges inevitably hold on to them, and hold tight, no matter how marginal the advantage involved, until compelled to bow to superior power of one sort or another.

Thus, the question of women's equality—in art as in any other realm—devolves not upon the relative benevolence or ill-will of individual men, nor the self-confidence or abjectness of individual women, but rather on the very nature of our institutional structures themselves and the view of reality which they impose on the human beings who are part of them. As John Stuart Mill pointed out more than a century ago: "Everything which is usual appears natural. The subjection of women to men being a universal custom, any departure from it quite naturally appears unnatural."[5] Most men, despite lip service to equality, are reluctant to give up this "natural" order of things in which their advantages are so great; for women, the case is further complicated by the fact that, as Mill astutely pointed out, unlike any other oppressed groups or castes, men demand of them not only submission but unqualified affection as well; thus, women are often weakened by the internalized demands of the male-dominated society itself, as well as by a plethora of material goods and comforts: the middle-class woman has a great deal more to lose than her chains.

The question "Why have there been no great women artists?" is simply the top tenth of an iceberg of misinterpretation and misconception; beneath lies a vast dark bulk of shaky *idées reçues* about the nature of art and its situational concomitants, about the nature of human abilities in general and of human excellence in particular, and the role that the social order plays in all of this. While the "woman problem" as such may be a pseudo-issue, the misconceptions involved in the question "Why have there been no great women artists?" points to major areas of intellectual obfuscation beyond the specific political and ideological issues involved in the subjection of women. Basic to the question are many naive, distorted, uncritical assumptions about the making of art in general, as well as the making of great art. These assumptions, conscious or unconscious, link such unlikely superstars as Michelangelo and van Gogh, Raphael and Jackson Pollock under the rubric of "Great"—an honorific attested to by the number of scholarly monographs devoted to the artist in question—and the Great Artist is, of course, conceived of as one who has "Genius"; Genius, in turn, is thought of as an atemporal and mysterious power somehow embedded in the person of the Great Artist.[6] Such ideas are related to unquestioned, often unconscious, meta-historical premises that make Hippolyte Taine's race-milieu-moment formulation of the dimensions of historical thought seem a model of sophistication. But these assumptions are intrinsic to a great deal of art-historical writing. It is no accident that the crucial question of the conditions *generally* productive of great art has so rarely been investigated, or that attempts to investigate such general problems have, until fairly recently, been dismissed as unscholarly, too broad, or the province of some other discipline, like sociology. To encourage a dispassionate, impersonal, sociological, and institutionally oriented approach would reveal the entire romantic, elitist, individual-glorifying, and monograph-producing substructure upon which the profession of art history is based, and which has only recently been called into question by a group of younger dissidents.

Underlying the question about woman as artist, then, we find the myth of the Great Artist—subject of a hundred monographs, unique, godlike—bearing within his person since birth a mysterious essence, rather like the golden nugget in Mrs. Grass's chicken soup, called Genius or Talent, which, like murder, must always out, no matter how unlikely or unpromising the circumstances.

The magical aura surrounding the representational arts and their creators has, of course, given birth to myths since the earliest times. Interestingly enough, the same magical abilities attributed by Pliny to the Greek sculptor Lysippos in antiquity—the mysterious inner call in early youth, the lack of any teacher but Nature herself—is repeated as late as the 19th century by Max Buchon in his biography of Courbet. The supernatural powers of the artist as imitator, his control of strong, possibly dangerous powers, have functioned historically to set him off from others as a godlike creator, one who creates Being out of nothing. The fairy tale of the discovery by an older artist or discerning patron of the Boy Wonder, usually in the guise of a lowly shepherd boy, has been stock-in-trade of artistic mythology ever since Vasari immortalized the young Giotto, discovered by the great Cimabue while the lad was guarding his flocks, drawing sheep on a stone; Cimabue, overcome with admiration for the realism of the drawing, immediately invited the humble youth to be his pupil.[7] Through some mysterious coincidence, later artists including Beccafumi, Andrea Sansovino, Andrea del Castagno, Mantegna, Zurbarán, and Goya were all discovered in similar pastoral circumstances. Even when the young Great Artist was not fortunate enough to come equipped with a flock of sheep, his talent always seems to have manifested itself very early, and independent of any external encouragement: Filippo Lippi and Poussin, Courbet and Monet are all reported to have drawn caricatures in the margins of their schoolbooks instead of studying the required subjects—we never, of course, hear about the youths who neglected their studies and scribbled in the margins of their notebooks without ever becoming anything more elevated than department-store clerks or shoe salesmen. The great Michelangelo himself, according to his biographer and pupil, Vasari, did more drawing than studying as a child. So pronounced was his talent, reports Vasari, that when his master, Ghirlandaio, absented himself momentarily from his work in Santa Maria Novella, and the young art student took the opportunity to draw "the scaffolding, trestles, pots of paint, brushes and the apprentices at their tasks" in this brief absence, he did it so skillfully that upon his return the master exclaimed: "This boy knows more than I do."

As is so often the case, such stories, which probably have some truth in them, tend both to reflect and perpetuate the attitudes they subsume. Even when based on fact, these myths about the early manifestations of genius are misleading. It is no doubt true, for example, that the young Picasso passed all the examinations for entrance to the Barcelona, and later to the Madrid, Academy of Art at the age of fifteen in but a single day, a feat of such difficulty that most candidates required a month of preparation. But one would like to find out more about similar precocious qualifiers for art academies who then went on to achieve nothing but mediocrity or failure—in whom, of course, art historians are uninterested—or to study in greater detail the role played by Picasso's art professor father in the pictorial precocity of his son.

What if Picasso had been born a girl? Would Señor Ruiz have paid as much attention or stimulated as much ambition for achievement in a little Pablita?

What is stressed in all these stories is the apparently miraculous, nondetermined, and asocial nature of artistic achievement; this semi-religious conception of the artist's role is elevated to hagiography in the 19th century, when art historians, critics, and, not least, some of the artists themselves tended to elevate the making of art into a substitute religion, the last bulwark of higher values in a materialistic world. The artist, in the 19th-century Saints' Legend, struggles against the most determined parental and social opposition, suffering the slings and arrows of social opprobrium like any Christian martyr, and ultimately succeeds against all odds—generally, alas, after his death—because from deep within himself radiates that mysterious, holy effulgence: Genius. Here we have the mad van Gogh, spinning out sunflowers despite epileptic seizures and near-starvation; Cézanne, braving paternal rejection and public scorn in order to revolutionize painting; Gauguin, throwing away respectability and financial security with a single existential gesture to pursue his calling in the tropics; or Toulouse-Lautrec, dwarfed, crippled, and alcoholic, sacrificing his aristocratic birthright in favor of the squalid surroundings that provided him with inspiration.

Now, no serious contemporary art historian takes such obvious fairy tales at their face value. Yet it is this sort of mythology about artistic achievement and its concomitants which forms the unconscious or unquestioned assumptions of scholars, no matter how many crumbs are thrown to social influences, ideas of the times, economic crises, and so on. Behind the most sophisticated investigations of great artists—more specifically, the art-historical monograph, which accepts the notion of the great artist as primary, and the social and institutional structures within which he lived and worked as mere secondary "influences" or "background"—lurks the golden-nugget theory of genius and the free-enterprise conception of individual achievement. On this basis, women's lack of major achievement in art may be formulated as a syllogism: If women had the golden nugget of artistic genius, then it would reveal itself. But it has never revealed itself. Q.E.D. Women do not have the golden nugget of artistic genius. If Giotto, the obscure shepherd boy, and van Gogh with his fits could make it, why not women?

Yet as soon as one leaves behind the world of fairy tale and self-fulfilling prophecy and, instead, casts a dispassionate eye on the actual situations in which important art production has existed, in the total range of its social and institutional structures throughout history, one finds that the very questions which are fruitful or relevant for the historian to ask shape up rather differently. One would like to ask, for instance, from what social classes artists were most likely to come at different periods of art history, from what castes and subgroup. What proportion of painters and sculptors, or more specifically, of major painters and sculptors, came from families in which their fathers or other close relatives were painters and sculptors or engaged in related professions? As Nikolaus Pevsner points out in his discussion of the French Academy in the 17th and 18th centuries, the transmission of the artistic profession from father to son was considered a matter of course (as it was with the Coypels, the Coustous, the Van Loos, etc.); indeed, sons of academicians were exempted from the customary fees for lessons.[8] Despite the noteworthy and dramatically satisfying cases of the great father-rejecting *révoltés* of the 19th century, one might be forced to admit that a large proportion of artists, great and not-so-great, in the days when it was normal for sons to follow in their fathers' footsteps, had artist fathers. In the rank of major artists, the names of Holbein and Dürer, Raphael and Bernini, immediately spring to mind; even in our own times, one can cite the names of Picasso, Calder, Giacometti, and Wyeth as members of artist-families.

As far as the relationship of artistic occupation and social class is concerned, an interesting paradigm for the question "Why have there been no great women artists?" might well be provided by trying to answer the question "Why have there been no great artists from the aristocracy?" One can scarcely think, before the antitraditional 19th century at least, of any artist who sprang from the ranks of any more elevated class than the upper bourgeoisie; even in the 19th century, Degas came from the lower nobility—more like the haute bourgeoisie, in fact—and only Toulouse-Lautrec, metamorphosed into the ranks of the marginal by accidental deformity, could be said to have come from the loftier reaches of the upper classes. While the aristocracy has always provided the lion's share of the patronage and the audience for art—as, indeed, the aristocracy of wealth does even in our own more democratic days—it has contributed little beyond amateurish efforts to the creation of art itself, despite the fact that aristocrats (like many women) have had more than their share of educational advantages, plenty of leisure and, indeed, like women, were often encouraged to dabble in the arts and even develop into respectable amateurs, like Napoleon III's cousin the Princess Mathilde, who exhibited at the official Salons, or Queen Victoria, who, with Prince Albert, studied art with no less a figure than Landseer himself. Could it be that the little golden nugget—genius—is missing from the aristocratic makeup in the same way that it is from the feminine psyche? Or rather, is it not that the kinds of demands and expectations placed before both aristocrats and women—the amount of time necessarily devoted to social functions, the very kinds of activities demanded—simply made total devotion to professional art production out of the question, indeed unthinkable, both for upper-class males and for women generally, rather than its being a question of genius and talent?

When the right questions are asked about the conditions for producing art, of which the production of great art is a subtopic, there will no doubt have to be some discussion of the situational concomitants of intelligence and talent generally, not merely of artistic genius. Piaget and others have stressed in their genetic epistemology that in the development of reason and in the unfolding of imagination in young children, intelligence—or, by implication, what we choose to call genius—is a dynamic activity rather than a static essence, and an activity of a subject *in a situation*. As further investigations in the field of child development imply, these abilities, or this intelligence, are built up minutely, step by step, from infancy onward, and the patterns of adaptation-accommodation may be established so early within the subject-in-an-environment that they may indeed *appear* to be innate to the unsophisticated observer. Such investigations imply that, even aside from meta-historical reasons, scholars will have to abandon the notion, consciously articulated or not, of individual genius as innate, and as primary to the creation of art.[9]

The question "Why have there been no great women artists?" has led us to the conclusion, so far, that art is not a free, autonomous activity of a super-endowed individual, "influenced" by previous artists, and more vaguely and superficially, by "social forces," but, rather, that the total situation of art making, both in terms of the development of the art maker and in the nature and quality of the work of art itself, occur in a social situation, are integral elements of this social structure, and are mediated and determined by specific and definable social institutions, be they art academies, systems of patronage, mythologies of the divine creator, artist as he-man or social outcast.

The Question of the Nude

We can now approach our question from a more reasonable standpoint, since it seems probable that the answer to why there have been no great women artists lies not in the nature of individual genius or the lack of it, but in the nature of given social institutions and what they forbid or encourage in various classes or groups of individuals. Let us first examine such a simple, but critical, issue as availability of the nude model to aspiring women artists, in the period extending from the Renaissance until near the end of the 19th century, a period in which careful and prolonged study of the nude model was essential to the training of every young artist, to the production of any work with pretentions to grandeur, and to the very essence of History Painting, generally accepted as the highest category of art. Indeed, it was argued by defenders of traditional painting in the 19th century that there could be no great painting *with* clothed figures, since costume inevitably destroyed both the temporal universality and the classical idealization required by great art. Needless to say, central to the training programs of the academies since their inception late in the 16th and early in the 17th centuries, was life drawing from the nude, generally male, model. In addition, groups of artists and their pupils often met privately for life drawing sessions from the nude model in their studios. While individual artists and private academies employed the female model extensively, the female nude was forbidden in almost all public art schools as late as 1850 and after—a state of affairs which Pevsner rightly designates as "hardly believable."[10] Far more believable, unfortunately, was the complete unavailability to the aspiring woman artist of *any* nude models at all, male or female. As late as 1893, "lady" students were not admitted to life drawing at the Royal Academy in London, and even when they were, after that date, the model had to be "partially draped."[11]

A brief survey of representations of life-drawing sessions reveals: an all-male clientele drawing from the female nude in Rembrandt's studio; men working from male nudes in 18th-century representations of academic instruction in The Hague and Vienna; men working from the seated male nude in Boilly's charming painting of the interior of Houdon's studio at the beginning of the 19th century. Léon-Mathieu Cochereau's scrupulously veristic *Interior of David's Studio*, exhibited in the Salon of 1814, reveals a group of young men diligently drawing or painting from a male nude model, whose discarded shoes may be seen before the models' stand.

The very plethora of surviving "Academies"—detailed, painstaking studies from the nude male studio model—in the youthful oeuvre of artists down through the time of Seurat and well into the 20th century, attests to the central importance of this branch of study in the pedagogy and development of the talented beginner. The formal academic program itself normally proceeded, as a matter of course, from copying from drawings and engravings, to drawing from casts of famous works of sculpture, to drawing from the living model. To be deprived of this ultimate stage of training meant, in effect, to be deprived of the possibility of creating major art works, unless one were a very ingenious lady indeed, or simply, as most of the women aspiring to be painters ultimately did, restricting oneself to the "minor" fields of portraiture, genre, landscape, or still life. It is rather as though a medical student were denied the opportunity to dissect or even examine the naked human body.

There exist, to my knowledge, no historical representations of artists drawing from the nude model which include women in any role but that of the nude model itself, an interesting commentary on rules of propriety: that is, it is all right for a ("low," of course) woman to reveal herself naked-as-an-object for a group of men, but forbidden to a woman to participate in the active study and recording of naked-man-as-an-object or even of a fellow woman. An amusing example of this taboo on confronting a dressed lady with a naked man is embodied in a group portrait of the members of the Royal Academy of London in 1772, represented by Johan Zoffany as gathered in the life room before two nude male models; all the distinguished members are present with but one noteworthy exception—the single female member, the renowned Angelica Kauffmann, who, for propriety's sake, is merely present in effigy, in the form of a portrait hanging on the wall. A slightly earlier drawing, *Ladies in the Studio* by the Polish artist Daniel Chodowiecki, shows the ladies portraying a modestly dressed member of their sex. In a lithograph dating from the relatively liberated epoch following the French Revolution, the lithographer Marlet has represented some women sketchers in a group of students working from the male model, but the model himself has been chastely provided with what appears to be a pair of bathing trunks, a garment hardly conducive to a sense of classical elevation; no doubt such license was considered daring in its day, and the young ladies in question suspected of doubtful morals, but even this liberated state of affairs seems to have lasted only a short while. In an English stereoscopic color view of the interior of a studio of about 1865, the standing, bearded male model is so heavily draped that not an iota of his anatomy escapes from the discreet toga, save for a single bare shoulder and arm: even so, he obviously had the grace to avert his eyes in the presence of the crinoline-clad young sketchers.

The women in the Women's Modeling Class at the Pennsylvania Academy were evidently not allowed even this modest privilege. A photograph by Thomas Eakins of about 1885 reveals these students modeling from a cow (bull? ox? the nether regions are obscure in the photograph), a naked cow to be sure, perhaps a daring liberty when one considers that even piano legs might be concealed beneath panta-lettes during this era. (The idea of introducing a bovine model into the artist's studio stems from Courbet, who brought a bull into his short-lived studio academy in the 1860s). Only at the very end of the 19th century, in the relatively liberated and open atmosphere of Repin's studio and circle in Russia, do we find representations of women art students working uninhibitedly from the nude—the female model, to be sure—in the company of men. Even in this case, it must be noted that certain photographs represent a private sketch group meeting in one of the women artists' homes; in another, the model is draped; and the large group portrait, a cooperative effort by two men and two women students of Repin's, is an imaginary gathering together of all of the Russian realist's pupils, past and present, rather than a realistic studio view.

I have gone into the question of the availability of the nude model, a single aspect of the automatic, institutionally maintained discrimina-tion against women, in such detail simply to demonstrate both the universality of this discrimination and its consequences, as well as the institutional rather than individual nature of but one facet of the neces-sary preparation for achieving mere proficiency, much less greatness, in the realm of art during a long period. One could equally well exam-ine other dimensions of the situation, such as the apprenticeship sys-tem, the academic educational pattern which, in France especially, was almost the only key to success and which had a regular progression and set competitions, crowned by the Prix de Rome which enabled the young winner to work in the French Academy in that city—un-thinkable for women, of course—and for which women were unable to compete until the end of the 19th century, by which time, in fact, the whole academic system had lost its importance anyway. It seems clear, to take France in the 19th century as an example (a country which probably had a larger proportion of women artists than any other—that is to say, in terms of their percentage in the total number of artists exhibiting in the Salon), that "women were not accepted as professional painters."[12] In the middle of the century, there were only a third as many women as men artists, but even this mildly encouraging statistic is deceptive when we discover that out of this relatively meager number, *none* had attended that major stepping-stone to artistic success, the École des Beaux-Arts, only 7 percent had ever received any official commission or had held any official office—and these might include the most menial sort of work—only 7 percent had ever received any Salon medal, and *none* had ever received the Legion of Honor.[13] Deprived of encouragements, educational facilities, and rewards, it is almost incredible that a certain percentage of women did persevere and seek a profession in the arts.

It also becomes apparent why women were able to compete on far more equal terms with men—and even become innovators—in literature. While art making traditionally has demanded the learning of specific techniques and skills, in a certain sequence, in an institutional setting outside the home, as well as becoming familiar with a specific vocabulary of iconography and motifs, the same is by no means true for the poet or novelist. Anyone, even a woman, has to learn the language, can learn to read and write, and can commit personal experiences to paper in the privacy of one's room. Naturally this oversimplifies the real difficulties and complexities involved in creating good or great literature, whether by man or woman, but it still gives a clue as to the possibility of the existence of an Emily Brontë or an Emily Dickinson and the lack of their counterparts, at least until quite recently, in the visual arts.

Of course we have not gone into the "fringe" requirements for major artists, which would have been, for the most part, both psychically and socially closed to women, even if hypothetically they could have achieved the requisite grandeur in the performance of their craft: in the Renaissance and after, the great artist, aside from participating in the affairs of an academy, might well be intimate with members of humanist circles with whom he could exchange ideas, establish suitable relationships with patrons, travel widely and freely, perhaps politic and intrigue; nor have we mentioned the sheer organizational acumen and ability involved in running a major studio-factory, like that of Rubens.

An enormous amount of self-confidence and worldly knowledgeability, as well as a natural sense of well-earned dominance and power, was needed by the great *chef d'école*, both in the running of the production end of painting, and in the control and instruction of the numerous students and assistants.

The Lady's Accomplishment

In contrast to the single-mindedness and commitment demanded of a *chef d'école*, we might set the image of the "lady painter" established by 19th-century etiquette books and reinforced by the literature of the times. It is precisely the insistence upon a modest, proficient, self-demeaning level of amateurism as a "suitable accomplishment" for the well-brought-up young woman, who naturally would want to direct her major attention to the welfare of others—family and husband—that militated, and still militates, against any real accomplishment on the part of women. It is this emphasis which transforms serious commitment to frivolous self-indulgence, busy work, or occupational therapy, and today, more than ever, in suburban bastions of the feminine mystique, tends to distort the whole notion of what art is and what kind of social role it plays. In Mrs. Ellis's widely read *The Family Monitor and Domestic Guide*, published before the middle of the 19th century, a book of advice popular both in the United States and in England, women were warned against the snare of trying too hard to excel in any one thing:

> It must not be supposed that the writer is one who would advocate, as essential to woman, any very extraordinary degree of intellectual attainment, especially if confined to one particular branch of study. "I should like to excel in something" is a frequent and, to some extent, laudable expression; but in what does it originate, and to what does it tend? To be able to do a great many things tolerably well, is of infinitely more value to a woman, than to be able to excel in any one. By the former, she may render herself generally useful; by the latter, she may dazzle for an hour. By being apt, and tolerably well skilled in everything, she may fall into any situation in life with dignity and ease—by devoting her time to excellence in one, she may remain incapable of every other.

So far as cleverness, learning, and knowledge are conducive to woman's moral excellence, they are therefore desirable, and no further. All that would occupy her mind to the exclusion of better things, all that would involve her in the mazes of flattery and admiration, all that would tend to draw away her thoughts from others and fix them on herself, ought to be avoided as an evil to her, however brilliant or attractive it may be in itself.[14]

Lest we are tempted to laugh, we may refresh ourselves with more recent samples of exactly the same message cited in Betty Friedan's *Feminine Mystique*, or in the pages of recent issues of popular women's magazines.

The advice has a familiar ring: propped up by a bit of Freudianism and some tag-lines from the social sciences about the well-rounded personality, preparation for woman's chief career, marriage, and the unfemininity of deep involvement with work rather than sex, it is still the mainstay of the Feminine Mystique. Such an outlook helps guard men from unwanted competition in their "serious" professional activities and assures them of "well-rounded" assistance on the home front, so that they can have sex and family in addition to the fulfillment of their own specialized talents at the same time.

As far as painting specifically is concerned, Mrs. Ellis finds that it has one immediate advantage for the young lady over its rival branch of artistic activity, music—it is quiet and disturbs no one (this negative virtue, of course, would not be true of sculpture, but accomplishment with the hammer and chisel simply never occurs as a suitable accomplishment for the weaker sex); in addition, says Mrs. Ellis, "it [drawing] is an employment which beguiles the mind of many cares. . . . Drawing is, of all other occupations, the one most calculated to keep the mind from brooding upon self, and to maintain that general cheerfulness which is a part of social and domestic duty. . . . It can also," she adds, "be laid down and resumed, as circumstance or inclination may direct, and that without any serious loss."[15] Again, lest we feel that we have made a great deal of progress in this area in the past one hundred years, I might bring up the remark of a bright young doctor who, when the conversation turned to his wife and her friends "dabbling" in the arts, snorted: "Well, at least it keeps them out of trouble!" Now as in the 19th century, amateurism and lack of real commitment, as well as snobbery and emphasis on chic on the part of women, in their artistic "hobbies" feeds the contempt of the successful, professionally committed man, who is engaged in "real" work and can, with a certain justice, point to his wife's lack of seriousness in her artistic activities. For such men, the "real" work of women is only that which directly or indirectly serves the family; any other commitment falls under the rubric of diversion, selfishness, egomania, or, at the unspoken extreme, castration. The circle is a vicious one, in which philistinism and frivolity mutually reenforce each other.

In literature, as in life, even if the woman's commitment to art was a serious one, she was expected to drop her career and give up this commitment at the behest of love and marriage: this lesson is, today as in the 19th century, still inculcated in young girls, directly or indirectly, from the moment they are born. Even the determined and successful heroine of Mrs. Craik's mid-19th-century novel about feminine artistic success, *Olive*, a young woman who lives alone, strives for fame and independence, and actually supports herself through her art—such unfeminine behavior is at least partly excused by the fact that she is a cripple and automatically considers that marriage is denied to her—even Olive ultimately succumbs to the blandishments of love and marriage. To paraphrase the words of Patricia Thomson in *The Victorian Heroine*, Mrs. Craik, having shot her bolt in the course of her novel, is content, finally, to let her heroine, whose ultimate greatness the reader has never been able to doubt, sink gently into matrimony. "Of Olive, Mrs. Craik comments imperturbably that her husband's influence is to deprive the Scottish Academy of 'no one knew how many grand pictures.'"[16] Then as now, despite men's greater "tolerance," the choice for women seems always to be marriage *or* a career, i.e., solitude as the price of success *or* sex and companionship at the price of personal renunciation.

That achievement in the arts, as in any field of endeavor, demands struggle and sacrifice is undeniable; that this has certainly been true after the middle of the nineteenth century, when the traditional institutions of artistic support and patronage no longer fulfilled their customary obligations, is also undeniable. One has only to think of Delacroix, Courbet, Degas, van Gogh, and Toulouse-Lautrec as examples of great artists who gave up the distractions and obligations of family life, at least in part, so that they could pursue their artistic careers more single-mindedly. Yet none of them was automatically denied the pleasure of sex or companionship on account of this choice. Nor did they ever conceive that they had sacrificed their manhood or their sexual role on account of their single-mindedness in achieving professional fulfill-ment. But if the artist in question happened to be a woman, one thou-sand years of guilt, self-doubt, and objecthood would have been added to the undeniable difficulties of being an artist in the modern world.

The unconscious aura of titillation that arises from a visual represen-tation of an aspiring woman artist in the mid-19th century, Emily Mary Osborn's heartfelt painting, *Nameless and Friendless* (1857), a canvas representing a poor but lovely and respectable young girl at a London art dealer nervously awaiting the verdict of the pompous proprietor about the worth of her canvases while two ogling "art lovers" look on, is really not too different in its underlying assumptions from an overtly salacious work like Bompard's *Debut of the Model*. The theme in both is innocence, delicious feminine innocence, exposed to the world. It is the charming *vulnerability* of the young woman artist, like that of the hesitating model, which is really the subject of Osborn's painting, not the value of the young woman's work or her pride in it: the issue here is, as usual, sexual rather than serious. Always a model but never an artist might well have served as the motto of the seriously aspiring young woman in the arts of the 19th century.

Successes

But what of the small band of heroic women, who, throughout the ages, despite obstacles, have achieved preeminence, if not the pinnacles of grandeur of a Michelangelo, a Rembrandt, or a Picasso? Are there any qualities that may be said to have characterized them as a group and as individuals? While I cannot go into such an investigation in great detail in this article, I can point to a few striking characteristics of women artists generally: they all, almost without exception, were either the daughters of artist fathers, or, generally later, in the 19th and 20th centuries, had a close personal connection with a stronger or more dominant male artistic personality. Neither of these characteris-tics is, of course, unusual for men artists, either, as we have indicated above in the case of artist fathers and sons: it is simply true almost *without exception* for their feminine counterparts, at least until quite recently. From the legendary sculptor Sabina von Steinbach, in the 13th century, who, according to local tradition, was responsible for South Portal groups on the Cathedral of Strasbourg, down to Rosa Bonheur, the most renowned animal painter of the 19th century, and including such eminent women artists as Marietta Robusti (daughter of Tintoretto), Lavinia Fontana, Artemisia Gentileschi, Elizabeth Chéron, Mme. Vigée-Lebrun, and Angelica Kauffmann—all, without exception, were the daughters of artists. In the 19th century, Berthe Morisot was closely associated with Manet, later marrying his brother, and Mary Cassatt based a good deal of her work on the style of her close friend Degas. Precisely the same breaking of traditional bonds and discarding of time-honored practices that permitted men artists to strike out in directions quite different from those of their fathers in the second half of the nineteenth century enabled women, with additional difficulties, to be sure, to strike out on their own as well. Many of our more recent women artists, like Suzanne Valadon, Paula Modersohn-Becker, Käthe Kollwitz, or Louise Nevelson, have come from nonartistic backgrounds, although many contemporary and near-contemporary women artists have married fellow artists.

It would be interesting to investigate the role of benign, if not outright encouraging, fathers in the formation of women professionals: both Käthe Kollwitz and Barbara Hepworth, for example, recall the influence of unusually sympathetic and supportive fathers on their artistic pursuits. In the absence of any thoroughgoing investigation, one can only gather impressionistic data about the presence or absence of rebellion against parental authority in women artists, and whether there may be more or less rebellion on the part of women artists than is true in the case of men or vice versa. One thing, however, is clear: for a woman to opt for a career at all, much less for a career in art, has required a certain amount of unconventionality, both in the past and at present; whether or not the woman artist rebels against or finds strength in the attitude of her family, she must in any case have a good strong streak of rebellion in her to make her way in the world of art at all, rather than submitting to the socially approved role of wife and mother, the only role to which every social institution consigns her automatically. It is only by adopting, however covertly, the "masculine" attributes of single-mindedness, concentration, tenaciousness, and absorption in ideas and craftsmanship for their own sake, that women have succeeded, and continue to succeed, in the world of art.

Rosa Bonheur

It is instructive to examine in greater detail one of the most successful and accomplished women painters of all time, Rosa Bonheur (1822–1899), whose work, despite the ravages wrought upon its estimation by changes of taste and a certain admitted lack of variety, still stands as an impressive achievement to anyone interested in the art of the 19th century and in the history of taste generally. Rosa Bonheur is a woman artist in whom, partly because of the magnitude of her reputation, all the various conflicts, all the internal and external contradictions and struggles typical of her sex and profession, stand out in sharp relief.

The success of Rosa Bonheur firmly establishes the role of institutions, and institutional change, as a necessary, if not a sufficient, cause of achievement in art. We might say that Bonheur picked a fortunate time to become an artist if she was, at the same time, to have the disadvantage of being a woman: she came into her own in the middle of the 19th century, a time in which the struggle between traditional history painting as opposed to the less pretentious and more freewheeling genre painting, landscape and still-life was won by the latter group hands down. A major change in the social and institutional support for art itself was well under way: with the rise of the bourgeoisie and the fall of the cultivated aristocracy, smaller paintings, generally of everyday subjects, rather than grandiose mythological or religious scenes were much in demand. To cite the Whites: "Three hundred provincial museums there might be, government commissions for public works there might be, but the only possible paid destinations for the rising flood of canvases were the homes of the bourgeoisie. History painting had not and never would rest comfortably in the middle-class parlor. 'Lesser' forms of image art—genre, landscape, still-life—did."[17] In mid-century France, as in 17th-century Holland, there was a tendency for artists to attempt to achieve some sort of security in a shaky market situation by specializing, by making a career out of a specific subject: animal painting was a very popular field, as the Whites point out, and Rosa Bonheur was no doubt its most accomplished and successful practitioner, followed in popularity only by the Barbizon painter Troyon (who at one time was so pressed for his paintings of cows that he hired another artist to brush in the backgrounds). Rosa Bonheur's rise to fame accompanied that of the Barbizon landscapists, supported by those canny dealers, the Durand-Ruels, who later moved on to the Impressionists. The Durand-Ruels were among the first dealers to tap the expanding market in movable decoration for the middle classes, to use the Whites' terminology. Rosa Bonheur's naturalism and ability to capture the individuality—even the "soul"—of each of her animal subjects coincided with bourgeois taste at the time. The same combination of qualities, with a much stronger dose of sentimentality and pathetic fallacy to be sure, likewise assured the success of her *animalier* contemporary, Landseer, in England.

Daughter of an impoverished drawing master, Rosa Bonheur quite naturally showed her interest in art early; at the same time, she exhibited an independence of spirit and liberty of manner which immediately earned her the label of tomboy. According to her own later accounts, her "masculine protest" established itself early; to what extent *any* show of persistence, stubbornness, and vigor would be counted as "masculine" in the first half of the 19th century is conjectural. Rosa Bonheur's attitude toward her father is somewhat ambiguous: while realizing that he had been influential in directing her toward her life's work, there is no doubt that she resented his thoughtless treatment of her beloved mother, and in her reminiscences, she half affectionately makes fun of his bizarre form of social idealism. Raimond Bonheur had been an active member of the short-lived Saint-Simonian community, established in the third decade of the nineteenth century by "Le Père" Enfantin at Menilmontant. Although in her later years Rosa Bonheur might have made fun of some of the more farfetched eccentricities of the members of the community, and disapproved of the additional strain which her father's apostolate placed on her overburdened mother, it is obvious that the Saint-Simonian ideal of equality for women—they disapproved of marriage, their trousered feminine costume was a token of emancipation, and their spiritual leader, Le Père Enfantin, made extraordinary efforts to find a Woman Messiah to share his reign—made a strong impression on her as a child, and may well have influenced her future course of behavior.

"Why shouldn't I be proud to be a woman?" she exclaimed to an interviewer. "My father, that enthusiastic apostle of humanity, many times reiterated to me that woman's mission was to elevate the human race, that she was the Messiah of future centuries. It is to his doctrines that I owe the great, noble ambition I have conceived for the sex which I proudly affirm to be mine, and whose independence I will support to my dying day. . . ."[18] When she was hardly more than a child, he instilled in her the ambition to surpass Mme. Vigée-Lebrun, certainly the most eminent model she could be expected to follow, and he gave her early efforts every possible encouragement. At the same time, the spectacle of her uncomplaining mother's slow decline from sheer overwork and poverty might have been an even more realistic influence on her decision to control her own destiny and never to become the slave of a husband and children. What is particularly interesting from the modern feminist viewpoint is Rosa Bonheur's ability to combine the most vigorous and unapologetic masculine protest with unabashedly self-contradictory assertions of "basic" femininity.

In those refreshingly straightforward pre-Freudian days, Rosa Bonheur could explain to her biographer that she had never wanted to marry for fear of losing her independence. Too many young girls let themselves be led to the altar like lambs to the sacrifice, she maintained. Yet at the same time that she rejected marriage for herself and implied an inevitable loss of selfhood for any woman who engaged in it, she, unlike the Saint-Simonians, considered marriage "a sacrament indispensable to the organization of society."

While remaining cool to offers of marriage, she joined in a seemingly cloudless, lifelong, and apparently Platonic union with a fellow woman artist, Nathalie Micas, who evidently provided her with the companionship and emotional warmth which she needed. Obviously the presence of this sympathetic friend did not seem to demand the same sacrifice of genuine commitment to her profession which marriage would have entailed: in any case, the advantages of such an arrangement for women who wished to avoid the distraction of children in the days before reliable contraception are obvious.

Yet at the same time that she frankly rejected the conventional feminine role of her times, Rosa Bonheur still was drawn into what Betty Friedan has called the "frilly blouse syndrome," that innocuous version of the feminine protest which even today compels successful women psychiatrists or professors to adopt some ultra-feminine item of clothing or insist on proving their prowess as pie-bakers.[19] Despite the fact that she had early cropped hair and adopted men's clothes as her habitual attire, following the example of George Sand, whose rural Romanticism exerted a powerful influence over her imagination, to her biographer she insisted, and no doubt sincerely believed, that she did so only because of the specific demands of her profession. Indignantly denying rumors to the effect that she had run about the streets of Paris dressed as a boy in her youth, she proudly provided her biographer with a daguerreotype of herself at sixteen, dressed in perfectly conventional feminine fashion, except for her shorn hair, which she excused as a practical measure taken after the death of her mother; "Who would have taken care of my curls?" she demanded.[20]

As far as the question of masculine dress was concerned, she was quick to reject her interlocutor's suggestion that her trousers were a symbol of emancipation. "I strongly blame women who renounce their customary attire in the desire to make themselves pass for men," she affirmed. "If I had found trousers suited my sex, I would have completely gotten rid of my skirts, but this is not the case, nor have I ever advised my sisters of the palette to wear men's clothes in the ordinary course of life. If, then, you see me dressed as I am, it is not at all with the aim of making myself interesting, as all too many women have tried, but simply in order to facilitate my work. Remember that at a certain period I spent whole days in the slaughterhouses. Indeed, you have to love your art in order to live in pools of blood. . . . I was also fascinated with horses, and where better can one study these animals than at the fairs . . . ? I had no alternative but to realize that the garments of my own sex were a total nuisance. That is why I decided to ask the Prefect of Police for the authorization to wear masculine clothing.[21] But the costume I am wearing is my working outfit, nothing else. The remarks of fools have never bothered me. Nathalie [her companion] makes fun of them as I do. It doesn't bother her at all to see me dressed as a man, but if you are even the slightest bit put off, I am completely prepared to put on a skirt, especially since all I have to do is to open a closet to find a whole assortment of feminine outfits."[22]

At the same time Rosa Bonheur was forced to admit: "My trousers have been my great protectors. . . . Many times I have congratulated myself for having dared to break with traditions which would have forced me to abstain from certain kinds of work, due to the obligation to drag my skirts everywhere. . . ." Yet the famous artist again felt obliged to qualify her honest admission with an ill-assumed "femininity": "Despite my metamorphoses of costume, there is not a daughter of Eve who appreciates the niceties more than I do; my brusque and even slightly unsociable nature has never prevented my heart from remaining completely feminine."[23]

It is somewhat pathetic that this highly successful artist, unsparing of herself in the painstaking study of animal anatomy, diligently pursuing her bovine or equine subjects in the most unpleasant surroundings, industriously producing popular canvases throughout the course of a lengthy career, firm, assured, and incontrovertibly masculine in her style, winner of a first medal in the Paris Salon, Officer of the Legion of Honor, Commander of the Order of Isabella the Catholic and the Order of Leopold of Belgium, friend of Queen Victoria—that this world-renowned artist should feel compelled late in life to justify and qualify her perfectly reasonable assumption of masculine ways, for any reason whatsoever, and to feel compelled to attack her less modest trouser-wearing sisters at the same time, in order to satisfy the demands of her own conscience. For her conscience, despite her supportive father, her unconventional behavior, and the accolade of worldly success, still condemned her for not being a "feminine" woman.

The difficulties imposed by such demands on the woman artist continue to add to her already difficult enterprise even today. Compare, for example, the noted contemporary, Louise Nevelson, with her combination of utter, "unfeminine" dedication to her work and her conspicuously "feminine" false eyelashes, her admission that she got married at seventeen despite her certainty that she couldn't live without creating because "the world said you should get married."[24] Even in the case of these two outstanding artists—and whether we like *The Horse Fair* or not, we still must admire Rosa Bonheur's professional achievement—the voice of the feminine mystique with its potpourri of ambivalent narcissism and guilt, internalized, subtly dilutes and subverts that total inner confidence, that absolute certitude and self-determination, moral and aesthetic, demanded by the highest and most innovative work in art.

Conclusions

I have tried to deal with one of the perennial questions used to challenge women's demand for true, rather than token, equality, by examining the whole erroneous intellectual substructure upon which the question "Why have there been no great women artists?" is based; by questioning the validity of the formulation of so-called problems in general and the "problem" of women specifically; and then, by probing some of the limitations of the discipline of art history itself. By stressing the *institutional*—that is, the public—rather than the *individual*, or private, preconditions for achievement or the lack of it in the arts, I have tried to provide a paradigm for the investigation of other areas in the field. By examining in some detail a single instance of deprivation or disadvantage—the unavailability of nude models to women art students—I have suggested that it was indeed *institutionally* made impossible for women to achieve artistic excellence, or success, on the same footing as men, *no matter what* the potency of their so-called talent, or genius. The existence of a tiny band of successful, if not great, women artists throughout history does nothing to gainsay this fact, any more than does the existence of a few superstars or token achievers among the members of any minority groups. And while great achievement is rare and difficult at best, it is still rare and more difficult if, while you work, you must at the same time wrestle with inner demons of self-doubt and guilt and outer monsters of ridicule or patronizing encouragement, neither of which have any specific connection with the quality of the art work as such.

What is important is that women face up to the reality of their history and of their present situation, without making excuses or puffing mediocrity. Disadvantage may indeed be an excuse; it is not, however, an intellectual position. Rather, using as a vantage point their situation as underdogs in the realm of grandeur, and outsiders in that ideology, women can reveal institutional and intellectual weaknesses in general, and, at the same time that they destroy false consciousness, take part in the creation of institutions in which clear thought—and true greatness—are challenges open to anyone, man or woman, courageous enough to take the necessary risk, the leap into the unknown.

NOTES

1. Kate Millett's *Sexual Politics* (Doubleday, 1970) and Mary Ellman's *Thinking about Women* (Harcourt, Brace and World, 1968) provide notable exceptions.

2. "Women Artists," review of *Die Frauen in die Kunstgeschichte* by Ernst Guhl, *The Westminster Review* (American edition), 70 (July 1858), 91–104. I am grateful to Elaine Showalter for having brought this review to my attention.

3. See, for example, Peter S. Walch's excellent studies of Angelica Kauffmann or his unpublished doctoral dissertation, "Angelica Kauffmann," Princeton University, 1968, on the subject; for Artemisia Gentileschi, see R. Ward Bissell, "Artemisia Gentileschi—A New Documented Chronology," *Art Bulletin*, 50 (June 1968), 153–68.

4. New York, 1968.

5. John Stuart Mill, *The Subjection of Women* (1869) in *Three Essays by John Stuart Mill* (World Classics Series, 1966), 441.

6. For the relatively recent genesis of the emphasis on the artist as the nexus of aesthetic experience, see M. H. Abrams, *The Mirror and the Lamp: Romantic Theory and the Critical Tradition* (Norton, 1953), and Maurice Z. Shroder, *Icarus: The Image of the Artist in French Romanticism* (Harvard University Press, 1961).

7. A comparison with the parallel myth for women, the Cinderella story, is revealing: Cinderella gains higher status on the basis of a passive, "sex-object" attribute—small feet—whereas the Boy Wonder always proves himself

through active accomplishment. For a thorough study of myths about artists, see Ernst Kris and Otto Kurz, *Die Legende vom Künstler: Ein Geschichtlicher Versuch* (Krystall Verlag, 1934).

8. Nikolaus Pevsner, *Academies of Art, Past and Present* (Da Capo Press, 1973 [1940]), 96f.

9. Contemporary directions—earthworks, conceptual art, art as information, etc.—certainly point *away* from emphasis on the individual genius and his salable products; in art history, Harrison C. and Cynthia A. White's *Canvases and Careers: Institutional Change in the French Painting World* (Wiley, 1965) opens up a fruitful new direction of investigation, as did Nikolaus Pevsner's pioneering *Academies of Art*. Ernst Gombrich and Pierre Francastel, in their very different ways, always have tended to view art and the artist as part of a total situation rather than in lofty isolation.

10. Female models were introduced in the life class in Berlin in 1875, in Stockholm in 1839, in Naples in 1870, at the Royal College of Art in London after 1875. Pevsner, *Academies of Art*, 231. Female models at the Pennsylvania Academy of the Fine Arts wore masks to hide their identity as late as about 1866—as attested to in a charcoal drawing by Thomas Eakins—if not later.

11. Pevsner, *Academies of Art*, 231.

12. H. C. and C. A. White, *Canvases and Careers*, 51.

13. Ibid., Table 5.

14. Mrs. Ellis, "The Daughters of England: Their Position in Society, Character, and Responsibilities," in *The Family Monitor and Domestic Guide* (1844), 35.

15. Ibid., 38–39.

16. Patricia Thomson, *The Victorian Heroine: A Changing Ideal* (Oxford University Press, 1956), 77.

17. H. C. and C. A. White, *Canvases and Careers*, 91.

18. Anna Klumpke, *Rosa Bonheur: Sa vie, son oeuvre* (E. Flammarion, 1908), 311.

19. Betty Friedan, *The Feminine Mystique* (Norton, 1963), 158.

20. Klumpke, *Rosa Bonheur*, 166.

21. Paris, like many cities even today, had laws against cross-dressing on its books.

22. Klumpke, *Rosa Bonheur*, 308–9.

23. Ibid., 310–11.

24. Cited in Elizabeth Fisher, "The Woman as Artist: Louise Nevelson," *Aphra* 1 (Spring 1970), 32.

The Female Experience
and Artistic Creativity

JOELYNN SNYDER-OTT

The arts of a society mirror man's values and attitudes, but what about woman's values and attitudes? Western civilization's culture and arts are *male*-dominated and *male*-oriented. Women's highest artistic achievements are off the scene, seldom heard, or if heard, devalued, and finally viewed, but not observed. If you doubt this, there is a simple test: Name just five women artists and their contributions to history.

What is the "female experience"? Why distinguish between male and female experience? You might argue that one creates as an individual regardless of sex. However, we know the sum total of our experiences reflects in our individual statements as artists, but as women artists we have been forced to see the world, ourselves, and other women as men see us. Simply because we as women still believe our experiences, as Virginia Woolf states in *A Room of One's Own*, are "trivial"! The "male perception" has become accepted as the "universal vision." At one time, I too believed that being referred to as a "woman" artist was an unjustified prefix to place before my name. As a woman art student I had always had great confidence in what was *male*. I sought male approval for my work. As a woman I believed that being told that I painted "like a man" or "thought like a man" was the ultimate compliment and goal. Even semantics became important to me concerning my exhibitions. My exhibits were carefully listed as "one-man." There was always the possibility that someone wouldn't take my work (or me) seriously if the prefix "woman" were attached to my name. This of course was not an unfounded fear. An example of this sexism can be documented in the following review concerning the work of the great living sculptor Louise Nevelson. This review appeared in *Cue Magazine* on October 4, 1941:

> We learned the artist is a woman, in time to check our enthusiasm. Had it been otherwise we might have hailed these sculptural expressions as by surely a great figure among moderns. See them by all means—painted plaster figures and continuous line drawings that take much knowledge from Picasso and Ozenfant and from Mayan and Indian expressions. I suspect that the artist is clowning—but with what excellent equipment artistically.

So, if *I* was not to be taken seriously either, because I was a woman, I concluded that I would disguise my sex. I internalized the male value structure as well. My work became eclectically *male*, influenced as it were by male artists. I truly believed that if I succeeded as an artist, it would have to be in spite of my sex. I hoped that I would have the stamina to become one of those courageous women in history who broke with convention and dared to use her talent and intellect. I had a rude awakening.

Marcia Tucker, an associate curator of the Whitney Museum, stated in an article appearing in *Ms. Magazine*, entitled "By-Passing the Gallery System," that of ten leading New York galleries, 96.4 percent of their artists were male. The Guggenheim Museum has had no major woman's exhibit, and the Museum of Modern Art had only four shows by women between 1942 and 1969.

We can change this situation. Naturally, the first step in solving the problem is an awareness and acceptance that it does exist. Secondly, we must become knowledgeable concerning women's contributions in the arts. By education we will destroy the stereotype that artists are always of the male gender. This education will have a long-reaching effect on future generations of museum directors, art educators, curators, and most importantly, the future art patrons and collectors. We must encourage research concerning women's contributions. Libraries today carry a limited number of books dealing with women's contributions, and even fewer visual examples of their work such as slides or posters. I have found that women's historical contributions have been buried so well that I sometimes feel like an archaeologist, crying out in delight (to the annoyance of the librarian) as I "excavate" some small reference to a woman painter or architect such as Elisabeth Vigée-Lebrun or Angelica Kauffmann buried or wedged in between page-long articles and huge color reproductions of male artists' work.

Where do we begin? Elizabeth Gould Davis, in her book *The First Sex*, states:

> According to mythology women are given credit for inventing the flute, chariot, wheel, ship, art of numbers, fire, cooking, weaving and spinning. In other words women invented ceramics, agriculture, land transportation, animal domestication, commerce, math, handicrafts, domestic economy, and industry.

In addition, in certain cultures all the art is and was made by women. All Navaho blankets are woven by women; almost all American basketry and pottery is done by women. The huts of the Australian, the black camel-hair tents of the Bedouin, the yurta of the nomads of Central Asia, the earth lodges of the Omaha, and the pueblos of the Hopi were all the exclusive work of women.

If we search diligently we may discover an extensive contribution by women in the fine arts also. In the 16th century there was a painter named Sofonisba Anguisciola who was most famous for her portraits. The 16th century also recorded Catherine Van Hemessen, a painter whose patron was the Queen of Hungary. Van Hemessen was also listed by her married name, "Sanders," and was most famous as a miniaturist. Artemisia Gentileschi, a 17th-century Italian, was trained by her father, who was also a painter. His paintings are represented in several school poster art reproductions, but unfortunately her work is not. Judith Leyster, who lived from 1609 to 1660, became a pupil of Frans Hals in Haarlem. Many of her paintings have been attributed to the Dutch painter (Hals)—something that happened to other women in history as well. There was Rosalba Carriera, a 17th-century painter. Angelica Kauffmann, born in 1741 in Switzerland, was a founding member of the Royal Academy in England. Elisabeth Vigée-Lebrun, a French 18th-century painter, was a favorite painter of Marie-Antoinette, and painted at least twenty versions of the Queen and her children. She was a great favorite at the French court and, after the French Revolution, at other courts in Europe as well. Rosa Bonheur, a

French 19th-century painter, was best known for her animal paintings. Trained by her father (the only way girls received art training), she early showed great determination in the pursuit of her career and achieved early success as an animal painter. Later she was criticized for painting only animals, but it must be understood that girls were not permitted to draw from the life model.

In 1893 there was a building at the Chicago World Fair Columbian Exposition, designed by the woman architect Sophia Hayden, which was established and run by a board of women managers. Emily Sartain of Philadelphia was chairwoman of the board from Pennsylvania. She was also one of the founders and first dean of Moore College of Art, the oldest art school for women in the country. The building contained artwork by women from around the world, including a large mural by Mary Cassatt, and Mrs. (Mary Fairchild) Macmonnies, whose full name was not mentioned. William Walton's comment in *World's Columbian Exposition, Art and Architecture*, concerning the mural was typical of the descriptions concerning women's work. He referred to Cassatt's mural as "overly sentimental," and the following statement appeared in the Exposition's program:

> Both [Cassatt and Macmonnies] placed their figures in long pleasant landscapes, though by so doing Mary Cassatt seems rather to have missed the point of her symbolism, as the occupation in which she has represented her "modern woman"—gathering fruit—is scarcely that which best corresponds to the high claims put forth for their share in modern civilization. Mrs. Macmonnies' primitive women were more appropriate in their household and domestic labors.

The female experience in visual perception can best be described by comparing a painting of a mother and child by Renoir to that of a work with the same subject by Mary Cassatt. Renoir painted many women, and one might imagine that he was, ideally, in love with women as we gaze at his many works. The following is a letter written by Renoir to his friend, the poet Catulle Mendès:

> I consider that women are monsters who are authors, lawyers, and politicians, like George Sand, Madam Adam, and other bores who are nothing more than five-legged beasts. The woman who is an artist is merely ridiculous. Graceful-

ness is woman's domain and even her duty. I know very well
that today things have become worse, but what can we do?

This statement by Renoir hardly reflects the idea of respect and equality, and certainly not "love" for women. What do Renoir's paintings
of women reflect about women? If we examine the three versions and
numerous drawings of Renoir's wife, Aline, nursing their son Pierre,
we can make an interesting observation. In each painting, Renoir focuses on his wife's exposed breast and the little boy's naked lower half.
Aline gazes at the painter. She is not depicted as emotionally involved
with little Pierre; Renoir paints his wife as a passive, decorative fruit-
cake, gazing soulfully at the artist.

Cassatt's mother and child, on the other hand, are depicted as actively involved with each other. In paintings and drawings by Cassatt
having a mother-and-child theme, the mothers are caring for, nursing,
engaged with, and generally portrayed as emotionally involved with
their children.

Another example of painting from the "female experience" can be
observed in the paintings by the French painter Berthe Morisot. In
her work we observe women as self-contained beings actively involved
in "doing things" rather than depicted as passive subjects splayed out
frontally for male appreciation as is Manet's *Olympia*.

Women as well as men can find culturally relevant information in all
aspects of Western culture, but the belittlement of women's contributions in the arts can no longer be tolerated. It is not true that there
have been no great women artists. We must no longer accept the "male-
oriented" vision and perception as "universal" vision and perception,
no longer be forced to see the world from a single perspective—as men
see it. As long as the male artist's perception is taught as the "universal"
vision, no women's work that challenges those perceptions can be
rightfully valued and honored.

The female experience becomes the "feminist" experience as we
search through old periodicals and library basements, "excavating" tiny
fragments of information concerning women's contributions. We have
a great amount of "excavation" ahead of us. Women's historical contributions are buried in books on shelves throughout the libraries of the
world. The time has come to blow away the dust and cobwebs from
them as well as from our minds.

An Aesthetic of Blackness: strange and oppositional

bell hooks

This is the story of a house. It has been lived in by many people. Our grandmother, Baba, made this house living space. She was certain that the way we lived was shaped by objects, the way we looked at them, the way they were placed around us. She was certain that we were shaped by space. From her I learn about aesthetics, the yearning for beauty that she tells me is the predicament of heart that makes our passion real. A quiltmaker, she teaches me about color. Her house is a place where I am learning to look at things, where I am learning how to belong in space. In rooms full of objects, crowded with things, I am learning to recognize myself. She hands me a mirror, showing me how to look. The color of wine she has made in my cup, the beauty of the everyday. Surrounded by fields of tobacco, the leaves braided like hair, dried and hung, circles and circles of smoke fill the air. We string red peppers fiery hot, with thread that will not be seen. They will hang in front of a lace curtain to catch the sun. Look, she tells me, what the light does to color! Do you believe that space can give life, or take it away, that space has power? These are the questions she asks which frighten me. Baba dies an old woman, out of place. Her funeral is also a place to see things, to recognize myself. How can I be sad in the face of death, surrounded by so much beauty? Death, hidden in a field of tulips, wearing my face and calling my name. Baba can make them grow. Red, yellow, they surround her body like lovers in a swoon, tulips everywhere. Here a soul on fire with beauty burns and passes, a soul touched by flame. We see her leave. She has taught me how to look at the world and see beauty. She has taught me "we must learn to see."

Years ago, at an art gallery in San Francisco near the Tassajara restaurant, I saw rooms arranged by Buddhist monk Chögyam Trungpa. At a moment in my life when I had forgotten how to see, he reminds me to look. He arranges spaces. Moved by an aesthetic shaped by old beliefs. Objects are not without spirit. As living things they touch us in unimagined ways. On this path one learns that an entire room is a space to be created, a space that can reflect beauty, peace, and a harmony of being, a spiritual aesthetic. Each space is a sanctuary. I remember. Baba taught me "we must learn to see."

Aesthetics then is more than a philosophy or theory of art and beauty; it is a way of inhabiting space, a particular location, a way of looking and becoming. It is not organic. I grew up in an ugly house. No one there considered the function of beauty or pondered the use of space. Surrounded by dead things, whose spirits had long ago vanished since they were no longer needed, that house contained a great engulfing emptiness. In that house things were not to be looked at, they were to be possessed—space was not to be created but owned—a violent anti-aesthetic. I grew up thinking about art and beauty as it existed in our lives, the lives of poor black people. Without knowing the appropriate language, I understood that advanced capitalism was affecting our capacity to see, that consumerism began to take the place of that predicament of heart that called us to yearn for beauty. Now many of us are only yearning for things.

In one house I learned the place of aesthetics in the lives of agrarian poor black folks. There the lesson was that one had to understand beauty as a force to be made and imagined. Old folks shared their sense that we had come out of slavery into this free space and we had to create a world that would renew the spirit, that would make it life-giving. In that house there was a sense of history. In the other house, the one I lived in, aesthetics had no place. There the lessons were never about art or beauty, but always only to possess things. My thinking about aesthetics has been informed by the recognition of these houses: one which cultivated and celebrated an aesthetic of existence, rooted in the idea that no degree of material lack could keep one from learning how to look at the world with a critical eye, how to recognize beauty, or how to use it as a force to enhance inner well-being; the other which denied the power of abstract aestheticism. Living in that other house where we were so acutely aware of lack, so conscious of materiality, I could see in our daily life the way consumer capitalism ravaged the black poor, nurtured in us a longing for things that often subsumed our ability to recognize aesthetic worth or value.

Despite these conditions, there was in the traditional southern racially segregated black community a concern with racial uplift that continually promoted recognition of the need for artistic expressiveness and cultural production. Art was seen as intrinsically serving a political function. Whatever African-Americans created in music, dance, poetry, painting, etc., it was regarded as testimony, bearing witness, challenging racist thinking which suggested that black folks were not fully human, were uncivilized, and that the measure of this was our collective failure to create "great" art. White supremacist ideology insisted that black people, being more animal than human, lacked the capacity to feel and therefore could not engage the finer sensibilities that were the breeding ground for art. Responding to this propaganda, 19th-century black folks emphasized the importance of art and cultural production, seeing it as the most effective challenge to such assertions. Since many displaced African slaves brought to this country an aesthetic based on the belief that beauty, especially that created in a collective context, should be an integrated aspect of everyday life, enhancing the survival and development of community, these ideas formed the basis of African-American aesthetics. Cultural production and artistic expressiveness were also ways for displaced African people to maintain connections with the past. Artistic African cultural retentions survived long after other expressions had been lost or forgotten. Though not remembered or cherished for political reasons, they would ultimately be evoked to counter assertions by white supremacists and colonized black minds that there remained no vital living bond between the culture of African-Americans and the cultures of Africa. This historical aesthetic legacy has proved so powerful that consumer capitalism has not been able to completely destroy artistic production in underclass black communities.

Even though the house where I lived was ugly, it was a place where I could and did create art. I painted, I wrote poetry. Though it was an environment more concerned with practical reality than art, these aspirations were encouraged. In an interview in *Callaloo* painter Lois Mailou Jones describes the tremendous support she received from black folks: "Well I began with art at a very early stage in my life. As a child, I was always drawing. I loved color. My mother and father, realizing that I had talent, gave me an excellent supply of crayons and pencils and paper—and encouraged me." Poor black parents saw artistic cultural production as crucial to the struggle against racism, but they were also cognizant of the link between creating art and pleasure. Art was necessary to bring delight, pleasure, and beauty into lives that were hard, that were materially deprived. It mediated the harsh conditions of poverty and servitude. Art was also a way to escape one's plight. Protestant black churches emphasized the parable of the talents, and commitment to spirituality also meant appreciating one's talents and using them. In our church if someone could sing or play the piano and they did not offer these talents to the community, they were admonished.

Performance arts—dance, music, and theater—were the most accessible ways to express creativity. Making and listening to black music, both secular and sacred, was one of the ways black folks developed an aesthetic. It was not an aesthetic documented in writing, but it did inform cultural production. Analyzing the role of the "talent show" in segregated black communities, which was truly the community-based way to support and promote cultural production, would reveal much about the place of aesthetics in traditional black life. It was both a place for collective display of artistry and a place for the development of aesthetic criteria. I cite this information to place African-American concern with aesthetics in a historical framework that shows a continuity of concern. It is often assumed that black folks first began to articulate an interest in aesthetics during the 1960s. Privileged black folks in the 19th and early 20th centuries were often, like their white counterparts, obsessed with notions of "high art." Significantly, one of the important dimensions of the artistic movement among black people, most often talked about as the Harlem Renaissance, was the call for an appreciation of popular forms. Like other periods of intense focus on the arts in African-American culture, it called attention to forms of artistic expression that were simply passing away because they were not valued in the context of a conventional aesthetic focusing on "high art." Often African-American intellectual elites appropriated these forms, reshaping them in ways suited to different locations. Certainly the spiritual as it was sung by Paul Robeson at concerts in Europe was an aspect of African-American folk culture evoked in a context far removed from small, hot, Southern church services, where poor black folks gathered in religious ecstasy. Celebration of popular forms ensured their survival, kept them as a legacy to be passed on, even as they were altered and transformed by the interplay of varied cultural forces.

Conscious articulation of a "black aesthetic" as it was constructed by African-American artists and critics in the 1960s and early '70s was an effort to forge an unbreakable link between artistic production and revolutionary politics. Writing about the interconnectedness of art and politics in the essay "Frida Kahlo and Tona Modottit," Laura Mulvey describes the way an artistic avant-garde

> . . . was able to use popular form not as a means of communication but as a means of constructing a mythic past whose effectiveness could be felt in the present. Thereby it brought itself into line with revolutionary impetus towards constructing the mythic past of the nation.

A similar trend emerged in African-American art as painters, writers, musicians worked to imaginatively evoke black nationhood, a homeland, re-creating bonds with an African past while simultaneously evoking a mythic nation to be born in exile. During this time Larry Neal declared the Black Arts Movement to be "the cultural aim of the black revolution." Art was to serve black people in the struggle for liberation. It was to call for and inspire resistance. One of the major voices of the black aesthetic movement, Maulana Karenga, in his *Thesis on Black Cultural Nationalism*, taught that art should be functional, collective, and committed.

The black aesthetic movement was fundamentally essentialist. Characterized by an inversion of the "us" and "them" dichotomy, it inverted conventional ways of thinking about otherness in ways that suggested that everything black was good and everything white bad. In his introduction to the anthology *Black Fire*, Larry Neal set the terms of the movement, dismissing work by black artists which did not emerge from black power movement:

> A revolutionary art is being expressed today. The anguish and aimlessness that attended our great artists of the forties and fifties and which drove most of them to early graves, to dissipation and dissolution, is over. Misguided by white cultural references (the models the culture sets for its individuals), and the incongruity of these models with black reality, men like Bird were driven to willful self-destruction. There

was no program. And the reality-model was incongruous. It was a white reality-model. If Bird had had a black reality-model, it might have been different. . . . In Bird's case, there was a dichotomy between his genius and the society. But that he couldn't find the adequate model of being was the tragic part of the whole thing.

Links between black cultural nationalism and revolutionary politics led ultimately to the subordination of art to politics. Rather than serving as a catalyst promoting diverse artistic expression, the Black Arts Movement began to dismiss all forms of cultural production by African-Americans that did not conform to movement criteria. Often this led to aesthetic judgments that did not allow for recognition of multiple black experience or the complexity of black life, as in the case of Neal's critical interpretation of jazz musician Charlie Parker's fate. Clearly, the problems facing Parker were not simply aesthetic concerns, and they could not have been resolved by art or critical theories about the nature of black artistic production. Ironically, in many of its aesthetic practices the Black Arts Movement was based on the notion that a people's art, cultural production for the masses, could not be either complex, abstract, or diverse in style, form, content, etc.

Despite its limitations, the Black Arts Movement provided useful critique based on radical questioning of the place and meaning of aesthetics for black artistic production. The movement's insistence that all art is political, that an ethical dimension should inform cultural production, as well as the encouragement of an aesthetic which did not separate habits of being from artistic production, were important to black thinkers concerned with strategies of decolonization. Unfortunately, these positive aspects of the black aesthetic movement should have led to the formation of critical space where there could have been more open discussion of the relevance of cultural production to black liberation struggle. Ironically, even though the Black Arts Movement insisted that it represented a break from white western traditions, much of its philosophical underpinning re-inscribed prevailing notions about the relationship between art and mass culture. The assumption that naturalism or realism was more accessible to a mass audience than abstraction was certainly not a revolutionary position. Indeed the paradigms for artistic creation offered by the Black Arts Movement were most often restrictive and disempowering. They stripped many artists of creative agency by dismissing and devaluing their work because it was either too abstract or did not overtly address a radical politic. Writing about socialist attitudes toward art and politics in *Art and Revolution*, John Berger suggests that the relationship between art and political propaganda is often confused in the radical or revolutionary context. This was often the case in the Black Arts Movement. While Berger willingly accepts the truism "that all works of art exercise an ideological influence—even works by artists who profess to have no interest outside art," he critiques the idea that simplicity of form or content necessarily promotes critical political consciousness or leads to the development of a meaningful revolutionary art. His words of caution should be heeded by those who would revive a prescriptive black aesthetic that limits freedom and restricts artistic development. Speaking against a prescriptive aesthetic, Berger writes:

> When the experience is "offered up," it is not expected to be in any way transformed. Its apotheosis should be instant, and as it were invisible. The artistic process is taken for granted: it always remains exterior to the spectator's experience. It is no more than the supplied vehicle in which experience is placed so that it may arrive safely at a kind of cultural terminus. Just as academicism reduces the process of art to an apparatus for artists, it reduces it to a vehicle for the spectator. There is absolutely no dialectic between experience and expression, between experience and its formulation.

The black aesthetic movement was a self-conscious articulation by many of a deep fear that the power of art resides in its potential to transgress boundaries.

Many African-American artists retreated from black cultural nationalism into a retrogressive posture where they suggested there were no links between art and politics, evoking outmoded notions of art as transcendent and pure to defend their position. This was another step backwards. There was no meaningful attempt to counter the black aesthetic with conceptual criteria for creating and evaluating art which would simultaneously acknowledge its ideological content even as it allowed for expansive notions of artistic freedom. Overall the impact of these two movements, black aesthetics and its opponents, was a stifling of artistic production by African-Americans in practically every medium with the exception of music. Significantly, avant-garde jazz musicians, grappling with the artistic expressivity that demanded experimentation, resisted restrictive mandates about their work, whether they were imposed by a white public saying their work was not really music or a black public which wanted to see more overt links between that work and political struggle.

To re-open the creative space that much of the black aesthetic movement closed down, it seems vital for those involved in contemporary black arts to engage in a revitalized discussion of aesthetics. Critical theories about cultural production, about aesthetics, continue to confine and restrict black artists, and passive withdrawal from a discussion of aesthetics is a useless response. To suggest, as Clyde Taylor does in his essay "We Don't Need Another Hero: Anti-Theses On Aesthetics," that the failure of black aesthetics or the development of white western theorizing on the subject should negate all African-American concern with the issue is to once again repeat an essentialist project that does not enable or promote artistic growth. An African-American discourse on aesthetics need not begin with white western traditions and it need not be prescriptive. Cultural decolonization does not happen solely by repudiating all that appears to maintain connection with the colonizing culture. It is really important to dispel the notion that white western culture is "the" location where a discussion of aesthetics emerged, as Taylor suggests; it is only one location.

Progressive African-Americans concerned with the future of our cultural production seek to critically conceptualize a radical aesthetic that does not negate the powerful place of theory as both that force which sets up criteria for aesthetic judgment and as vital grounding that helps make certain work possible, particularly expressive work that is transgressive and oppositional. Hal Foster's comments on the importance of an anti-aesthetic in the essay "Postmodernism: A Preface" present a useful paradigm African-Americans can employ to interrogate modernist notions of aesthetics without negating the discourse on Aesthetics. Foster proposes this paradigm to critically question "the idea that aesthetic experience exists apart, without 'purpose,' all but beyond history, or that art can now affect a world at once (inter) subjective, concrete, and universal—a symbolic totality." Taking the position that an anti-aesthetic "signals a practice, cross-disciplinary in nature, that is sensitive to cultural forms engaged in a politic (e.g., feminist art) or rooted in a vernacular—that is, to forms that deny the idea of a privileged aesthetic realm," Foster opens up the possibility that work by marginalized groups can have a greater audience and impact. Working from a base where difference and otherness are acknowledged as forces that intervene in western theorizing about aesthetics to reformulate and transform the discussion, African-Americans are empowered to break with old ways of seeing reality that suggest there is only one audience for our work and only one aesthetic measure of its value. Moving away from narrow cultural nationalism, one leaves behind as well racist assumptions that cultural productions by black people can only have "authentic" significance and meaning for a black audience.

Black artists concerned with producing work that embodies and reflects a liberatory politic know that an important part of any decolonization process is critical intervention and interrogation of existing repressive and dominating structures. African-American critics and/or artists who speak about our need to engage in ongoing dialogue with dominant discourses always risk being dismissed as assimilationist. There is a grave difference between that engagement with white culture which seeks to deconstruct, demystify, challenge, and transform and gestures of collaboration and complicity. We cannot participate in dialogue that is the mark of freedom and critical agency if we dismiss all work emerging from white western traditions. The assumption that the crisis of African-Americans should or can only be addressed by us must also be interrogated. Much of what threatens our collective well-being is the product of dominating structures. Racism is a white issue as much as it is a black one.

Contemporary intellectual engagement with issues of "otherness and difference" manifest in literary critique, cultural studies, feminist theory, and black studies indicates that there is a growing body of work that can provide and promote critical dialogue and debate across boundaries of class, race, and gender. These circumstances, coupled with a focus on pluralism at the level of social and public policy, are creating a cultural climate where it is possible to interrogate the idea that difference is synonymous with lack and deprivation, and simultaneously call for critical re-thinking of aesthetics. Retrospective examination of the repressive impact a prescriptive black aesthetic had on black cultural production should serve as a cautionary model for African-Americans. There can never be one critical paradigm for the evaluation of artistic work. In part, a radical aesthetic acknowledges that we are constantly changing positions, locations, that our needs and concerns vary, that these diverse directions must correspond with shifts in critical thinking. Narrow limiting aesthetics within black communities tend to place innovative black artistry on the margins. Often this work receives little or no attention. Whenever black artists work in ways that are transgressive, we are seen as suspect, by our group and by the dominant culture. Rethinking aesthetic principles could lead to the development of a critical standpoint that promotes and encourages various modes of artistic and cultural production.

As artist and critic, I find compelling a radical aesthetic that seeks to uncover and restore links between art and revolutionary politics, particularly black liberation struggle, while offering an expansive critical foundation for aesthetic evaluation. Concern for the contemporary plight of black people necessitates that I interrogate my work to see if it functions as a force that promotes the development of critical consciousness and resistance movement. I remain passionately committed to an aesthetic that focuses on the purpose and function of beauty, of artistry in everyday life, especially in the lives of poor people, one that seeks to explore and celebrate the connection between our capacity to engage in critical resistance and our ability to experience pleasure and beauty. I want to create work that shares with an audience, particularly oppressed and marginalized groups, the sense of agency artistry offers, the empowerment. I want to share the aesthetic inheritance handed down to me by my grandmother and generations of black ancestors, whose ways of thinking about the issue have been globally shaped in the African diaspora and informed by the experience of exile and domination. I want to reiterate the message that "we must learn to see." Seeing here is meant metaphysically as heightened awareness and understanding, the intensification of one's capacity to experience reality through the realm of the senses.

Remembering the houses of my childhood, I see how deeply my concern with aesthetics was shaped by black women who were fashioning an aesthetic of being, struggling to create an oppositional worldview for their children, working with space to make it livable. Baba, my grandmother, could not read or write. She did not inherit her contemplative preoccupation with aesthetics from a white western literary tradition. She was poor all her life. Her memory stands as a challenge to intellectuals, especially those on the left, who assume that the capacity to think critically, in abstract concepts, to be theoretical, is a function of class and educational privilege. Contemporary intellectuals committed to progressive politics must be reminded again and again that the capacity to name something (particularly in writing terms like aesthetics, postmodernism, deconstruction, etc.) is not synonymous with the creation or ownership of the condition or circumstance to which such terms may refer.

Many underclass black people who do not know conventional academic theoretical language are thinking critically about aesthetics. The richness of their thoughts is rarely documented in books. Innovative African-American artists have rarely documented their process, their critical thinking on the subject of aesthetics. Accounts of the theories that inform their work are necessary and essential; hence my concern with opposing any standpoint that devalues this critical project. Certainly many of the revolutionary, visionary critical perspectives on music that were inherent to John Coltrane's oppositional aesthetics and his cultural production will never be shared because they were not fully documented. Such tragic loss retards the development of reflective work by African-Americans on aesthetics that is linked to enabling politics. We must not deny the way aesthetics serves as the foundation for emerging visions. It is, for some of us, critical space that inspires and encourages artistic endeavor. The ways we interpret that space and inhabit it differ.

As a grown black woman, a guest in my mother's house, I explain that my interior landscape is informed by minimalism, that I cannot live in a space filled with too many things. My grandmother's house is only inhabited by ghosts and can no longer shelter or rescue me. Boldly I declare that I am a minimalist. My sisters repeat this word with the kind of glee that makes us laugh, as we celebrate together that particular way language, and the "meaning" of words is transformed when they fall from the hierarchical space they inhabit in certain locations (the predominantly white university setting) into the mouths of vernacular culture and speech, into underclass blackness, segregated communities where there is much illiteracy. Who can say what will happen to this word "minimalist." Who knows how it will be changed, refashioned by the thick patois that is our Southern black tongue. This experience cannot be written. Even if I attempt description it will never convey process.

One of my five sisters wants to know how it is I come to think about these things, about houses, and space. She does not remember long conversations with Baba. She remembers her house as an ugly place, crowded with objects. My memories fascinate her. She listens with astonishment as I describe the shadows in Baba's house and what they meant to me, the way the moon entered an upstairs window and created new ways for me to see dark and light. After reading Tanizaki's essay on aesthetics *In Praise of Shadows*, I tell this sister in a late-night conversation that I am learning to think about blackness in a new way. Tanizaki speaks of seeing beauty in darkness and shares this moment of insight: "The quality that we call beauty, however, must always grow from the realities of life, and our ancestors, forced to live in dark rooms, presently came to discover beauty in shadows, ultimately to guide shadows toward beauty's end." My sister has skin darker than mine. We think about our skin as a dark room, a place of shadows. We talk often about color politics and the ways racism has created an aesthetic that wounds us, a way of thinking about beauty that hurts. In the shadows of late night, we talk about the need to see darkness differently, to talk about it in a new way. In that space of shadows we long for an aesthetic of blackness—strange and oppositional.

The Point of View: Universal or Particular?

MONIQUE WITTIG

I have gathered here a number of reflections on writing and language, which I wrote while translating Spillway *by Djuna Barnes, and which are related to Djuna Barnes's work and to my own work.*

1.

That there is no "feminine writing" must be said at the outset, and one makes a mistake in using and giving currency to this expression. What is this "feminine" in "feminine writing"? It stands for Woman, thus merging a practice with a myth, the myth of Woman. "Woman" cannot be associated with writing because "Woman" is an imaginary formation and not a concrete reality; it is that old branding by the enemy now flourished like a tattered flag refound and won in battle. "Feminine writing" is the naturalizing metaphor of the brutal political fact of the domination of women, and as such it enlarges the apparatus under which "femininity" presents itself: that is, Difference, Specificity, Female Body/Nature. Through its adjacent position, "writing" is captured by the metaphor in "feminine writing" and as a result fails to appear as work and a production process, since the words "writing" and "feminine" are combined in order to designate a sort of biological production peculiar to "Woman," a secretion natural to "Woman."

Thus, "feminine writing" amounts to saying that women do not belong to history, and that writing is not a material production. The (new) femininity, feminine writing, and the lauding of difference are the backlash of a political trend[1] very much concerned with the questioning of the categories of sex, those two great axes of categorization for philosophy and social science. As always happens, when something new appears, it is immediately interpreted and turned into its opposition. Feminine writing is like the household arts and cooking.

2.

Gender is the linguistic index of the political opposition between the sexes. Gender is used here in the singular because indeed there are not two genders. There is only one: the feminine, the "masculine" not being a gender. For the masculine is not the masculine but the general.[2] The result is that there are the general and the feminine, or rather, the general and the mark of the feminine. It is this which makes Nathalie Sarraute say that she cannot use the feminine gender when she wants to generalize (and not particularize) what she is writing about. And since what is crucial for Sarraute is precisely abstracting from every concrete material, the use of the feminine is impossible when its presence distorts the meaning of her undertaking, due to the a priori analogy between feminine gender/sex/nature. Only the masculine as general is the abstract. The feminine is the concrete (sex in language). Djuna Barnes makes the experiment (and succeeds) by universalizing the feminine. (Like Proust she makes no difference in the way she describes male and female characters.) In doing so she succeeds in removing from the feminine gender its "smell of hatching," to use an expression of Baudelaire's about the poet Marceline Desbordes-Valmore. Djuna Barnes cancels out the genders by making them obsolete. I find it necessary to suppress them. That is the point of view of a lesbian.

3.

The signifieds of 19th-century discourse have soaked the textual reality of our time to the saturation point. So, "'the genius of suspicion has appeared on the scene.'" So, "we have now entered upon an age of suspicion."[3] "Man" has lost ground to such an extent that he is barely acknowledged as the subject of discourse. Today they are asking: what is *the* subject? In the general debacle which has followed the calling of meaning into question, there is room for so-called minority writers to enter the privileged (battle) field of literature, where attempts at constitution of the subject confront each other. For since Proust we know that literary experimentation is a favored way to bring a subject to light. This experimentation is the ultimate subjective practice, a practice of the cognitive subject. Since Proust, the subject has never been the same, for throughout *Remembrance of Things Past* he made "homosexual" the axis of categorization from which to universalize. The minority subject is not self-centered as is the straight subject. Its extension into space could be described as being like Pascal's circle, whose center is everywhere and whose circumference is nowhere. This is what explains Djuna Barnes's angle of approach to her text—a constant shifting which, when the text is read, produces an effect comparable to what I call an out-of-the-corner-of-the-eye perception; the text works through fracturing. Word by word, the text bears the mark of that "estrangement" which Barnes describes with each of her characters.

4.

All minority writers (who are conscious of being so) enter into literature obliquely, if I may say so. The important problems in literature which preoccupy their contemporaries are framed by their perspective. They are as impassioned about problems of form as are straight writers, but also they cannot help but be stirred heart and soul by their subject—"that which calls for a hidden name," "that which dares not speak its name," that which they find everywhere although it is never written about. Writing a text which has homosexuality among its themes is a gamble. It is taking the risk that at every turn the formal element which is the theme will overdetermine the meaning, monopolize the whole meaning, against the intention of the author who wants above all to create a literary work. Thus the text which adopts such a theme sees one of its parts taken for the whole, one of the constituent elements of the text taken for the whole text, and the book becomes a symbol, a manifesto. When this happens, the text ceases to operate at the literary level; it is subjected to disregard, in the sense of ceasing to be regarded in relation to equivalent texts. It becomes a committed text with a social theme and it attracts attention to a social problem. When this happens to a text, it is diverted from its primary aim, which is to change the textual reality within which it is inscribed. In fact, by reason of its theme it is dismissed from the textual reality, it no longer has access to it, it is banned (often simply by the silent treatment or by failure to reprint), it can no longer operate as a text in relationship to other past or contemporary texts. It is interesting only to homosexuals. Taken as a symbol or adopted by a political group, the text loses its polysemy, it becomes univocal. This loss of meaning and lack of grip on the textual reality prevents the text from carrying out the only political action that it could: introducing into the textual tissue of the times by way of literature that which it embodies. Doubtless this is why Djuna Barnes dreaded that the lesbians should make her *their* writer, and that by doing this they should reduce her work to one dimension. At all events, and even if Djuna Barnes is read first and widely by lesbians, one should not reduce and limit her to the lesbian minority. This would not only be no favor to her, but also no favor to us. For it is within literature that the work of Barnes can better act both for her and for us.

5.

There are texts which are of the greatest strategic importance both in their mode of appearance and their mode of inscription within literary reality. This is true of the whole oeuvre of Barnes, which from this point of view functions as a single, unique text, for *Ryder, Ladies Almanack, Spillway,* and *Nightwood* are linked by correspondences and permutations. Barnes's text is also unique in the sense that it is the first of its kind, and it detonates like a bomb where there has been nothing before it. So it is that, word by word, it has to create its own context, working, laboring with nothing against everything. A text by a minority writer is effective only if it succeeds in making the minority point of view universal, only if it is an important literary text. *Remembrance of Things Past* is a monument of French literature *even though* homosexuality is *the* theme of the book. Barnes's oeuvre is an important literary oeuvre *even though* her major theme is lesbianism. On the one hand the work of these two writers has transformed, as should all important work, the textual reality of our time. But as the work of members of a minority, their texts have changed the angle of categorization as far as the sociological reality of their group goes, at least in affirming its existence. Before Barnes and Proust how many times had homosexual and lesbian characters been chosen as the theme of literature in general? What had there been in literature between Sappho and Barnes's *Ladies Almanack* and *Nightwood?* Nothing.

6.

The unique context for Djuna Barnes, if one chooses to look at it from a minority angle, was the work of Proust, whom she refers to in *Ladies Almanack*. It is Djuna Barnes who is our Proust (and not Gertrude Stein). A different sort of treatment, nevertheless, was accorded the work of Proust and the work of Barnes: that of Proust more and more triumphant until becoming a classic, that of Barnes appearing like a flash of lightning and then disappearing. Barnes's work is little known, unrecognized in France, but also in the United States. One could say that strategically Barnes is nevertheless more important than Proust. And as such constantly threatened with disappearance. Sappho also has disappeared. But not Plato. One can see quite clearly what is at stake and "dares not speak its name," the name which Djuna Barnes herself abhorred. Sodom is powerful and eternal, said Colette, and Gomorrah doesn't exist. The Gomorrah of *Ladies Almanack*, of *Nightwood*, of "Cassation" and "The Grande Malade" in *Spillway* is a dazzling refutation of Colette's denials, for what is written *is*. "Raise high the roof beam, carpenter,/for here comes the lesbian poet,/rising above the foreign contestants." This poet generally has a hard battle to wage, for, step by step, word by word, she must create her own context in a world which, as soon as she appears, bends every effort to make her disappear. The battle is hard because she must wage it on two fronts: on the formal level with the questions being debated at the moment in literary history, and on the conceptual level against the that-goes-without-saying of the straight mind.

7.

Let us see the word *letter* for what is generally called the signifier and the word *meaning* for what is called the signified (the sign being the combination of the letter and the meaning). Using the words *letter* and *meaning* in place of *signified* and *signifier* permits us to avoid the interference of the referent prematurely in the vocabulary of sign. (For *signified* and *signifier* describe the sign in terms of the reality being referred to, while *letter* and *meaning* describe the sign solely in relation to language). In language, only the meaning is abstract. In a work of literary experimentation there can be an equilibrium between letter and meaning. Either there can be an elimination of meaning in favor of the letter ("pure" literary experimentation), or there can be the production of meaning first and foremost. Even in the case of "pure" literary experimentation, it can happen, as Roland Barthes pointed out, that certain meanings are overdetermined to such an extent that the letter is made the meaning and the signifier becomes the signified, whatever the writer does. Minority writers are menaced by the meaning even while they are engaged in formal experimentation: what for them is only a theme in their work, a formal element, imposes itself as meaning *only*, for straight readers. But also it is because the opposition between letter and meaning, between signifier and signified has no *raison d'être* except in an anatomical description of language. In the practice of language, letter and meaning do not act separately. And, for me, a writer's practice consists in constantly reactivating letter and meaning, for, like the letter, meaning vanishes. Endlessly.

8.

Language for a writer is a special material (compared to that of painters or musicians), since it is used first of all for quite another thing than to produce art and discover forms. It is used by everybody all the time, it is used for speaking and communicating. It is a special material because it is the place, the means, the medium for bringing meaning to light. But meaning hides language from sight. For language, like the purloined letter of Poe's tale, is constantly there, although totally invisible. For one sees, one hears only the meaning. Then isn't meaning language? Yes, it is language, but in its visible and material form, language is form, language is letter. Meaning is not visible, and as such appears to be outside of language. (It is sometimes confused with the referent when one speaks of the "content.") Indeed, meaning is language, but being its abstraction it cannot be seen. Despite this, in the current use of language one sees and hears *only* meaning. It is because the use of language is a very abstract operation, in which at every turn in the production of meaning its forms disappears. For when language takes form, it is lost in the literal meaning. It can only reappear abstractly as language while redoubling itself, while forming a figurative meaning, a figure of speech. This, then, is writers' work—to concern themselves with the letter, the concrete, the visibility of language, that is, its material form. Since the time that language has been perceived as material, it has been worked word by word by writers. This work on the level of the words and of the letter reactivates words in their arrangement, and in turn confers on meaning its full meaning: in practice this work brings out in most cases—rather than one meaning—polysemy.

But whatever one chooses to do on the practical level as a writer, when it comes to the conceptual level, there is no other way around—one must assume both a particular *and* a universal point of view, at least to be part of literature. That is, one must work to reach the general, even while starting from an individual or from a specific point of view. This is true for straight writers. But it is true as well for minority writers.

NOTES

1. The beginning of the women's liberation movement in France and everywhere else was in itself a questioning of the categories of sex. But afterwards only radical feminists and lesbians continued to challenge on political and theoretical grounds the use of sexes as categories and as classes. For the theoretical aspects of this question, see *Questions féministes* between 1977 and 1980, and *Feminist Issues* since its first number.
2. See Colette Guillaumin, "The Masculine: Denotations/Connotations," *Feminist Issues* 5.1 (1985).
3. Nathalie Sarraute, *The Age of Suspicion* (George Braziller, 1963), 57.

The Artist as Woman

PATRICIA MEYER SPACKS

*This story . . . bears witness to my desire to
escape from my familiar surroundings
and become an omnipotent woman,
or fairy, in a supernaturally free domain.*
                    —Marie Bonaparte
*Art to me was a state; it didn't need
to be an accomplishment.*
                    —Margaret Anderson

Like the adolescent, the artist is a dreamer and a revolutionary; like the adolescent, he often finds his accomplishment inadequate to his imaginings. But his dream, setting him apart, helps him to escape the burden of the real. To some women, as to some men, the idea of art seems to solve all problems. They may insistently describe themselves as artists without actually creating much art, using the self-designation to express wish rather than fact, trying to transform reality by refusing to accept the given conditions of life as definitive. When they write about themselves directly, as many have done, they reveal the complex purposes that the condition of being an artist—unlike adolescence, a *chosen* state—may serve.

To say that the artist has something in common with the adolescent is not to derogate the artist. The comparison suggests both the high aspiration and the characteristic frustration of the artist's life. When the artist is a woman, both the function of aspiration and the nature of frustration assume characteristic forms. In many ways woman artists' self-depictions corroborate the implications of the more indirect testimony offered by fictional accounts of female adolescence.

What artists protest resembles what adolescents find intolerable. Isadora Duncan remembers a past dominated by "the constant spirit of revolt against the narrowness of the society in which we lived, against the limitations of life." Confronting a restrictive environment while powerless to effect significant change in it, a woman may find herself driven inward, to a realm where she can assert the omnipotence life denies her. Art externalizes the inward; imagining oneself an artist, one imagines *using* precious fantasies. The woman's most potent fear is likely to be of abandonment, her most positive vision, of love: the child who fancies herself a fairy princess fancies also the throng of admirers at her feet. She dreams of herself as beautiful, therefore beloved; as powerful because beloved. Her narcissism, too, may seem more acceptable if it belongs to an artist. But what of her dreams of accomplishment? Some women imagine that accomplishment is one more means to love; some fear that it is love's enemy. Almost all seem to understand that publicly acknowledged achievement is a mode of power. The puzzle of how power relates to love in a woman's experience is central to the dilemma of the woman as artist—as it is central to Emma Woodhouse and Catherine Linton. The woman as artist may help to illuminate the woman as woman.

For Isadora Duncan, the function of art was to assert power, the function of power, to demand love. The dancer provides an illuminating example of what it means to "think of oneself as an artist," precisely because words are not her chosen artistic medium. Her writings pour forth her imaginings. A dancer with the world at her feet, she can simultaneously assert her femininity and her artistic genius. Given her history of spectacular public success, she need not rely on her imagination for sustenance; yet her autobiography testifies that a fantasy of pseudo-divine power remains the foundation of her existence. When she bears a child, she imagines the act of procreation as defining her greatness:

> Oh, women, what is the good of us learning to become lawyers, painters or sculptors, when this miracle [of birth] exists? Now I know this tremendous love, surpassing the love of men. I was stretched and bleeding, torn and helpless, while the little being sucked and howled. Life, life, life! Give me

life! Oh, where was my Art? My Art or any Art? What did
I care for Art! I felt I was a God, superior to any artist.

But she describes herself as artist—twelve pages later—in equally extravagant terms:

> . . . I was possessed by the dream of Promethean creation
> that, at my call, might spring from the Earth, descend from
> the Heavens, such dancing figures as the world had never
> seen. Ah, proud, enticing dream that has led my life from
> one catastrophe to another! Why did you possess me? Lead-
> ing, like the light of Tantalus, only to darkness and despair.
> But no! Still flickering, that light in the darkness must eventu-
> ally lead me to the Glorious Vision, at last realised. Small
> fluttering light, just ahead of my stumbling footsteps, I still
> believe, I still follow you.

Art and motherhood, in Isadora's view, are alike metaphors for
power. The "Promethean creation" of art defines one mode in conventional romantic rhetoric, the act of giving birth, another ("a God,
superior to any artist"). Parturition temporarily generates feelings of
superiority, but before long dreams of artistic triumph entice the
dancer once more. Both art and motherhood involve ambiguities about
control of the outer world. The mother is "helpless" while "the little
being" sucks and howls; yet she claims godlike power. The artist is
"possessed" by her dream, itself "proud," dominating and controlling
her life; but her own pride emerges as she imagines calling new creations from earth and heaven. Such ambiguity is inherent in the concept
of "genius," which possesses its possessor in unpredictable ways, and it
requires little imagination to see it also in motherhood. This particular
analogy between two forms of feminine creativity is particularly significant in Isadora Duncan's account of herself because it suggests why
she could receive ultimate satisfaction from neither. Seeking always
ways to control her own life and the responses of others (her childhood
experience of the father's desertion, the family's bitter poverty and
insecurity may hint why), she thus engages in a search destined never
to achieve success. Her autobiography ends with invocation of "the
dream" associated with Buddha, Christ, "all great artists," Lenin: "I
was entering now into this dream that my work and life might become
a part of its glorious promise." Only through dreams can she sustain

her sense of possibility. She resolves the potential conflict between "art" and "life" by acts of imaginative assertion that subordinate the value of all activity to that of the actor. Gazing at Botticelli's *Primavera*, the dancer decides, "I will dance this picture and give to others this message of love, spring, procreation of life which has been given to me with such anguish. I will give to them, through the dance, such ecstasy." Her extravagant assessment of the power of art to bring "ecstasy" to all the world depends on her exalted self-image: the power, finally, is not art's but Isadora's. She sees herself as the giver of unimaginable gifts, exercising her power benevolently as dancer, mother, teacher, lover, her own expressiveness the sole focus of her attention.

"Art" and "Life" alike aid her endless self-caressing. Other women may imagine lovers who will be their own mirror images; Isadora finds one. "Here, at last, was my mate; my love; my self—for we were not two, but one, that one amazing being of whom Plato tells in the Phaedrus, two halves of the same soul. This was not a young man making love to a girl. This was the meeting of twin souls." She is speaking of Gordon Craig. Earlier, she missed an opportunity to be seduced by Rodin. "What a pity! How often I have regretted this childish miscomprehension which lost to me the divine chance of giving my virginity to the Great God Pan himself, to the Mighty Rodin. Surely Art and all Life would have been richer thereby!" Her attribution of universal significance to her own sex life is another instance of her imaginative transformation of experience. People become souls or pagan gods in her mythology, a seduction can transfigure the universe, a man does not make love to a woman—even when he *does*—but enacts a symbolic union. It is impossible for her to look at things as they are; everything must feed on her sense of her own unique significance. "I could not do anything without seeming extravagantly different from other people": the boast and the doom of the artist.

The patterns of Isadora's experience lend themselves readily to her myth-making. Her difficulty in making full commitments, her inability to be satisfied, ensure a sequence of constant change. Nothing lasts. One lover yields to another, or to a period of celibacy which astonishes her, so conscious is she of her seductive body. She starts a school of the dance, loves its students, leaves it. She and her siblings decide to build a temple on a Greek mountain. They drink goat's milk, dress in tunics, convince the countryside of their madness. Then Isadora goes away, leaving her brother to discover the impossibility of finding water and to abandon the undertaking. The tragic death of her two children corroborates the impermanence of all her commitments. She does not, of course, see it that way—nor is there any literal connection between her inability to sustain anything but the conviction of her own uniqueness and the accident that deprived her of her children. From her point of view, she is a victim of Fate, heroine of a compelling tragic drama. The disproportion between the way she sees and the way she reveals herself creates much of the interest of her autobiography, testimony to a mind that refuses to accept the domination of external circumstance. Her vision more compelling than any conceivable reality, she declares her ultimate power to deny facts, transforming them into myth.

Her tawdry prose both defines and undermines her way of seeing herself, always demanding more interest than it justifies. Isadora, trying to control Life (and Art), cannot control language because she lacks critical capacity, capacity for judgment, capacity to deal in realities. In fact, her vocation as artist expresses her discontent with the real. Only the impossible—the perfectly expressive dance, the ideally fulfilling love, the Greek myth come to life—is adequate. Dreaming of herself as creator and apostle of perfect art, perfect life, she collides with reality, successful as an artist, constantly disappointed by life. Her self-dramatizing, self-loving writing about herself tries to heighten her experience by grandiose metaphor but repeatedly reveals the final falseness of such metaphors, the necessary unhappiness of a life so fundamentally founded on a dream of uniqueness.

Dancing, realizing her art, her audience before her, Isadora experiences the arrangement of the universe for which she longs—herself at its center. Here she achieves that unity of fantasy and fact which art demands, able to sustain in action her larger than life-size imagining of herself, winning the applause that attests her stature. As a dancer she expends disciplined energy in the service of her dream. Her real artistic achievement as a physical performer contrasts with the aesthetic inadequacy of her autobiography as a verbal accomplishment. Yet however real her achievement as a dancer, it was not equivalent to her vision of herself as dancer: she may have delighted millions, but she did not bring millions the experience of ecstasy. The power of the dancer is less than that of the dreamer, who can assert and believe her universal power, universal love. As an autobiographer, Isadora Duncan is dreamer rather than observer of her life: not an artist despite all her assertions of artistry.

Although she sometimes recognizes that art and life may make conflicting demands, Isadora characteristically insists on her capacity to
reconcile their claims through sheer genius. She refuses to admit that
the desire for power may clash with the yearning for love; her denial
probably conceals a potent fear. That fear emerges more clearly in other
woman artists, less able than she to use imaginative transformation as
a weapon against reality. The misery flaunted or concealed in the self-
depictions of woman artists often derives from their sense of the incompatibility of their desires. Two interesting cases in point are Dora
Carrington, who, after adopting various temporary expedients, killed
herself when "love" no longer justified her artistic achievement; and
Margaret Anderson, who resolved her conflict by rejecting "life" in
favor of an art which existed only in her self-conception.

Carrington's discomfort with her female nature was loud and consistent. "You know I have always hated being a woman. I think I mind
much more than most women. The Fiend [her telling metaphor for
menstruation] which most women hardly notice, fills me with such
disgust and agitation every time, I cannot get reconciled to it. I am
continually depressed by effeminacy [a word which clearly implies that
masculinity is the standard of excellence]. It is true *au fond* I have a
female inside which is proved by ~ [her symbol for sexual intercourse]
but afterwards a sort of rage fills me because of that very pleasure ~.
And I cannot literally bear to let my mind think of ~ again, or of
my femaleness."

Carrington had lovers, a husband, a strange prolonged relationship
with Lytton Strachey, after whose death her own life seemed so meaningless that she ended it at thirty-nine. She tested the meaning of relationship and of artistic endeavor, finding it impossible to value art
more highly than people, feeling that only great artistic creation could
compensate for human failure, recognizing her own artistic inadequacy. Love, she believed, was the fundamental means of fulfillment,
art only a kind of *pis aller*. But she was doomed to want to be an
artist, and doomed to feel inadequate both as artist and as woman. She
did not write an autobiography, but her letters, collected by David
Garnett, attest her condition. "The pleasures of being loved and loving
and having friends and the pains and sordidness of the same relations. . . . One year I would like to take an average of the days one is
happy against the wretched days. Perhaps it's absurd ever to think
about it. If one painted pictures it wouldn't matter and one probably
wouldn't think about it. But I can't see the use of painting pictures 'as

good as' those at the London Group." "Gerald [Brenan, her lover], I think I am unfitted . . . to have a relation with anyone. . . . The alternative is to try and be a serious artist." If she is self-dramatizing in presenting herself as hopelessly miserable, she also reveals genuine unhappiness, even desperation, for the alternatives she perceives are equally impossible. She cannot by taking thought make herself happy rather than wretched, increase the proportion of cheerful days or her own capacity for fruitful relationship; nor can she by will make herself an adequate artist by her own standards. Sometimes she claims that her painting is more important to her than anything else, though characteristically she measures it by comparison with emotional realities: "I think you know that the discovery of a person, of an affection, of a new emotion, is to me *next to my painting* [my italics], the greatest thing I care about." More typical is her moan to Rosamond Lehmann: "Your reproaches towards yourself for not writing more, make my cheeks *burn* with shame. For really I used every excuse not to do any proper painting. It's partly I have such high standards that I can't bear going on with pictures when I can see they are amateurish and dull."

Like Isadora, Carrington feels the "specialness" of the artist, the degree to which she is set apart, and she feels it as tragic. Her wish to love and to be loved conflicts daily with her wish to paint, and she is unable to resolve the conflict in fantasy or in reality. Her image of herself as artist, stressing the terrible split and its inevitability, suggests also that the emotional energies of love may be the source as well as the enemy of art.

> The importance above everything [that] a work of art, and a creator of such works, has for me. And yet do you know, this morning I felt these conflicting emotions are destroying my purpose for painting. That perhaps that feeling which I have had ever since I came to London years ago now, that I am not strong enough to live in this world of people, and paint, is a feeling which has complete truth in it. And yet when I envision leaving you [Strachey] and going like Gerald into isolation, I feel I should be so wretched that I should never have the spirit to work.

To paint while living in a world of people is impossible, but it is equally impossible to isolate oneself. Carrington decided to marry Ralph Partridge largely to avoid constituting an emotional drain on Strachey, to whom she writes a heart-rending letter declaring her undying love and her determination not to allow herself the dependency of love. She can imagine avoiding dependency only by creating new dependencies. She cannot paint without loving, she cannot love in "normal" heterosexual ways (her attempt at a sexual relation with Strachey was disastrous); she finds in Strachey the homosexual lover who makes painting and life possible for her, providing love without too many associated demands; without him, quite simply, she cannot exist. "What does anything mean to me now without you. I see my paints and think it is no use, for Lytton will never see my pictures now, and I cry."

The problem she dramatizes, the conflicts between the yearning for artistic expression and the desire for relationship, is not peculiar to women, but women are likely to experience it with special intensity. Feminine narcissism as traditionally defined centers on love for one's own body and involves the desire to attract men sexually. The artist's narcissism, on the other hand, connects itself with the sense of creative power, the need to express preceding the need to attract. In men, for whom ideas of conquest often mingle with those of love, artistic power, declaring the vitality of the personality, may seem identical with sexual force. Norman Mailer is sexy despite his paunch; Picasso still clicked his goat hoofs at ninety. For a woman, the artist's power—assertive, insistent, dominating—combines uneasily with orthodox feminine modes of attraction. If she performs as dancer, singer, actress, the potential incompatibility may be resolved: offering herself as artistic product, she offers herself also as sexual being. The writer who writes only of herself (we shall encounter an example in Mary MacLane) attempts an equivalent resolution—risking, however, the totality of self-absorption which shuts out rather than attracts others. But the painter, the novelist, the sculptress or composer, whose separate creation demands attention for itself, faces a cruel dilemma of opposing needs. Carrington attempted to reconcile their conflict by declaring that she painted only for the sake of another; deprived of that rationalization, she could no longer live. Her belief that the feminine role is to serve others became an obsession which had to be gratified in order to make painting possible. If Isadora is the victim of her insistent self-glorification, which attempts to deny the incompatibility of power and love, Carrington was equally trapped in her devotion to the impossible Other, again, an effort to paper over the split in her desires.

The clash between the artist's narcissism, its need for power satisfied by creation, and the woman's need to attract others by her very nature may be resolved also by denial of an opposite kind, declaring art's transcendent importance at the cost of love's. Margaret Anderson's career—which she painstakingly records, often almost moment by moment, in three volumes—involves a systematic if not fully self-aware effort to deny her need for others or theirs for her. "My unreality is chiefly this: I have never felt much like a human being. It's a splendid feeling." "I have always had so little need of the humanity of people. Their humanity is always the same." "I can't imagine belonging to a group." The life she reports is one of increasing isolation and diminishing accomplishment: first vigorous activity in Chicago and New York, then twenty-one years in France with a beloved older woman, finally solitude, in which she sustains herself by her larger than life-size self-image. Like Isadora, she feels superior to others: "My impression was that I was one of the world's most favored beings, lifted through space from one rapturous event to another, possessing everything necessary for happiness and living like a lighted Christmas tree." And like Isadora's self-conception, her "impression" derives more from wish than from fact.

Yet she had some solid accomplishment to her credit, mainly as an editor. Founding *The Little Review* before she was twenty-one, she made it an important medium of artistic expression. Her work as editor had symbolic as well as literal significance, providing a metaphor for her orientation toward life. "I was born to be an editor," she observes. Shifting the metaphor in another volume, she makes the point clearer: "I always felt that I knew the score. From morning to night I lived like an orchestra conductor." Both images are of control. The conflicts implicit for most women in a commitment to art generate chaos, a grotesque disorder of clashing impulses and purposes. The release of this disorder drove Carrington to her death; the control of disorder was the center of Margaret Anderson's life. Her impulse, as she points out, was always toward revision—of other people's expression, and of her own. She insists on dominating experience, on dominating her own consciousness: "I tried never to let a day go by without turning it into a trance." Controlling her experience, she limits it more and more. It becomes less interesting to the reader with whom she shares it—she had difficulty finding a publisher for her autobiography after the first volume. There is pathos in her claim to have achieved self-knowledge with the aid of the mystic Gurdjieff, who helps her to see "that fixed point about which my life movement had revolved . . . : self-love." The insight is all too convincing—but insight appears to have brought no end to the self-obsession, expressed in ever more frequent claims of the author's superiority to others, her rare sensibilities, the isolation that testifies to her magnificent difference.

An artist only in self-conception, not in accomplishment, a failure at human relations, Margaret Anderson announces defiantly, "I won't be cornered and I won't stay suppressed." But she avoids the restrictions of society only by self-constriction, depriving herself of the satisfactions both of art and of relationship, demonstrating that her editorship of her own life has produced a very cramped volume. The "power" she achieves focuses mainly on herself, and its most conspicuous result is an autobiography which, like Isadora's, testifies to the substitution of self-flattery for self-confrontation. The need to think of herself as an artist is far more intense than the need to be one.

Isadora Duncan believed that the power of artistic success was a means to love, and that she had achieved both to the highest degree. Carrington and Margaret Anderson, understandably less secure in their sense of themselves as artists, doubted whether artistic power could coexist with fulfilled love. A third possibility is represented by Marie Bashkirtseff, who shared Isadora's conviction without her achievement and identified herself as artist at least partly on the basis of her passionate yearning for fame and love.

A young woman of Russian birth whose adolescence passed mainly in Paris, Marie Bashkirtseff died of tuberculosis at the age of twenty-four, leaving diaries (clearly intended for publication) which record her experience from the time she was twelve to a few days before her death. Both adolescent and aspiring artist, she wanted desperately to be a great painter. Early in her teens, she had hoped to be a singer, but there was little evidence that she could sing. She transferred her aspiration to the visual arts, dedicating herself passionately to her effort to achieve recognition for her artistic production, ignoring her gathering illness in her full commitment to her studies. For her the connection between fame and love seemed perfectly clear. "What is necessary to my very existence is to have it acknowledged that I possess great talent. I never shall be happy like all the world. As Balzac wrote: 'To be celebrated and to be loved, that is happiness!' And yet, to be loved is only an accessory, or, rather, the natural result of being celebrated."

Over and over, in a way that by now must seem familiar, the diarist reiterates her distinction between herself and "all the world," insisting that she is different, that she can escape from the tedious restrictions of daily life into romantic unhappiness or the equally romantic special happiness of fame. Social restrictions, she realizes, are particularly limiting for women. She cannot go anywhere without a chaperone, she has no freedom of movement, people talk about her if she tries to assert her difference, and she seems as fearful as Hedda Gabler of the strictures of public opinion. But if people talked about her *as an artist*, everything would be wonderful. The self-image of artist is one of freedom and of ultimate justification. It is difficult, she knows, really to *be* an artist. When she paints real pictures, she necessarily risks judgment. She can protect herself by the knowledge that she is only a student; page after page of her journal records her obsessive comparisons of herself with her contemporaries. She has had less training, less experience than they; less should be expected of her. Intensely competitive, absorbed in rituals of comparative judgment, she is subject to violent discouragement over the impossibility of adequate artistic achievement. The remedy for such discouragement is the retreat inward. She can imagine herself as flawlessly beautiful (beauty, she explains, is "everything for a woman") and control of self-presentation to impose this self-image on the world. "I take great pride in appearing radiant and proud, impregnable in every way." She is literally impregnable: her relations with men take place only in her imagination. On one occasion she allows herself to be kissed, by a cardinal's nephew; nothing comes of the relationship, and she feels humiliated by having made herself momentarily vulnerable. Far safer to dream of ideal men, confiding to her diary that she would be unable to marry a man with corns, a man possessed of actual human frailties. Her dreams of herself as artist serve a similar defensive function.

There is no way for Marie Bashkirtseff to reconcile fantasy with fact: the fantasies are too extreme. She cannot be as beautiful as she imagines herself being, no real lover will be devoid of corns, no picture that she paints will win as much fame and love as she demands. The omnipotence possible in a world devoid of real opposition is more triumphant than literal power could conceivably be. The only way to preserve an inviolable sense of power is never to test it: fantasy is the best protection against the imperfections of reality.

All Marie Bashkirtseff's fantasies—of beauty, of fame, of perfect romance, of artistic achievement—reflect her intense desire for love. But the tragic result of her dedication to a larger than life-size self-image, larger than life-size demands on the world, is necessary isolation. No lover, no mother, no friend, no art critic can satisfy her needs. She is forced finally back on herself: "I know one person who loves me, understands me, pities me, who employs every hour in efforts to make me happier; someone who will do everything for me and will succeed; someone who will never betray me again—although that happened once [when she kissed the cardinal's nephew]—and that person is *myself*." Her recognition that only she can gratify herself is perhaps ironic in tone; it is nonetheless true.

Mortality, the condition in which all human achievement must be measured, the ineluctable reality, is the final enemy of fantasy. As the psychoanalyst Marion Milner puts it, "Certainly the greatest disillusion, the greatest discrepancy between one's wish and the external facts, is the fact of death." Marie Bashkirtseff, like the rest of us, was dying; but faster than most. She avoids the ultimate disillusionment by attempting to incorporate death itself into her structure of romantic illusion, dreaming of death as she dreams of love: the seal of uniqueness. "I can not live; I am not constituted like other people. . . . Were I a goddess, and had the whole universe at my service, I would find the service bad." "I should like to see everything, to possess everything, to embrace everything, to become absorbed in everything, and to die . . .; to die in an ecstasy of joy at the thought of solving the last mystery." In some moods she enjoys thinking of herself as romantically doomed; in others, she declares herself "amused" by the possibility of death and unwilling to take measures against it. Although she reports symptoms of illness and worries of doctors, the threat of death is never real to her; her imagination converts it into further justification for her narcissism.

But the young woman's early death, throwing a special glamour over an externally uneventful life, also becomes a powerful emblem of the limitations against which she struggled. If she was unable fully to confront this unavoidable final limitation except through the rosy lens of fantasy, she was equally unable to confront the other limitations of her life. Her only power was the power to imagine what she wished to be, what she wished of others; to try to impose her imaginings on reality. Her artistic talent suggested the possibility of fulfilling simultaneously her yearning for love and her yearning for power; or perhaps the strength of those yearnings itself generated what talent she possessed. By thinking of herself as an artist, she could escape full realization of the world's unwillingness to take her as seriously as she took herself.

At a dinner party once I met a young woman who had kept a daily journal since her early adolescence. I asked her what sort of material she included in it. "Oh," she replied, "I lie."

She might have said that she wrote fiction in her journal, but she was too conscious of the need her fictions served: to re-create her experience in a way that made it tolerable.

Mary MacLane was such a liar: and her lies, revealing the familiar wish for power and love, reveal also the degree to which she feels confined to the world of her imagination in order to achieve them. Another adolescent, she resembles Martha Quest and Esther Greenwood in her inability to commit herself to meaningful activity. Like Isadora, she interprets her life in terms of a myth of herself. Like Marie Bashkirtseff, she offers virtually no external accomplishment to substantiate the myth. She confesses in a second edition of her account of herself that she lied in the first. A nineteen-year-old girl of no external distinction whatever, living in Butte, Montana, she remakes her experience to suit her image of a remarkable Self. What she writes is no journal but a "story": a narrative imagined in a form that substantiates her grandest claim, the claim to be an artist. Her evocation of the large personality of artist, her self-justification through sensibility, generated her extraordinary books.

Here is the opening sequence of *The Story of Mary MacLane*, published in 1902, now long out of print, remarkably revealing of the psyche of one variety of woman-as-artist:

> I of womankind and of nineteen years, will now begin to set down as full and frank a Portrayal as I am able of myself, Mary MacLane, for whom the world contains not a parallel.
> I am convinced of this, for I am odd.
> I am distinctly original innately and in development.
> I have in me a quite unusual intensity of life.
> I can feel.
> I have a marvelous capacity for misery and for happiness.
> I am broad-minded.
> I am a genius.

Her first self-definition sets the tone of the book and prepares for her later claims, her description of herself as Romantic artist, comparable to Lord Byron and Marie Bashkirtseff although, she decides finally, "deeper" and "more wonderful" than her Russian predecessor. In many respects her comparisons are accurate: she is indeed Byronic in her insistence on her grand isolation and her superiority to conventional moral norms (although she doesn't actually *do* anything unconventional); and she resembles Marie Bashkirtseff in the intensity of her youthful narcissism and its focus on the self-image of artist.

Unlike the Russian woman, though, Mary MacLane is richly aware of her environment. Her triumph and her limitation as an artist derive from her need to define herself against her surroundings, animate and inanimate: to distinguish herself vividly from her mother, who, she says, feels for her daughter what a hen might feel for her egg; to defy the commonplace through exact rendition of observed detail, the exactness itself declaring her superiority. She sees precisely what surrounds her, praying to the devil, to deliver her from her milieu, with its lisle stockings, people who refer to a woman's "shape," fried eggplant, talk of "a nice young man." Even a toothbrush provides her with a means of differentiation. Hers has a silver handle, but it hangs in the bathroom with five more matter-of-fact brushes. When she removes it, she feels overwhelmed by the ordinary; when she lets it stay, she must contemplate evidence of her separation from her kind. Everything she sees, everything she hears, refers to her. Her literary transformation of experience fills Butte with interest while declaring her frustration, making meaningful for the reader exactly what the writer experiences as meaningless. Her meticulous examination of banality is an act of triumph over it.

Marie Bashkirtseff worked hard at the study of art, making at least that much attempt to realize her dream of herself as artist. Her Montana imitator creates nothing beyond her personality to justify her self-designation, but her personality, as rendered in prose, becomes a work of art. Toward the end of her self-portrayal, she explains the nature of that "genius" she has insistently claimed: "I am merely and above all a creature of intense passionate *feeling*. I feel—everything. It is my genius. It burns me like fire." (One may recall Catherine, from *Wuthering Heights*.) But she "would give up this genius eagerly, gladly—at once and forever—for one dear, bright day free from loneliness."

It's the familiar dilemma: does the artist, even the artist of feeling, win love or lose it? Mary MacLane is not concerned with fame, but she is obsessed with the problem of winning love. And she recognizes the alienating effect of her self-obsession. "I know I am not lovable," she confesses," . . . There is no one to love me now." "My wailing, waiting soul burns with but one desire: *to be loved—oh, to be loved.*" Although she protects herself by irony in much of her self-description, all protection vanishes here: one cannot avoid the reality of her pain. Self-mockery returns as she expresses her desire to be loved in more specific terms, but it does not disguise her genuine emotion. Mary MacLane imagines two lovers: the devil and Napoleon. Their meaning for her is identical: *strength* makes both attractive. Her longing for Napoleon has particular poignance because much earlier she has declared, "I have the personality, the nature, of a Napoleon, albeit a feminine translation. . . . Had I been born a man I would by now have made a deep impression of myself on the world—on some part of it. But I am a woman." Unable to sustain her imagination of herself as a Napoleon, she falls back on a feminine transformation: if she cannot be a great man, let her be loved by one. But such love is punishment: "I would have you conquer me, crush me, know me." "Treat me cruelly, brutally." The ultimate fantasy demands neither Satan nor Napoleon, only "any man so that he is strong and thoroughly a villain, and so that he fascinates me." She sounds more and more like Catherine, inventing her Heathcliff, but unable to discover him.

Although she speaks of falling in love with the devil and with Napoleon, her imagery of being overwhelmed, possessed, denies her active participation in love. When she thinks of herself as feminine, her stress is on being loved; conversely, her own capacity to love seems to her masculine. Much of her anguish focuses in her feeling that she is not, after all, "a real woman"—specifically because, she says, she is unable ever to "go beyond *self*" like such noble beings as Charlotte Corday. Marie Bashkirtseff had a less self-punishing version of the same fantasy, concluding that she herself was a woman only "on the outside." She took pride in the sense of her fundamental maleness, one more fantasy of escape from the reality of social restriction. For Mary MacLane, on the other hand, the self-image of bisexuality was a tragic rather than triumphant mark of her difference from others. Unable to feel herself a real woman, she was obviously not a real man either. Lacking the satisfaction of either sex, she envied both; her desire to be an artist marked her to herself as a sexual anomaly; and it doubtless would have been scant comfort to her to learn that modern psychoanalysts find bisexuality characteristic of the artist's temperament.

Jonathan Swift's famous contrast between the spider "which feeding and engendering on it self, turns all into Excrement and Venom; producing nothing at all, but Fly-bane and a Cobweb" and the bee "which, by an universal Range, with long Search, much Study, true Judgment, and Distinction of Things, brings home Honey and Wax," defined the difference between supporters of the Moderns and the Ancients in *The Battle of the Books*. The spider "Spins and Spits wholly from himself" because of his pride. But many a woman has been forced by fate rather than temperament to compose like the spider, deprived of the range, search, and study made possible for the certainly masculine (this bee being metaphor rather than insect) honeybee. Feeding and engendering on herself, Mary MacLane creates her story, herself its heroine and its victim. Her subject is always herself—a compelling subject for reader as well as writer. The woman who dreams of the artist's power exercises it in describing it: she has literally become an artist of self-concentration. Her artistic energy throbs with the pressure generated by confinement. With no subject but herself, she justifies by force of her prose her demand to be taken seriously.

"Nothing is easier to pardon than the mistakes and excesses of self-love," Lionel Trilling has written. "If we are quick to condemn them, we take pleasure in forgiving them. . . . But we distinguish between our response to the self-love of men and the self-love of women. No woman could have won the forgiveness that has been so willingly given (after due condemnation) to the self-regard of, say, Yeats and Shaw." The observation may be out-of-date, but it certainly applies to Mary MacLane's era, when to be a woman was to be severely restricted. Allowed not even the open indulgence of self-love, the writer could escape by denying actuality in the construction of a powerful self-image. Her most trivial acts, even her flaws—like Marie Bashkirtseff, she claims to tell *everything* about herself—are glamorized or manufactured. Thus, she claims her *eating* an index of her artistic gifts. Her story converts eating into an aesthetic activity, rhapsodizing over olives, steak and onions, brown sugar fudge, maintaining that her consumption of them amounts to an artistic achievement. "I have uncovered for myself the art that lies in obscure shadows. I have discovered the art of the day of small things." Cooking, for most women a way of taking care of others, becomes for Mary MacLane a means to sustain herself metaphorically as well as literally. Avid for experience, confined in opportunity, she greedily takes in to herself what she can, savors what is available, pathetically boasts her responsiveness to a green onion as an index of her imaginative gifts. Similarly, she brags of stealing three dollars in order to buy chrysanthemums for an impoverished neighbor: thus she declares her difference from her family and acquaintances. In the second edition of her book, she admits that the entire story was invented; the admission of lying becomes another element in her vision of herself as extraordinary. But the fascination of Mary MacLane's books is not primarily that of falsification. It comes from the purity of her focus on herself, the brilliance and ingenuity with which she finds meanings and declares her right to attention, not for her accomplishments, only for herself. Mary MacLane declares the supreme relevance of only her own standards, demanding not merely to be forgiven her self-love but to be justified by it. She is her own creation, the truth of falsity of her record finally irrelevant.

Yet that record has the undeniable flavor of truth, in its obsessive concentration on external detail: it cannot be dismissed as the product only of a young woman's wishes, her daydreams of how she might be seen. For Marie Bashkirtseff, the link between the real world and that of dreams is her literal activity as an aspiring painter. By working at her art she defends against the temptation to abandon reality in favor of total commitment to the inner world. Mary MacLane does as little as possible in the real world; or so she tells us. She protests the restrictions of her female lot by going through minimal motions—making her bed, talking with a neighbor, cooking a meal—but refusing to invent more meaningful activity. Her mind, however, reflects steadily on external reality: observation is the stuff of her curious prose-poetry. Her toothbrush with a silver handle sounds like something she made up; but it is actually something she looks at. The significance with which she invests it is from within, but her commitment to the outer world remains, when she writes best, the foundation of her extravagances.

Mary MacLane's cobwebs, often compelling in their intricacy and ingenuity, become flimsy at the moments when they lose that firm connection to actuality: her writing doesn't always have the discipline of art. Her imaginings can be grandiose, empty, self-indulgent, her prose unbearably self-caressing ("My heart, my soul, my mind go wandering—wandering; ploughing their way through darkness with never a ray of light; groping with helpless hands; asking, longing, wanting things pursued by a Demon of Unrest") when she abandons all actuality beyond her emotions, answerable to no demand for exactness. Clichés multiply as she asserts the intensity of her feeling, demonstrating the destructive paradox of self-concentration: literary obsession with the self may end by weakening the self's actuality. Mary MacLane's midnight onions are more real than all her groping with helpless hands.

Hers is, of course, a version of the dilemma faced by all Romantic artists. Alienated from their environment, possessed by a sense of their own uniqueness, they may exploit their powers of perception yet feel that their surroundings are not worthy of them. Often they are gripped by what the critic Gabriel Josipovici has called "the paralysing euphoria of the Imagination," all conceivable reality less satisfying than the contemplation of infinite possibility. Economic necessity has forced action on most men since the early nineteenth century; and one may wonder whether the lack of it was an advantage to Shelley and Byron, although certainly it was to Wordsworth. It is hard to imagine a male Emily Dickinson in any era. If our poets are also insurance executives or doctors or college teachers, their work seems not to suffer as a result; one may even posit a certain profit. For women, on the other hand, until the very recent past, inertia was a social possibility. The world might not only allow but actively encourage women—as it has never encouraged men—simply to wallow in their inner lives. Mary MacLane's fate appears to have been near-paralysis. The art of her journal remained a compelling preoccupation, but her later life, more than her early years, has an unnerving aspect of parable.

"Later," in this case, means her early thirties. She herself again provides testimony. *I, Mary MacLane* appeared in 1917, fifteen years after the first book, to which it is a sequel. A war was going on; it is mentioned once, as Mary MacLane fantasizes briefly about exchanging her "two black dresses for two white ones with red crosses on the sleeves." She is back in Butte, having left it for eight years in Boston and New York made possible by the fame of her earlier book which, as she observes in its second edition, brought her "an astounding notoriety and much good gold money." In the East she met other young women, other writers, men who were interested in her; she hints of at least one love affair. But she chose to return to Montana, and she writes once more of her life of spiritual impoverishment there—a life freely elected. Now she is the old maid daughter of the family, her external life confined to housework, solitary walks, reading. She makes her bed meticulously and picks lint from her blue rug. She eats dinner with the family, but she doesn't eat much. On the other hand, she makes midnight raids on the pantry, stealing a cold boiled potato or a green onion. Her picture gallery has been enlarged to include Marie Lloyd, Fanny Brawn, Nell Gwynn, Ty Cobb, Charlotte Corday, Susan B. Anthony, Queen Boadicea: earlier, it contained only thirteen pictures of Napoleon. John Keats's image presides; he is the central object of her adoration. She owns two black dresses, she listens to the voices of children, she takes luxurious baths. She laughs at William Jennings Bryan.

The choice of Butte over Boston is the choice of fantasy over reality. It enables Mary MacLane to retreat to a life obsessively private, a woman's life of external insignificance, inner power. She still defines herself as woman—meaning now something distinctly sexual—and as artist—meaning something rather peculiar.

> I am a true Artist, not as a writer but as a writing person. . . . It is not a literary but a personal art. . . .
>
> I once thought me destined to be a "writer" in the ordinary sense. And many good people visioned a writing career for me. It has a vapid taste, just to recall it. . . .
>
> My writing is to me a precious thing—and a rare bird—and a Babylonish jade. It demands gold in exchange for itself. But though it is my talent it is not my living. It is too myself, like my earlobes and my throat, to commercialize by the day.

From her point of view, her selfhood now *is* her writing. She cannot bear to think of herself as "a 'writer' in the ordinary sense" or to contemplate anything so "vapid" as a "writing career." The sparseness of her literary production and its total concentration on herself as subject distinguish her from the "ordinary" writer and declare the high value of the"precious thing," her writing. So she thinks of herself as a writer exactly because she doesn't write much, and her literary art has weird affinities with her rubbing cold cream into her face, her attention to the quality of her underwear. One chapter begins, "I love my shoes." The forms of self-adoration are various.

Mary MacLane's most impassioned claim is that she yearns for the real:

> I want to plunge headlong into life—not imitation life which is all I've yet known, but honest worldly life at its biggest and humanest and cruelest and damnedest: to be blistered and scorched by it if it be so ordered—so that only it's realness—from the outside of my skin to the deeps of my spirit. . . .

> I want to feel one big hot red bloody kiss-of-Life placed
> square and strong on my mouth and shot straight into me to
> the back wall of my Heart.

But her language betrays her: reality is her ultimate fantasy. Her actual
experience—Butte, Boston, New York—seems to her only "imitation
life"; her dream of erotic satisfaction identifies itself with wider, vaguer
kinds of fulfillment; her masochism emerges once more, in the eager-
ness to be "blistered and scorched," the yearning for the "hot red
bloody" kiss: clearly no literal event will ever seem sufficiently "real"
to satisfy her. Despite the fact that the book's compelling subject is
herself, even that self is so manifestly an image of her dreams that the
author becomes a fictional character: one finds it harder to believe in
her than in her observations of external fact. Did she really pick the
lint off the rug, did she really have a "picture gallery"? Such questions
rarely occur to the reader of autobiography in relation to such mundane
details. We may wonder whether a love affair took place exactly as
described, but why should we doubt whether a woman does the housework, what could be at stake to make her lie about such matters?
What's at stake for Mary MacLane is her own significance, denied by
the world outside her, therefore needing to be created in the most
minute detail.

Here she is, explaining why she enjoys the back of magazines:

I like the Revolvers, handsome plausible short-barreled Revolvers with
pictures of ordinary people in dim-lit midnight bedrooms, and ordinary expected-looking burglars climbing in windows—Revolvers of
ten shots and of six, and of different calibers, and all of them gleam-
ingly mystically desirable: . . . I like the foods—of miraculous spotless
purity and enticement—Biscuits and Chocolate and Figs, and Foie-
gras in thick glossy little pots, so richly pictured and sung that merely
to let my thoughts graze in their pasturage fattens my Heart: I like
the men's very thin Watches, and men's Garters—no metal can touch
you—, and men's fluffy-lathered shaving sticks, and men's trim smart
flawless tailored Suits, in none of which I have use or interest until I
find them in the Back of a magazine: I like the jars and boxes and tubes
and glasses of Cold Cream, Cold Cream fit for skins of goddesses, fit
for elves to feed on—a soft satiny scented snow-white elysium of wax
and vaseline and almond paste, pictured in forty alluring shapes till it
feels pleasantly ecstatic just to be living in the same world with be-

witching vases of Cold Cream, Cold Cream, Cold Cream—always bewitching and lovely but never so notably and festively as in the Back of a magazine: and I like the Pencils: and Book-cases: and Silver: and Jewels: and Glass: and Gloves. . . .

The self-awareness of this account is as striking as its sense of detail. Mary MacLane understands that she has no "use or interest" for the appurtenances she glorifies until they are transformed into fantasy. Real revolvers, real men's suits, are tedious. The advertisements which picture them distance them, provide a kind of allegory of the transforming operations of the artist's mind. Real cold cream is alluring, imagined cold cream—like Keats's unheard melodies—more so. And of course the operations of the artist's mind are much in evidence here: in the precision of language ("notably and festively"), the comedy of conjunctions ("Fit for the skin of goddesses, fit for elves to feed on"), the irony of perspective ("ordinary expected-looking burglars"), even the delight in commercial jargon ("no metal can touch you"). Real advertisements, after all, are tedious too. Enjoying the play of her mind over what is intended only to encourage buying and selling, not bothering about the "real," the writer uncovers the poetry of the prosaic.

Here, clearly, she is not lying: her professed subject and her real one are the same, the capacity of her imagination to reconcile her to the actual by converting it to the fantastic. One admires and wonders at the force of that imagination; temporarily one may even share the author's high self-assessment. But Mary MacLane's compulsion always to transform actuality or reject it or deny its claim to reality, as when she terms her own experience "imitation life," finally limits the scope of her artistic achievement. She is alienated from her own life, as she is alienated from her fellows by her tormenting awareness of being unique. Her dilemma as an artist is that of all artists, all adolescents, all human beings: to reconcile the inner and the outer world. Her compulsive, selective eating, a primitive act of incorporation, enables her to possess what she wants from outside—though only, of course, by destroying it. Her compulsive writing, attempting equivalent incorporation, likewise risks destroying objective reality. Marion Milner remarks "the primitive hating that results from the inescapable discrepancy between subjective and objective, between the unlimited possibilities of one's dreams and what the real world actually offers us." Such hating seems the dominant fact of Mary MacLane's experience—her contempt for other people is almost total; she protects herself against the probability of receiving less love than she yearns for by declaring her total superiority to everyone who might offer love. As an imaginative woman, she faces a vaster discrepancy between subjective and objective than a male counterpart would probably endure because the possibilities of real existence are so severely limited by social expectation. In Butte, the limitation is obvious: she is supposed to sweep the floor and wash the dishes. In Boston and New York, which seem to offer relative freedom, limitation is only more subtle: she still feels herself exploited by a rigid set of conventions, even if those conventions belong to the Bohemian world. Everywhere, objective reality is a terrible threat to imaginative freedom. So Mary MacLane, like Isadora Duncan, struggles to impose her dreams on the world, working to promulgate that self-image she must treasure as the best compensation for a limited experience. Sometimes her persona is as compelling for the reader as for the author; sometimes it seems only a figment of the writer's imagination, a solipsistic avoidance of communication.

Relatively few women have asserted themselves unambiguously as shaping artists in the act of writing about themselves; even Anaïs Nin, whose self-glorification as artist and as woman parallels Isadora Duncan's, publishes diaries rather than formal autobiography. Mary McCarthy, insisting explicitly on the *art* of autobiography, masters life by describing it. In a fashion rare among women artists describing themselves, she achieves a harmonious interchange of subjective and objective, recognizing and dealing with her own desire for an imaginative heightening of experience, understanding that fantasy precedes art but is not identical with it.

The fusion Mary McCarthy achieves between inner wishes and outer reality depends on artistic control. Unlike Isadora, she does not have to assert her total power over the external world or to revel in her ultimate lovability. Unlike Mary MacLane, she need not cut herself off from actual experience in order to avoid damaging her image of her own specialness. Yet "specialness" and "lovability" are important to her, too. She claims them on the basis of her literary accomplishment, and makes that accomplishment a demonstration of her life's struggle and achievement. Her awareness of herself as artist—as a writer converting her life into a work of art—is unrelenting in *Memories of a Catholic Girlhood*. It is, indeed, her fundamental subject. Unlike women whose self-definition as artist defends them from the necessity of accomplishment, Mary McCarthy shows the artist as worker. Her "work" is to control her experience not only by converting it to myth but by commenting on her own myth-making: criticism the crucial dimension.

The child Mary's early experience, shared with three brothers, was of glamorous parents who gratified every desire. When she was six years old both parents died, victims of a flu epidemic, leaving their children to a dismal existence as charges of an ineffectual, infatuated aunt and her brutal husband. A few years later Mary (but not her brothers) was rescued, moving from Minneapolis austerity to Seattle luxury, cared for by a loving Protestant grandfather and his mysterious Jewish wife. She attends now an elegant convent school run by French nuns; she "loses her faith" in dramatic fashion and "regains" it equally dramatically; she moves on to a Protestant boarding school, has daring friends, successfully tricks her grandparents. Her narrative ends with her high-school experience, although there are references to her going east to Vassar and to her first unsuccessful marriage.

Adolescence contemplated from the vantage point of maturity looks very different from adolescence being endured; it is no wonder that Mary McCarthy's account of her teen-age years bears little resemblance to Marie Bashkirtseff's or Mary MacLane's. But she shares with them, and with most other adolescents, certain problems. "It was the idea of being noticed that consumed all my attention; the rest, it seemed to me, would come of itself." To be noticed is, in youthful fantasy, to be loved—that is "the rest" that will come of itself. It is not fame that she wants, not even a single lover; she yearns rather to be loved by everyone. Achieving minor notoriety, she finds it a precarious state. The security of love eludes her, nor can she even confess directly her need for it.

The autobiographer's apparent reluctance to admit openly her deep desire for love may be accounted for by the fact that the desire conflicts cruelly with the effort to control experience by understanding it, this memoir's more explicit theme. Commitment to others decreases one's possibilities for control, yet remains vitally necessary. A child orphaned at six must feel the need for relationship, and Mary's early guardians provide virtually no emotional security. Moreover, they make "success" seem the opposite of love: Uncle Myers beats the girl to prevent her getting "stuck up" when she wins an essay contest. Successful at school in Minneapolis, admired by her classmates for her intellect and her wit, she is not loved; she feels alienated from her fellows by her pitiable condition as neglected orphan. In Seattle, burning to be noticed, she is never noticed enough; although she learns to follow the devious social laws that govern her classmates, she cannot extract emotional satisfaction from them.

When she finds temporary emotional gratification, it is often at the cost of intellectual clarity: her memoir abounds in illustrative episodes. Twelve-year-old Mary, having stained her bedsheets slightly with blood from a cut on her leg, tries desperately to explain to successive nuns that she has not started menstruating. The nuns comfort away her putative fears about "becoming a woman"; she, finally helpless, accepts the offered solace and tries in succeeding months to produce a show of blood to mark the sanitary napkins inexorably issued to her. It is a comedy of mutual incomprehension permeated with pathos. Miss McCarthy sees her girlish self as pulsating with energy, "excited," forever "crying out," "chafing" to be heard, "breaking in," "fighting the convent." On the other side are the forces of constraint and paralysis. The nuns are "soothing, and yet firm." Their function is to calm, to hush, to reassure. "'And you, Mary, have lost your dear mother, who could have made this easier for you.' Rocked on Madame MacIllvra's lap, I felt paralysis overtake me, and I lay, mutely listening, against her bosom, my face being tickled by her white, starched, fluted wimple, while she explained to me how babies were born, all of which I had heard before."

The image of the child rocked on a maternal bosom, simultaneously reminded of the loss of her real mother and provided with a substitute, is both reassuring and frightening. Its positive aspect is the ease of being taken care of. But the cost is helpless passivity, the victim forced to listen to what she already knows. How does Mary get herself into such a position? She asks the question, dimly recognizing her own concealed complicity, but she cannot answer it. "It was just that I did not fit into the convent pattern: the simplest thing I did, like asking for a clean sheet, entrapped me in consequences that I never could have predicted." "There I was, a walking mass of lies . . . ; yet all this had come about without my volition and even contrary to it." The trouble comes when she asks for help—for a clean sheet, for rescue from her pretended loss of faith. She wishes to be taken care of, to be loved, but (like everyone) she also wants the opposite: to be independent, self-sufficient. So she is repeatedly "entrapped in consequences" she cannot anticipate, forced to deceit by her internal conflict—for she cannot risk rejection by fully declaring her independence, revealing that her loss of faith has become real and irreversible, telling the nuns unequivocally that they are deluded by false assumptions.

Her clarity of perception, her demanding logical faculty, clash with her yearning for love and make internal conflict perpetual. She allows the nuns to be deceived, yet feels the full horror of deception; allows them to believe her restored to the bosom of the Church while driven by logic to reject the Church's comfort. When she visits the Brent sisters in Medicine Springs, Montana, they supply an instant boyfriend—married, to be sure, but that's not the real problem. The real problem is that even as an adolescent, Mary cannot avoid the consequences of her own perception. She wishes—or thinks she wishes—only to enjoy herself. Yet, "When I saw him in the drugstore, with his white coat and ripply hair, I was embarrassed for him, just because I could see him so clearly *from the outside*, as a clerk, who would always be a clerk, limited, like his kisses, flat, like the town." Although she's excited by the fact that this particular clerk is "sweet on her," she must struggle with her perception that the man is unworthy, the situation ridiculous; there is no way to resolve the incompatibility. The spririt's capacity to see, in McCarthy's autobiography as in her novel *The Company She Keeps*, generates possible salvation, but also wretchedness.

For Marie Bashkirtseff and Mary MacLane, emotional isolation seems a proof of uniqueness; they sustain their self-images partly by reflection on how inevitably they misunderstood. Mary McCarthy, wishing desperately to be understood, wishes equally intensely to be unique. Her self-depiction repeatedly concentrates on her difference from the rest of mankind, the subject recurring in every chapter. Such "differentness," of course, is another obstacle to love. As in classic versions of the myth of artistic specialness (Prometheus, Daedalus), the writer's story reveals the special anguish of being set apart.

The defining episode of Mary's early youth was the tin buttterfly contretemps. Accused of stealing the trinket, the girl makes self-righteous proclamations of innocence which convince her aunt but not her uncle, who beats her into a false confession (promptly rescinded) when the butterfly appears pinned beneath the tablecloth at her place. Subsequent beatings elicit from her "wild cries," but no further admission of guilt. "I finally limped up to bed, with a crazy sense of inner victory, like a saint's, for I had not recanted, despite all they had done or could do to me." Years later, her brother tells her "that on the famous night of the butterfly, he had seen Uncle Myers steal into the dining room from the den and lift the tablecloth, with the tin butterfly in his hand." Or perhaps he tells her nothing of the sort; perhaps the idea was suggested by a playwriting instructor in college.

Mary McCarthy's deliberate introduction of the possibility that this dramatic episode contains fiction as well as fact emphasizes the mythic aspect of the tale. Ernst Kris has documented the theory that artists' biographies often incorporate anecdotes belonging to traditional mythology of the artist: the story, for example, that the youth's talents were discovered as he drew pictures in the sand while tending his sheep. Autobiographers also draw upon mythology, recalling or reshaping events that validate their claim of perceived significance in their experience. Mary McCarthy's butterfly story closely resembles Rousseau's account of refusing to confess falsely to breaking a comb as a child. In both instances, the triumphant protagonist considers the episode a testimony of his moral superiority to those around him, who misunderstand but cannot destroy him. Rousseau generalizes the effect of such misunderstanding, claiming that the event produced his lasting hatred of injustice in all its forms. McCarthy draws no general conclusions, allowing the encounter with adult unfairness to be one among many of her efforts to come to terms with an incomprehensible world. But the real point is that she does *not* come to terms. The artist-as-hero-or-heroine never comes to terms; he defies the realm of things-as-they-are to claim his difference. If anecdotes to prove it did not exist, he would be forced to invent them. Looking back on his life, he sees a sequence of proofs that he is not like other people.

Of course no one sees himself as altogether "like other people," but not everyone is comfortable making the assertion of superiority hidden in the claim of difference. Many who cry that they are set apart base their self-esteem on production, achievement, performance. For Mary McCarthy, the self-justifying performance is the artful autobiography itself. The form and style of *Memories of a Catholic Girlhood* largely define its meaning, as the book constantly calls attention to its own artifice, manipulating the reader's doubt about whether "true" autobiography is possible. Of course not, Mary McCarthy says, if what you mean is "literal." No one has total recall; we are far too sophisticated, in an age of analysis, to believe that memory is to be trusted without question. This author publicly questions her own memory. Did events really happen as she claims? Perhaps not. Her father couldn't really have threatened the conductor with a gun when the man wished to put his flu-stricken family off the train; Uncle Myers is probably not as detestable as his niece needs to think. Memory reforms experience; the writer reforms it further. But she is not writing fiction, which would force her to provide motives, for people who seem to her adult mind as incomprehensible as they appeared to her as a child. The experience she records, however transmuted, is real; it has shaped her before she can shape it.

Similar statements could be made of all autobiographies, but not all demand them. This book makes such a demand by its form: the alternation of narrated experience with interpolated comment on both the experience and the narration. Calling constant attention to the fact of writing, the author triumphs over the arbitrary, unjust world by describing it. Thus she gives to memory more order than exists in experience. She controls her past in retrospect as she could not control it while living it; the child's helplessness yields to the domination of the adult artist, as her life turns into a work of art. An artist offers her specialness as a gift to the world, expecting love in return—a pattern duplicating one she describes repeatedly in her childhood, when she is declared by a nun to resemble Lord Byron, brilliant but unsound, and takes the declaration as an indication of "the fact that I was loved by Madame Barclay"; or she defies authority in an individualistic dramatic portrayal of Catiline which emerges from and contributes to her devotion to her Latin teacher; or she loses her faith and pretends to regain it in order to capture the attention of others. As an adult, she reports with emphasis that many of her readers have written to testify that they have relatives, experiences, relationships to Catholicism exactly like hers. By reporting her unique experience, she has declared her common humanity; the reward is testimony of kinship. The dream of universal love is the center of her emotional life as it is of Marie Bashkirtseff's; but she has the power to channel it more richly into successful creativity.

Is it important that this memoir is by a woman? Some of the experiences it relates are peculiarly female: the false menstruation, the excursion into dissipation with the Brent sisters. But Mary McCarthy, never made to feel that boys can do what girls cannot, reports little suffering as a special result of her sex. The crucial problems of her life—the effort to reconcile the need for distinction with the need for relationship, the struggle to gain the understanding that offers control of experience—are not peculiar to women; indeed, the analogies I have suggested are all to men, mythical or real: Daedalus, Prometheus, Rousseau. Inasmuch as Mary McCarthy understands her experience as a sequence of efforts to gain the intellectual mastery that will defeat disorder, she denies the importance of her womanhood: her brain is meaningful, not her body. Yet her self-depiction is not really so simple as all that. The final chapter, about her grandmother, adds another dimension to the entire narrative.

"She never says anything about how she may be fabricating about her grandmother, it's different from the rest of the book."

Indeed it is: and the author wishes no suspicion of fictionalizing to touch this crucial concluding portrait, in which the intricate configuration of emotions directed toward the grandmother suggests also the intricacies of complex self-perception.

In narrative form, *Memories of a Catholic Girlhood* has stressed the theme of developing awareness, deviating from chronology in order to emphasize more complex principles of growth. (Its intricate formal pattern, a comparative rarity in autobiographies by women, itself testifies to the author's deliberate artistic intent.) The final chapter in this respect recapitulates the whole, tracing a child's increasingly complex responses to a mysterious older woman. In all obvious respects, Mary McCarthy's grandmother seems very different from her descendant. The old lady holds grudges, has an almost paranoid passion for privacy, resents the idea of being written about, has little interest in her own past. Physically vain, she spends her life in self-adornment. Totally unintrospective, she cannot even respond to questions about her feelings; her days run by truisms. She has little capacity for or interest in relationship. Most important, she is intensely feminine, treating all the world as her suitors. "Life itself was obliged to court her." Living a luxurious, highly scheduled life, the world around her responsive to her whims, she yet repeatedly suffers terrible hurt: a botched face-lifting operation mars her beauty, her daughter dies, then her husband. Against such hurt, her recourse is retreat, cutting her off from meaningful contact with others. Like Mary, she endures conflicting needs for "specialness" and for community; she resolves the conflict mainly on the side of specialness, glorifying almost to the point of self-worship the physical beauty that remains to her.

Her granddaughter's increasing comprehension moves from the small child's perception of her grandmother as a fairy princess to the grown woman's shocked realization that the old lady is senile. But the chapter's deeper principle of organization depends on the gradual, never stated awareness of some deep identity between narrator and subject and the learning that results from this awareness. Mary McCarthy's search for intellectual control, like the desire for power in other woman artists, is at least partly a response to problems inherent in being a woman. The older woman's life is more miserable than she realizes, restricted in possibility to the exercise of feminine tricks and to narcissistic self-contemplation. She makes drama out of the buying of hats and she tells funny stories in which she is always the victim. "She is always the loser in these anecdotes; she never gets the better of the situation with a biting retort, as she often did in real life. But because she is the heroine, she is usually rescued, in the nick of time." In real life, verbal dexterity can save a woman; she is none the less tempted to present a version of herself in which, dependent on others, she is rescued (i.e., loved) by them.

The same temptation faces Mary McCarthy, who, thinking of her grandmother, finds a warning of the dangers of self-definition by femininity. Her narrative has included stories of her own victimization—presentations of herself emotionally at the mercy of priests, nuns, relatives, drugstore clerks, crippled boys—in which she, like her grandmother, asks for love by presenting herself as baffled and helpless. But now, contemplating the older woman, Mary McCarthy asserts definitively her mastery of her own past: she refuses to be only a victim. The "uncontrollable event" lies in wait for her as well as her grandmother, but she will not merely wait for a rescuer: her version of the gift for "a biting retort" is the clarity of an irony often self-directed, often directed outward, always assertive of intellectual mastery. To worship the mirror, as the grandmother does, is to declare one's beauty the primary instrument of control; but other modes of self-contemplation may create more dependable power. Mary McCarthy's grandmother has no sense of future possibility; her obsession with the mirror derives from her fearful attempt to deny the power of time. Her descendant, also engaged in self-examination, is more capable of confronting the fourth dimension. Recognizing time as an element in the creation of the self rather than only as an enemy to the preservation of beauty, she turns to her history for sustenance and for self-assertion as well as for the winning of love. She has seen in her grandmother an image of women's limited possibilities for control and of the final futility of physical narcissism; she escapes into narcissism of another order, modified by the action of a cool intellect, and she asserts in her narcissism the mind's mastery of the past if not the present. The freedom created by her wit—"there is no wit without freedom, there is no freedom without wit," Heine said—allows her room for the creation of order.

Her literary accomplishment demonstrates her power: not the power to produce that man without corns for whom Marie Bashkirtseff longs or the environment of perfect acceptance which Mary MacLane craves, but the power retrospectively to control experience by understanding it. And it is a means to love: the esteem and acceptance of a body of readers rather than the limitless adoration that Isadora longs for. More fully than many autobiographers, Mary McCarthy commits herself to reality, dealing with the gap between inner and outer experience by turning a sharp eye on both, disciplining fantasy by fact. Like Isadora Duncan, she earns recognition as an artist, but she does not find it necessary to exaggerate what "art" means. Recognizing in herself conflicting desires for the power that elevates its possessor above her fellows and the love that unites her with them, she simply demands—and to a considerable extent achieves—both, reminding us that a woman's self-image as artist need not be dramatically at odds with the facts of her experience. She shows also that the artist can transcend her metaphoric adolescence. Like those old-fashioned fictional heroines, Elizabeth Bennet and Emma Woodhouse, she grows from irresponsibility to control, learning (and dramatizing the process of learning) not how to relinquish her critical perspective on the world around her but how to use it.

Variations on Negation
and the Heresy of
Black Feminist Creativity

MICHELE WALLACE

*In short, the image of black women writing in isolation,
across time and space, is conduced toward radical revision.
The room of one's own explodes its four walls to embrace
the classroom, the library, and the various mechanisms
of institutional and media life, including conferences, the
lecture platform, the television talk show, the publishing
house, the "best seller," and collections of critical essays.*
—Hortense Spiller, "Cross-currents,
Discontinuities: Black Women's Fiction"[1]

In the past seventeen years, or more, black women writers have begun
to produce a literature that transcends its intrinsic political boundaries
of invisibility to address the world. Yet despite the commercial success
of some books by some black women writers, most black women
writers are not well known. Their creativity—especially if it doesn't
fit the Book-of-the-Month Club/*New York Times* Best-Seller mold—
continues to suffer the fate of marginality. Perhaps the most persuasive
evidence of this predicament is the way black feminist interpretation
has been all but extinguished in mainstream and academic discourses,
despite the omnipresent mechanical reproduction of interpretation
through electronic media. Meanwhile, the highly visible success of

a few works—including my own *Black Macho and the Myth of the Superwoman* in 1979—sometimes obscures the revolutionary challenge black feminist creativity could pose to white male cultural hegemony.

Sadder still is that nobody in particular and everybody in general seems responsible for this situation. Universities, museums, and publishing houses, what Ishmael Reed calls "cultural detention centers," run by white men and their surrogates, remain the unrelenting arbiters of cultural standards, which exclude or erase the diverse creativity of nonelite populations. Post-modernists, new historicists, deconstructionists, Marxists, Afro-Americanists, feminists, and even some black female academics, for the most part, fail to challenge the exclusionary parlor games of knowledge production.

While I will focus on black women writers, my overall concern is with black feminist creativity in general and with the manner in which, in fields like popular music, opera, and modeling, media visibility may be allowed to substitute for black female economic and political power, whereas in more politically articulate fields such as film, theater, and TV news commentary, black feminist creativity is routinely gagged and "disappeared."

From the black woman whose face is featured on the cover of *Vogue* to the recordings of black female rappers to Sue Simmons interviewing rhythm 'n' blues singer "Wicked" Wilson Pickett on the New York TV talk show *Live at Five*, at some level, all black feminist creativity wants to make the world a place that will be safe for women of color, their men, and their children. Nevertheless, I will refer to black feminist creativity at its most profound—in the novels and poetry of writers like Toni Morrison, Alice Walker, and Ntozake Shange; in the performances of singers like Nina Simone, Miriam Makeba, and Betty Carter; and in the work of artists like Faith Ringgold (my mother) and Bettye Saar—as the "incommensurable," or "variations on negation," in order to characterize the precarious dialectic of a creative project that is forced to be "other" to the creativity of white women and black men, who are "other" themselves.[2] You've probably heard a great deal of talk about the "other"—lately the problem of choice in culture and politics. The question being posed here concerns the "other" of the "other" in public discourse: the culture's potential for the Rainbow Coalition in general, black feminist creativity in particular.

For Marxist historian Hayden White, the tropological—or the tendency of all written argument to rely on figurative language to persuade—is a good name for the perpetual gaps in that discourse which ordinarily describes itself as rational, logical, and therefore universally true. I would add that these tropes or gaps in the dominant discourse become a kind of road map of where the bodies—the bodies of those who have been ignore or negated—are buried. "There is no document of civilization which is not at the same time a document of barbarism," Walter Benjamin once pointed out. Moreover, as feminist philosopher Alison Jagger has said, "the myth of dispassionate investigation bolsters the epistemic authority of white men," a procedure that results in their "emotional hegemony." Therefore, in a subversive critical process, "outlaw emotions become a primary motivation for investigation," which is another way of saying that the personal becomes political yet again.[3]

In this light, what interests me is the problem of a black female cultural perspective, which for the most part is not allowed to become written in a society in which writing is the primary currency of knowledge. How then does feminist creativity finally surface as writing? Moreover, can it be self-critical?

Hayden White uses the tropological to diagnose the discontinuities in white male hegemony, while reconsolidating precisely the same hegemony. (This move is habitual among white male theorists, which continues to be the problem in using their work to other ends.) In *Blues, Ideology and Afro-American Literature*, Afro-American literary critic Houston Baker borrows the tropological from White to construct a black male cultural hegemony. Neither White nor Baker is concerned to read into the apparent gaps the disorderliness of sexuality.

Baker's key trope in describing the work of Richard Wright is a black hole, an area in which gravitation is so intense that no light can escape. Contrary to what we might expect, black holes are full not empty. They are unimaginably dense stars. "They are surrounded by an 'event horizon,' a membrane that prevents the unaltered escape of anything which passes through," Baker writes. "Light shone into a black hole disappears," it converts energy into mass that is infinitely compressed, and "all objects are 'squeezed' to zero volume."[4]

But a feminist physics major at the University of Oklahoma told me something else about black holes. Physicists now believe black holes may give access to other dimensions. An object or energy enters the black hole and is infinitely compressed to zero volume, as Baker reports; then it passes through to another dimension, whereupon the object and/or energy reassumes volume, mass, form, direction, velocity—all the properties of visibility and concreteness, but in another dimension. The idea of a black hole as a process—as a progression that appears differently, or not at all, from various perspectives—seems a useful way of illustrating how I conceive of incommensurability, or variations on negation, as characteristic of black feminist creativity.

The point in using this analogy of the black hole is not simply the obvious sexual one—nor even that if you add up all the cases of successful creative black women, you'll arrive at only a small fraction of black women engaged in creative acts—but rather that even successful creative black women have next to nothing to say about the nature of commentary and interpretation in their respective fields. So to the extent that the arts exist as a byproduct of diverse acts of interpretation and analysis, black feminist creativity is virtually nonexistent. Moreover, it is nonexistent precisely because everybody (including many black women) agrees that black women have no interest in criticism, interpretation, and theoretical analysis, and no capacity for it.

In other words, the black hole represents the dense accumulation, without explanation or inventory, of black feminist creativity. Prevented from assuming a commensurable role in critical theory and the production of knowledge by a combination of external and internal pressures, it is confined to the aesthetic and the commercial. To compensate for ghettoization, black feminist creativity's concentration in music and now literature has become provocatively intense. And yet it is still difficult, even for those who study this music and literature, to apprehend black feminist creativity as a continuous and coherent discourse.

What most people see of the black woman is a void, a black hole that appears empty, not full. The outsider sees black feminist creativity as a dark hole from which nothing worthwhile can emerge and in which everything is forced to assume the zero volume of nothingness, the invisibility, that results from the intense pressure of race, class, and sex.

Even when a media production is passed off as a translation of black feminist creativity—as in Steven Spielberg's translation of Alice Walker's *The Color Purple*—it is crucial to speak of its inadequacies and failures. To those of us hypnotized by the dominant discourse, as Ntozake Shange put it in *for colored girls who have considered suicide/ when the rainbow is enuf*, black feminist creativity sounds like "half-notes scattered/without rhythm/no tune."[5]

When I wrote "The Myth of the Superwoman" in 1977–78, I tried to subsume a lot of smaller, historically specific cultural myths about the strength of the black woman—such stereotypes as "mammy," "Sapphire," "matriarch," "Aunt Jemima"—under the rubric of one large, all-purpose myth. In the process, of course, I was defeating the very purpose of myth, which is to obscure contradiction and drown out history and the dialectical in a superficial (marketable) binary opposition. But that was not the way I saw things then.

It seemed to me that the evidence was everywhere in American culture that precisely because of their profound political and economic disadvantages, black women were considered to have a peculiar advantage. Not only did this premise seem basic to representations of black women in the dominant discourse, it was also becoming characteristic of a lot of Afro-American discourse.

No doubt, as Alice Walker said in her essay "To the Black Scholar,"[6] I thought my ideas were more original than they were. Moreover, while my role models for cultural criticism in 1978 were Tom Wolfe, Norman Mailer, Hunter Thompson, Joan Didion, and James Baldwin, an emergent feminist cultural studies approach has been instrumental in persuading me that style, or strategies of public address, has profound political implications in dealing with material concerning women of color because of their limited access to mainstream, academic, and "avant-garde" discourses.

Specifically, few black critics understood the rhetorical imperative— imposed by the combination of "white" media/marketplace and "black" audience—which produced *Black Macho and the Myth of the Superwoman*. A black woman writer who wants to write seriously about contemporary cultural issues and how they are socially constructed is faced with an almost insurmountable communication problem: if she takes a scholarly approach, she will be virtually ignored because black women have no power in that context; if she takes a colloquial "entertainment" approach—as I did in *Black Macho*—then she will be read, but she will be attacked and ostracized. Either way can cut the possibility of constructive commentary—in the work itself or in the criticism of that work—down to zero.[7] The trick may be to fall somewhere in between the academic and the entertaining, as did Walker in *In Search of Our Mothers' Gardens*. Yet her plain-spoken, "commonsense" style has its limits as well.

As for Walker's discussion of "The Myth of the Superwoman," she does not significantly disagree with my general thesis in her essay, originally written in 1979 as a letter to *The Black Scholar*. This issue of *The Black Scholar* responded to the controversy over the publication of my book and the connection between it and Shange's *for colored girls*, which was then on Broadway. Briefly, the controversy had to do with the problem of black images, and whether or not my work and Shange's work helped to perpetuate stereotypical images of the race. In a short prologue to the essay, Walker says that *The Black Scholar* refused to publish it because they considered the tone too "personal" and "hysterical."

What Walker takes exception to is my assertion that "the myth of the superwoman" is "unquestioned even by the occasional black woman writer or politician." "'It is a lie,'" she reports having written to my publishers." "'I can't speak for politicians but I can certainly speak for myself. I've been hacking away at that stereotype for years, and so have a good many other black women writers.' I thought not simply of Meridian, but of Janie Crawford, of Pecola, of Sula and Nell, of Edith Jackson, even of Iola Leroy and Medga, for God's sake. (Characters of black women writers Ms. Wallace is unacquainted with; an ignorance that is acceptable only in someone not writing a book about black women.)"[8]

I agree. But it wasn't true that I hadn't read Walker's second novel *Meridian* or Toni Morrison's *Sula* or Zora Neale Hurston's *Their Eyes Were Watching God*, although Frances Harper's *Iola Leroy* wasn't generally available then (and Megda and Edith Jackson I still don't know). Like many other black women of my generation, I eagerly awaited the publication or reissue of black women's books. But as a young black woman who was in search of feminist solidarity *and* a writing career, I wanted something very specific from the black women writers I read. I had grown up in Harlem, not in the rural South. My family had lived in Harlem for three generations. To me, the South these writers recollected was fragmented and nostalgic. My mother Faith Ringgold was an artist, my grandmother Willi Posey was a fashion designer, and I had been the beneficiary of a private school education, purchased with greater difficulty than I was then capable of understanding—an education that had acquainted me with the extent to which black women were customarily denied cultural participation. I felt rebuffed by the unwillingness of black women writers to deal with a contemporary urban context. Moreover, I wanted them to deal with the problem of being a black woman writer, which seemed to me overwhelming, and I wanted them to do so immediately and explicitly, to cease their endless deflecting in their lyrical way about a rural Afro-American purity forever lost.

Of course, this view was unfair in that it did not take into account the work of Louise Meriweather, Ann Petry, Toni Cade Bambara, and Paule Marshall, although I had read the black feminist anthology *The Black Woman* from cover to cover when it was published in 1971, and I had also read Petry's *The Street*, Meriweather's *Daddy Was a Numbers Runner*, and some of Bambara's short stories.[9] Yet none of this work had any particular impact on my misgivings about black women's fiction, because I saw this work, as well, as fundamentally continuous with the kind of mysticism about the power of "roots" that characterized their fictions in rural settings.

I read *Mules and Men* and *Their Eyes Were Watching God* by Zora Neale Hurston in 1971 and 1972, while I was a student majoring in English and writing at the City College of New York. Fascinated as much by Jane Austen and George Eliot as by Hurston, and already thinking of myself as a "black feminist" thanks to the encouragement and support of an actively feminist mother, I was in the front row of the first Women's Studies classes at City College.

I read *The Bluest Eye* in 1974, while working as a secretary at Random House, where Toni Morrison was then an editor. That summer Angela Davis often came to see Morrison to work on her autobiography. When it was published in 1975, I read it immediately. In 1975 I also attended the first conference of the National Black Feminist Organization in New York, at which Shirley Chisholm, Eleanor Holmes Norton, and Florynce Kennedy were keynote speakers. Alice Walker led a workshop discussion together with Faith, my mother, on black women in the arts.

It was around this time that I read Walker's first book of short stories, *In Love and Trouble*, as well as the essay "In Search of Our Mothers' Gardens," which immediately became essential reading for black feminists, but which struck me then as afflicted by the same nostalgia for and valorization of the rural and the anonymity of the unlettered that I considered so problematic in the work of black women novelists. In particular, the premise of the article—that black women writers should speak for previous generations of silenced black women—posed certain conceptual difficulties for me. First, no one can really speak *for* anybody else. Inevitably, we silence others that we may speak at all. This is particularly true of "speaking" in print. Second, there was an implicit denial of the necessity for generational conflict and critical dialectic, which I found totally paralyzing. Anyhow, my mother was a prominent artist, well educated and active in the Women's Movement. So how could I pursue Walker's proposal? Moreover, didn't it imply that black women writers would always "speak" from the platform of a silenced past?

Faith was then (and still is) involved on a daily basis in making a politically engaged black feminist art out of quilting, soft sculpture, sewing, painting, lettering, and performance. My interest in visual art and art criticism—which was shaped by Faith's involvement with artists on the left organizing to protest the Vietnam War and the racism and sexism of establishment museums—was perhaps the largest influence on my notion of what black feminist creativity could mean at that point.

So when I completed the manuscript of my book in 1978, my decision to make the statement that black women writers were reinforcing "the myth of the superwoman" was no accidental afterthought, nor was it made because I didn't think art was important, or because I didn't know of Pecola, Meridian, and Janie Crawford. Now I realize that I was reading too narrowly. My sense of these matters has changed mostly because of black feminist reinterpretations of Hurston's *Their Eyes Were Watching God* that foreground Janie's ascension to the posture of articulate storyteller, despite the obstacle of a twisted sexism coming from a black community besieged by racism.[10]

Moreover, the interpretation of deconstructivist critic Barbara Johnson makes the point that polar or binary oppositions are crucial to the logic of our culture's rhetoric about race and sex. That Hurston occupied the wrong end of each of these oppositions made inevitable the continuous splitting of the difference (it's sometimes called "waffling" in Baldwin's work) that marked Hurston's narrative and expositional style. Johnson divides the field of the dominant discourse into four realms: white men make statements of universality; white women make statements of "complementarity"; black men make statements of "the other"; and black female discourse is identified only by the lowercase "x" of radical negation. "The black woman is both invisible and ubiquitous," Johnson writes of the often paltry efforts of black men, white men, and white women to include her in their progressive political formulations, "never seen in her own right but forever appropriated by the others for their own ends."[11]

While Johnson's thesis is meant to be illuminating and suggestive rather than precisely sociological, there is no question in my mind that the unrelenting logic of dualism, or polar oppositions—such as black and white, good and evil, male and female—is basic to the discourse of the dominant culture and tends to automatically erase black female subjectivity. The "on the one hand/on the other hand" logic of most rational argumentation works out fine if you happen to fit neatly into one of the following categories: (1) the unified, universalizing subject, usually claimed by white men, or (2) the "other," usually spoken for by white women or men of color. But if you happen to have more then one feature disqualifying you from participation in the dominant discourse—if you are black and a woman, and perhaps lesbian and poor, as well—and you insist on writing about it, you're in danger of not making any sense, because you are attempting speech from the dangerously unspeakable posture of the "other" of the "other."

It was my view that black women writers were verifying "the myth of the superwoman" by creating perverse characterizations, which displayed inordinate strengths and abilities as the inevitable booby prize of a romanticized marginality. The problem with the myth of the superwoman, as I saw and still see it, is that it seems designed to cover up an inexorable process of black female disenfranchisement, exploitation, oppression, and despair. Even more important than whether black women believe the myth or whether some black women engage in superlative accomplishments (which they obviously do) is the way the dominant culture perpetuates the myth, not to celebrate the black woman but as a weapon against her. "She is already liberated" becomes an excuse for placing her needs last on every shopping list in town. Also very important is the way in which otherwise liberal or marginal constituencies, such as white progressives, white feminists, and ordinarily enlightened black male intellectuals, benignly consent to or actively conspire with the dominant discourse in this process.

The "other" of the "other," or incommensurability, is another approach to the same problem. Whereas the myth of the superwoman was a concept designed to describe the culture's general misapprehension about black women, the "other" of the "other" is an attempt to diagnose the black woman's relationship to the dominant discourse. It is more important to talk of the "other" of the "other" at this point, not because there is no longer a problem of myths (or stereotypes), but because myths are not dispelled by revelation. Rather the revelation of myth simply continues the process of myth. Or, as Claude Lévi-Strauss's reading of Freud's encounter with the Oedipus myth would imply,[12] the "revelation" becomes yet another version of the myth by not focusing on the politics of who speaks and who doesn't, which ultimately determines the power of knowledge and the knowledge of thus derived of the world. At the same time, the "other" of the "other" is resistant to theoretical articulation—hence the black feminist fear of theory, the invisibility of black feminist interpretation in the realm of the dominant discourse, and the way black feminist literature prioritizes variations on negation.

Another way of describing variations on negation would be to call them "negative images." But I prefer the phrase "variations on negation" because "negation" seems indispensable to a dialectical critical process. My liking for the term "variations" is more whimsical, based on an idea of musical performance. To me, "variations" suggest experimental approaches that delay closure almost indefinitely. Billie Holiday used to sing "The difficult I'll do right now, the impossible will take a little while." Variations on negation confront "the impossible," the radical being and not-being of women of color.

The capacity for rendering the negative substantial and dialectical has been a particular strength of fiction by black women writers—a point that Barbara Smith, Deborah McDowell, and other black feminist critics, in their pursuit of programmatic concerns, have minimized.[13] The way these variations on negation occur is twofold, as can be seen in Toni Morrison's *Sula*. On the level of content, the reader can't help but notice that the black community, called "The Bottom," comes to dislike Sula, even as Sula's best friend rejects her for "stealing her man." Neither Sula, nor her mother Hannah, nor her grandmother Eva fits anybody's notion of a good guy. But Nel, her mother Helene, and her grandmother are hardly positive images either. Rather, their characterizations seem a direct response to the imbalances of Sula, Hannah, and Eva, which bears upon the second way of reading, variations on negation.

It is the relationship (or gaps) between items in the text—description, character, plot, dialogue—that gives this book its force. The book's power lies in its willingness to contradict itself. In particular, one must look for moments that directly oppose one another in their construction of "reality."

The various oppositions of race, class, and sex only support the paramount opposition between Sula—the epitome of the "negative being," who will not marry or settle down and who breaks all the conventions of adult behavior by living, unhypocritically, for pleasure—and the "Bottom," whose sentiments are ultimately personified by Nel, who marries and settles down while Sula goes off to college. The tension between Sula and Nel is the level at which Morrison is problematizing issues of black feminist creativity. Sula's and Nel's individual characterizations are less important than the roles they play in the novel's larger problem of working out how black feminist creativity will become written.

Certainly, the undermining of facile dualisms or binary oppositions of class, race, and sex is a priority in fiction by black women. One intriguing possibility is that there may be a systematic disorder within language itself, which helps to explain the perpetual invisibility of women of color to the dominant discourse. Another provocative possibility is that the very process of radical negation, or doubling and tripling the difference, may provide a way to reformulate the problem of black female subjectivity and black female participation in culture.

Perhaps the most important book to look at in this regard is Morrison's *The Bluest Eye*. When I first read this book, I was deeply troubled by Pecola's characterization as a victim of incest and by her subsequent loss of the ability to communicate rationally. It seemed to me such a story was hopelessly negative, not transformational or transcendent in a manner I considered essential to creative acts. Now, however, I think that in the relationship between Pecola and Claudia, who serves as narrator for much of the book, we find a problemization of the conditions that plague the discourse of the "other" of the "other."

Pecola illustrates the path of those who will never recover, the ultimate victim who will never be able to speak for herself. Claudia is the survivor, who sees color and variety even in the somber, severe circumstances of her childhood. Her narration moves smoothly from childhood reminiscence to the occasional adult/editorial reflection of "the author," incorporating the pain and victimization of Pecola as a crucial factor in her need to be articulate, or to write. In the end— which is also where the book begins—Pecola is living on the edge of town, permanently isolated from the black community by her inability to rise above the crimes committed against her.

Without Claudia's and Morrison's storytelling, Pecola's marginalization and social death become a distinct possibility for anyone who challenges the present invisibility of black feminist interpretation by speaking the unspeakable hell of Pecola's real-life counterparts. Yet there isn't a character in *The Bluest Eye* who doesn't have more psychological resources than Pecola in combatting an internalization of self-hatred that might be considered routine in the black community.

Indeed, as much as this book is about the plight of the individual incest victim, it is also about the collective internalization of self-hatred, the cultural erasure of a people and their mostly unconscious battle with what Western civilization calls "madness." That political, economic, and cultural process of negation, which the sociologist Orlando Patterson calls "social death," and which we date from slavery, is where *The Bluest Eye* starts. It is announced by Morrison's use of the "Dick and Jane" primer text:

> Here is the House. It is green and white. It has a red door. It is very pretty. Here is the family. Mother, Father, Dick, and Jane live in the green-and-white house. They are very happy. See Jane. She has a red dress. She wants to play. Who will play with Jane?[14]

Countless American children have encountered this text—which lays out the world as classless, lily-white, sexually stratified but sexless, timeless and without history—as the single path to learning, to the achievement of knowledge. Morrison announces that the meaninglessness of this official text (and perhaps all unitary models) will be a primary focus in *The Bluest Eye* by repeating it a second time without punctuation—the law of the Father, or dominant discourse—and a third time without space between the words, undercutting the very basis of the alphabet's power to signify. In the process, Morrison suggests that Pecola's madness originates less in her individual psyche or the psyche of anyone else in the ghetto; rather, it is socially and linguistically constructed by the dominant discourse. The book then details the social construction of that "otherness" to Dick and Jane's world by systematically contrasting houses, families, mothers, fathers, siblings, and play in Pecola's community. Pecola's family is extremely dysfunctional; Claudia's family is much better. And there are other examples, although all belie the reality of the Dick and Jane model. Yet, everyone and everything is powerless to protect Pecola from tragedy.

Through Soaphead Church, Morrison designates one culprit as the European Judeo-Christian patriarchal tradition. When he takes God's place by pretending to grant Pecola blue eyes—the book's symbol of whiteness, safety, and madness—Morrison seems to be saying that

Soaphead Church is all the God that one can expect in a world that believes in binary oppositions.

At the same time, I haven't done justice to the compositional complexity of *The Bluest Eye* if I've given the impression that this novel explicitly advocates black feminist creativity as a corrective for what ails the black community. The richness of its variation on negation lies precisely in its unwillingness to advocate anything but the circular progress of its own logic. Perhaps the difficulty of identifying the novel's opinion of feminist engagement is clearest in the depiction of Marie, Poland, and China, the three prostitutes who live over the storefront occupied by Pecola's family. In distinct contrast to the variety of maternal images in the book, these women neither nurture nor protect children. They engage in (mostly pointless) resistances to local male authority, yet fail to understand victimization or the fact that Pecola is in danger. Their inclusion in the text seems to question the self-involvement of traditional modes of black female creativity, as well as posing a general critique of more recent feminist strategies of "man-hating" and self-love.

I now see that like many other people who read *The Bluest Eye* and other books by black women writers, I focused too much on the extent to which they mirrored certain obvious sociological realities.[15] This, too, is part of invisibility and the peculiar limitations of the "other" of the "other." From the perspective of dominance, a woman of color who insists on functioning as a speaking (writing) subject threatens the status of Truth itself. The indirection of fiction that seems essential to override reader resistance is, in fact, the shortest distance between two ideological points. Thus the Afro-American woman's talent for fictional narrative is steeped in what Susan Willis has called "the changes wrought by history."[16] As she suggests, black women writers show an uncanny ability for rendering a collective black history of migration, poverty, segregation, and exploitation singular and readable.

Further, black women writers not only make it possible to understand how a convergence of racism, sexism, and class antagonism marks the Third World woman's peculiar position in discourse, but their work calls into question the truth value of any unitary or dualistic apprehension of the world. Not only is it necessary that we focus on difference rather than on sameness or universality, but also, at every conceivable moment, we must choose and take responsibility for what we will emphasize in ourselves and others. And we must respond to Michel Foucault's question "What matter who's speaking?" with the recognition that it matters mostly because there's no variety.

I was struck by these issues most forcefully when I attended a performance of Lorraine Hansberry's *A Raisin in the Sun* about two years ago. The first time I saw *A Raisin in the Sun*—indeed, the first time I saw evidence that black women were capable of literature—was when I saw the movie in 1961. I was nine years old and I remember it well because my entire family went to the theater together. Like the movie of *The Color Purple*, it was a historic occasion.

Every time I see *A Raisin in the Sun* my attention is drawn to how the female characters—the mother, Walter Lee's wife, and Beneatha—represent more thoroughly than most other works of American literature the archetypal choices available to black women (except lesbians) in this culture, as well as the nature of those obstacles blocking critical self-expression. And it is interesting to me that what critics have considered inherent shortcomings in Hansberry's attempts to re-create Chicago tenement life realistically really have to do with her depicting her own complex relation to American intellectual and cultural life. In a family drama, and therefore conventionally, Hansberry explores the myriad tensions of race, class, and sex that plague the black community.

Nevertheless, there's no question that conventional form and conventional gender roles are a handicap in Hansberry's attempt to grapple with who Beneatha is/can be, and that conventionality, in general, limits black feminist explorations. I am also well aware that I lay myself open to the charge of elitism when I proceed as though cultural criticism were as crucial as health, the law, politics, economics, and the family to the condition of black women. But I am convinced that the major battle for the "other" of the "other" will be to achieve a voice, or voices, thus inevitably transforming the basic relations of dominant discourse. Only with those voices—written, published, televised, taped, filmed, staged, cross-indexed, and footnoted—will we approach control over our own lives.

NOTES

1. Marjorie Pryse and Hortense Spiller, eds., *Conjuring: Black Women, Fiction, and Literary Tradition* (Indiana University Press, 1985), 250.

2. See Michele Wallace, "Female Troubles: Ishmael Reed's Tunnel Vision," *Voice Literary Supplement* (December 1986), 10–11.

3. See Hayden White, *Tropics of Discourse: Essays in Cultural Criticism* (Johns Hopkins University Press, 1978); Walter Benjamin, *Illuminations* (Schocken Books, [1955] 1968), 256; Alison Jaggar, "Love & Knowledge: Emotions as an Epistemic Resource for Feminism," delivered at SUNY-Buffalo, November 11, 1987.

4. Houston Baker, *Blues, Ideology and Afro-American Literature* (University of Chicago Press, 1984), 145.

5. See Michele Wallace, "'The Color Purple': Blues for Mr. Spielberg," *Village Voice* (March 18, 1986), 21–24, 26; Ntozake Shange, *for colored girls who have considered suicide/when the rainbow is enuf* (Bantam, [1976] 1980), 1.

6. Alice Walker, *In Search of Our Mothers' Gardens* (Harcourt Brace/Jovanovich, 1983), 322.

7. Obviously, this is too broad a generalization and black women have engaged in constructive written commentary before. One could point to June Jordan's *Civil Wars*, Audre Lorde's *Sister Outsider*, Barbara Christian's *Black Feminist Criticism*, bell hooks' *Ain't I a Woman* and *Feminist Theory*, but this work remains marginal to every academic establishment except Women's Studies.

8. Walker, *In Search of Our Mothers' Gardens*, 324–25.

9. Toni Cade Bambara, ed., *The Black Woman* (Fawcett, 1971); *Gorilla, My Love* (Random House, 1972); Paule Marshall, *Brown Girls, Brownstones* (Beacon, 1960).

10. See Michele Wallace, "Who Owns Zora Neale Hurston? Critics Carve Up the Legend," *Village Voice Literary Supplement* 64 (April 1988), 18–21.

11. Barbara Johnson, *A World of Difference* (Johns Hopkins University Press, 1987), 166–71.

12. Claude Lévi-Strauss, "The Structural Study of Myth," in *The Structuralists from Marx to Lévi-Strauss*, ed. Richard and Fernande DeGeorge (Doubleday Anchor, 1972), 181.

13. Barbara Smith, "Toward a Black Feminist Criticism," 168–85; Deborah E. McDowell, "New Directions for Black Feminist Criticism," in *The New Feminist Criticism: Essays on Women, Literature & Theory*, ed. Elaine Showalter (Pantheon, 1985), 186–99.

14. Toni Morrison, *The Bluest Eye* (Holt, Rhinehart and Winston, 1970), 1.

15. Sociological misreading of black women writers are legend. See, for instance, Mel Watkins, "Sexism, Racism and Black Women Writers," *New York Times Book Review* (1 June 1986), 1, 35–36; Darryl Pinckney, "Black Victims, Black Villains," *New York Review of Books* (January 29, 1987): 17–20; Marlaine Gicksman, "Lee's Way," *Film* (October 1986): 46–49; Stanley Crouche, "Aunt Meda," *New Republic* (October 1987): 34–43.

16. Susan Willis, *Specifying: Black Women Writing the American Experience* (University of Wisconsin Press, 1987), 3.

·II·

ON
WOMEN
IN THE ARTS

Reflecting on
Why I Am an Artist

GEORGIA O'KEEFFE

The meaning of a word—to me—is not as exact as the meaning of color. Colors and shapes make a more definite statement than words. I write this because such odd things have been done about me with words. I have often been told what to paint. I am amazed at the spoken and written word telling me what I have painted. I make this effort because no one else can know how my paintings happen.

Where I was born and where and how I have lived is unimportant. It is what I have done with where I have been that should be of interest.

My first memory is of the brightness of light—light all around. I was sitting among pillows on a quilt on the ground—very large white pillows. The quilt was a cotton patchwork of two different kinds of material—white with very small red stars spotted over it quite close together, and black with a red and white flower on it. I was probably eight or nine months old. The quilt is partially a later memory, but I know it is the quilt I sat on that day.

The year I was finishing the eighth grade, I asked our washerwoman's daughter what she was going to do when she grew up. She said she didn't know. I said very definitely—as if I had thought it all out and my mind was made up—"I am going to be an artist."

I don't really know where I got my artist idea. The scraps of what I remember do not explain to me where it came from. I only know that by that time it was definitely settled in my mind. I hadn't seen many pictures and I hadn't a desire to make anything like the pictures I had seen. But in one of my mother's books I had found a drawing of a girl that I thought very beautiful. The title under it was "Maid of Athens." It was a very ordinary pen-and-ink drawing about two inches high. For me, it just happened to be something special—so beautiful. Maybe I could make something beautiful. . . . I think my feeling wasn't as articulate as that, but I believe that picture started as something moving in me that kept on going and has had to do with the everlasting urge that makes me keep on painting.

Up to that time—aside from the "Maid of Athens"—I can't remember any picture that interested me except a Mother Goose book printed on cloth, a little girl with pink roses in front of her on my table cover, and a painting that hung in my grandmother's parlor—some very fierce-looking Arabs on horseback crossing a stream.

I didn't have a very clear idea of what an artist would be. Later, when people asked what kind of an artist I would be, it always embarrassed me. I didn't know. Then they would ask, "Well, are you going to be an illustrator or a portrait painter or a designer, or what?" The idea of being an illustrator didn't mean much to me. I never associated my idea of being an artist with illustrations in books that we had and I didn't know what they meant by a designer. So I would say, "A portrait painter." I could grasp the idea of a portrait painter. There were two quite handsome portraits of my great-grandmother and great-grandfather at home. There was a crayon portrait of my mother, but I wondered how anyone could possibly imagine that it looked like her. The other two were dark and dignified, and great-grandmother wore a white lace collar and cuffs and a lace cap tied with a light blue ribbon that I thought very pretty. She wore a thin gold ring on her first finger. It looked very nice on her hand. But her face wasn't pretty to me, so the picture meant little to me.

The man was better looking. He was comfortable and rosy, with a queer collar that curved up near his ears. He held in his hands a newspaper attached to a long, dark polished stick. There was also a portrait of my grandmother. She looked old and sad. I didn't care for that one either. I think I had no desire at all to be a portrait painter. The portraits in the house didn't interest me enough to have made me think I would enjoy making them. I remember someone's saying that if I were going to be a portrait painter I would have to paint anyone who wanted to be painted. I emphatically insisted that I only intended to paint people whom I liked or thought beautiful.

The fall I was thirteen, I was taken to boarding school—a Dominican convent beyond Madison. The Sister who had charge of the art classes had beautiful large dark eyes and very white lovely hands, but she always felt a bit hot and stuffy to me. I felt the shrinking away from her.

My first day in the studio she placed a white plaster cast of a baby's hand on a table, gave me some charcoal, and told me to draw it. I worked laboriously—all in a cramp—drawing the baby's hand with a very heavy black line. I thought my drawing very nice and I liked doing it. When the Sister saw it she was very impatient. She said I had drawn the hand too small and my lines were all too black. She particularly emphasized the fact that it was too small. At the time I thought that she scolded me terribly. I was so embarrassed that it was difficult not to cry. The Sister sat down and drew a few light lines blocking in the way she thought the drawing should be started. It looked very strange to me—not at all beautiful like my own drawing. I wasn't convinced that she was right, but I said to myself that I would never have that happen again. I would never, never draw anything too small. So I drew the hand a little bit larger than she suggested and that whole year never made a heavy black line again. I worked mostly with a fairly hard lead pencil and always drew everything a little larger and a little lighter than I really thought it should be.

When my drawings were put up on the wall for exhibition in June, there was a whole wall of the pale drawing casts. The Sister wrote *G. O'Keeffe* on each of them in her big free hand—writing with a lead pencil much blacker than the tone of my drawings. I was shocked to see my name so big and black on my pale drawings. And it didn't seem like my name—it was someone quite apart from me. I had never thought much about having a last name.

It was in the fall of 1915 that I first had the idea that what I had been taught was of little value to me except for the use of my materials as a language—charcoal, pencil, pen and ink, watercolor, pastel, and oil. I had become fluent with them when I was so young that they were simply another language that I handled easily. But what to say with them? I had been taught to work like others and after careful thinking I decided that I wasn't going to spend my life doing what had already been done.

I hung on the wall the work I had been doing for several months. Then I sat down and looked at it. I could see how each painting or drawing had been done according to one teacher or another, and I said to myself, "I have things in my head that are not like what anyone has taught me—shapes and ideas so near to me—so natural to my way of being and thinking that it hasn't occurred to me to put them down." I decided to start anew—to strip away what I have been taught—to accept as true my own thinking. This was one of the best times of my life. There was no one around to look at what I was doing—no one interested me—no one to say anything about it one way or another. I was alone and singularly free, working into my own, unknown—no one to satisfy but myself. I began with charcoal and paper and decided not to use any color until it was impossible to do what I wanted to do in black and white. I believe it was June before I needed blue.

I find that I have painted my life—things happening in my life—without knowing. After painting the shell and shingle many times, I did a misty landscape of the mountain across the lake, and the mountain became the shape of the shingle—the mountain I saw out my window, the shingle on the other table in my room. I did not notice that they were alike for a long time after they were painted.

There are people who have made me see shapes—and others I thought of a great deal, even people I have loved, who make me see nothing. I have painted portraits that to me are almost photographic. I remember hesitating to show the paintings, they looked so real to me. But they have passed into the world as abstractions—no one seeing what they are.

It is surprising to me to see how many people separate the objective from the abstract. Objective painting is not good painting unless it is good in the abstract sense. A hill or tree cannot make a good painting just because it is a hill or a tree. It is lines and colors put together so that they say something. For me that is the very basis of painting. The abstraction is often the most definite form for the intangible thing in myself that I can only clarify in paint.

I am a dancer

MARTHA GRAHAM

I am a dancer.

I believe that we learn by practice. Whether it means to learn to dance by practicing dancing or to learn to live by practicing living, the principles are the same. In each it is the performance of a dedicated precise set of acts, physical or intellectual, from which comes shape of achievement, a sense of one's being, a satisfaction of spirit. One becomes in some area an athlete of God.

To practice means to perform, in the face of all obstacles, some act of vision, of faith, of desire. Practice is a means of inviting the perfection desired.

I think the reason dance has held such an ageless magic for the world is that it has been the symbol of the performance of living. Even as I write, time has begun to make today yesterday—the past. The most brilliant scientific discoveries will in time change and perhaps grow obsolete, as new scientific manifestations emerge. But art is eternal, for it reveals the inner landscape, which is the soul of man.

Many times I hear the phrase "the dance of life." It is an expression that touches me deeply, for the instrument through which dance speaks is also the instrument through which life is lived—the human body. It is the instrument by which all the primaries of life are made manifest. It holds in its memory all matters of life and death and love. Dancing appears glamorous, easy, delightful. But the path to the paradise of the achievement is not easier than any other. There is fatigue so great that the body cries, even in its sleep. There are times of complete frustration, there are daily small deaths. Then I need all the comfort that practice has stored in my memory, a tenacity of faith.

It takes about ten years to make a mature dancer. The training is twofold. First comes the study and practice of the craft which is the school where you are working in order to strengthen the muscular structure of the body. The body is shaped, disciplined, honored, and in time, trusted. The movement becomes clean, precise, eloquent, truthful. Movement never lies. It is a barometer telling the state of the soul's weather to all who can read it. This might be called the law of the dancer's life—the law which governs its outer aspects.

Then comes the cultivation of the being from which whatever you have to say comes. It doesn't just come out of nowhere, it comes out of a great curiosity. The main thing, of course, always is the fact that there is only one of you in the world, just one, and if that is not fulfilled then something has been lost. Ambition is not enough; necessity is everything. It is through this that the legends of the soul's journey are retold with all their tragedy and bitterness and sweetness of living. It is at this point that the sweep of life catches up with the mere personality of the performer, and while the individual becomes greater, the personal becomes less personal. And there is grace, I mean the grace resulting from faith . . . faith in life, in love, in people, in the act of dancing. All this is necessary to any performance in life which is magnetic, powerful, rich in meaning.

In a dancer, there is a reverence for such forgotten things as the miracle of the small beautiful bones and their delicate strength. In a thinker, there is a reverence for the beauty of the alert and directed and lucid mind. In all of us who perform there is an awareness of the smile which is part of the equipment, or gift, of the acrobat. We have all walked the high wire of circumstance at times. We recognize the gravity pull of the earth as he does. The smile is there because he is practicing living at the instant of danger. He does not choose to fall.

At times I fear walking that tightrope. I fear the venture into the unknown. But that is part of the act of creating and the act of performing. That is what a dancer does.

People have asked me why I chose to be a dancer. I did not choose. I was chosen to be a dancer, and with that, you live all your life. When any young student asks me, "Do you think I should be a dancer?" I always say, "If you have to ask, then the answer is no." Only if there is one way to make life vivid for yourself and for others should you embark upon such a career. . . . You will know the wonders of the human body because there is nothing more wonderful. The next time you look into the mirror, just look at the way the ears rest next to the head; look at the way the hairline grows; think of all the little bones in your wrist. It is a miracle. And the dance is a celebration of that miracle.

Rightness of My Being

LOUISE NEVELSON

I don't say I'm born with a perfect eye, but I'm born with the rightness of my being. I have a mind for what I need. That's why I can do so much. I just don't have any trouble. I feel maybe someone will say, "How sure she is of herself." So I restrain myself from saying it. But I am sure. Let's face it. You see, they said at four years old already I was creative. And so I use that and I understand it—maybe like Mozart knew his music. You are or you are not.

Well, I know I had it, and I also knew I had the energy of many people. I've always had it. So I'm prolific, to begin with; but I'm also prolific because I know how to use time. I prepare my materials for the next day. I get up, six in the morning. And I wear cotton clothes so that I can sleep in them or I can work in them—I don't want to waste time. I go to the studio, and usually I put in pretty much of a big day. And very often, almost all the time (I think I have a strong body), it wears me out. The physical body is worn out before the creative. When I finish, I come in and go to sleep if I'm tired, have something to eat. Time as such doesn't involve me. I think here I could really use time, feeling that a minute could be eternity, eternity could be a minute. So that is measured by man, not by creation. I think humans have measured things to the majority, but the person that is being on another level can't take the clock with him.

Sometimes I could work two, three days and not sleep and I didn't pay any attention to food, because . . . a can of sardines and a cup of tea and a piece of stale bread seemed awfully good to me. You know, I don't care about food and my diet has very little variety. I read once that in her old age Isak Dinesen only ate oysters and drank champagne, and I thought what an intelligent solution to ridding oneself of meaningless decision-making.

I gauge my dentist appointments or if I want to check up with a doctor or anything like that for a certain period of the year so as not to superimpose on me. That gives me a little rest period too. I spend a lot of time in the house, and I have folding tables. I may want to work here, or I may want to work in another studio. So nothing is too static. I don't like a chair that doesn't have a back. And I don't want anyone to come and park themselves. I have a way of living that suits me and I'm not pushing to make others comfortable. I want to make myself more comfortable, not only physically but in every state.

So you see, the economy of time is not only in the studio, but it is economy of all kinds of time. And if you regulate and understand it, can you imagine how the human mind clocks in? There's no waste of consciousness. So that is why and how I produce a lot, because I understand these things. And also how to use my mind, in the sense that I don't clutter it with things that don't pertain to the very *act* of doing it. I believe that we can clean our minds out and not carry too much waste. Anything that's cluttered is a constipation of some sort. Anything—a house, a closet. If it's clear you can put something in it, but if it's crowded you can't put anything in it. So I always started with that kind of a premise.

I take my mind out and put it on the table. I take silver polish or whatever and rags and sponges and clean it up and clear it up and keep it shiny. Look, if you get a little splinter in a finger, it can infest your whole hand and you get sick. I won't permit a thought to enter into my consciousness if I don't feel it's a healthy thought, and the good healthy thoughts I have for myself, for me. I feel that in my own life, I have made my own reality. I'm not seeking the concept truth. It does not interest me because I don't want to know everything, and I don't want to clutter myself. So I have *broken* the concept of a rigid truth or a yardstick. I have been able to make myself more comfortable by reorienting a thought or whatever to suit my kind of thinking. A truth isn't a truth to me, a lie isn't a lie. If I were to accept academically these words and what they stand for, it would kill me immediately. If a so-called lie will be a tool for me to fulfill myself, I'll use it and have no morals about it. And if a so-called truth can destroy me, the hell with it. I cling to my own standards as much as I can. I don't give a damn. If it is more comfortable for me, that's fine. That's my truth.

Maybe because so little of the other things on earth interest me, my total being is pretty much right in the work. I don't go to concerts or shows because I'm so tired of directors and man-made things. I've never gone in for many movies and still don't. You know, you have to go. And you have to sit with a lot of people and you see something that was manufactured. Even at that given time when it was an innovation, when I was young, I must say that I didn't move into those areas very much. Because my own life was very active. Very dramatic. It took all my emotions to survive and I couldn't go into a movie and lose myself even in Charlie Chaplin, or even in Buster Keaton. I just couldn't. The only one that *really* I felt great about was Greta Garbo. That's very interesting, but it's true. But I think that my work takes me to another place, and so I don't quite like sitting around. I'd rather be in the studio where the next thing is a new creation and wasn't planned.

Another thing about creation is that every day it is like it gave birth, and it's always kind of an innocent and refreshing. So it's always virginal to me, and it's always a surprise. I feel in principle or in the deep relationship of the vision and the object and the subject that there is a *unity* and that is *fresh* constantly. You make a living thing through your livingness. You move, you live, you breathe, so it enters . . . enters . . . enters. Each piece seems to have a life of its own. Every little piece or every big piece that I make becomes a very living thing to me, very living. I could make a million pieces; the next piece gives me a whole new thing. It is a new center. Life in total at that particular time. And that's why it's right. That reaffirms my life.

There isn't a thing I want to keep. I don't believe in keeping anything. Some artists don't want to give up a painting or a work, but I'm very fluid that way. I love to see my work move and be placed. I don't need it around me because I don't want my mind to be cluttered. I want my mind to be open and clear to do the next work. The excitement of my life is when I'm working and making decisions: when I put things together and *how* I put them together. I call that the livingness or the essence of aliveness. Because you are totally alive when you are doing it. You're tapping the real fibers of what life is all about.

Women Reconstructing
the World

ANAÏS NIN

I don't know what a "radical feminist" is, but I *am* a feminist. . . .
And what I discovered, when the diaries came out, were the thousands
of women in lonely little towns who had no one to share their aspirations with; who had some creative disturbance and restlessness and felt
that they had potentialities but did not know how to develop them
and were very much lacking in self-confidence; who were apt to invest
in the people around them the faith that they should have had for
themselves.

Now, it is true that I believe liberation is never achieved by one
segment of people; it has to be simultaneous and it has to happen to
all of us. But I also think that men have learned from woman's great
quest for her identity, have learned that we have to peel off the pro-
gramming, the conditioning, the education, the taboos, and the dogmas
that have been inculcated in us. The restrictions were stronger for
women because the pattern was very rigid and very limited, and she
was shut in within her personal world. A few women transcended that,
and the women that I used to read about—because I've always read
women writers, and they were a great inspiration to me—were the
women who were able to *free themselves*, who did not *demand* their
freedom, who were able to *create* it. I will tell you later the story of
a woman who achieved her wishes under amazing obstacles.

I became aware when the diaries came out that woman's problem
was deeper, that her self-confidence somehow had been damaged, that

she often looked to others for an image of herself. Men, as D. H. Lawrence said, were the ones who were making the pattern; men would decide one year if we had to be thin and another year if we had to be fat, or whatever. The pattern of our lives was really set by men. I think your response to the *Diary* is greatly due to the fact that we have had very few histories of the growth of women from the very beginning. In other words, I began with all the limitations and restrictions and taboos and dogmas which we all begin with, which were given to me by my culture—in this case straddling two cultures, the Latin and the American—which were given to me by religion: all the possible restrictions and limitations to growth . . .

So women have had greater handicaps. This I am very fully aware of. And I have been radical in that sense, that I have even argued with the analyst on therapy for woman. I have argued with the analyst about his image of me. I maintained a stubborn continuity of personality, but it was done through the diary. I don't know whether it would have happened without the diary, because the diary was not only the confessional, the mirror, it was also the log of the journey. It made me fully aware of the difficulties of the journey. It made me fully aware when my life was stagnant. I was fully aware of the trap that women fall into, the conventional marriage and life in the suburbs. So the *diary* was a reflector and didn't allow me for one minute to be blinded or to be diffused or to be confused by the outer images that were imposed on me. My concession was to play the roles that were demanded of me but to maintain my integrity for myself *somewhere* very strongly.

When the *Diary* came out and I heard from many women, I heard about their timidities, their lack of confidence, their reliance upon others. If someone criticized their work, for example, they would almost fall apart. Then I remembered my own vulnerabilities and my own hesitancies and my own timidities, and I wanted you to know that they can be overcome.

I want to stress this tremendous lack of confidence, this timidity and fear in woman, because I think that we have talked a great deal about the outer obstacles, the legal obstacles, the cultural obstacles, even the religious obstacles to her development and her growth. But we haven't focused enough on what happened to woman psychologically.

Otto Rank, in his book called *Truth and Reality*, stressed this very much when he spoke of two kinds of guilt that we have: a guilt for creating because we seem to be taking too much room or taking space from our fellows and asserting ourselves, and a guilt for not creating. By creating I don't mean only or specifically painting or composing music or writing books. I mean creating everything—creating a child, creating a garden, creating a house, creating a community, whatever it is. For me creativity is an all-encompassing word.

So we have guilt for creating and for not creating, and these women are caught really between the two: between the fear of asserting themselves, because then it would affect somehow the people near them, and the fear of not creating, of not realizing one's potential. I can give you an example of this. I am very obsessed with the idea of growth, and I used to think that if I grew too much I would overshadow my younger brothers or even some day overshadow my father, which was a terrifying thought. Now I don't know where I got the idea that I was growing into a giant redwood tree, or that I could possibly take the sunlight from other trees, but I really did. That was a tremendously erroneous concept, for I discovered that when a human being grows, this growth positively affects her environment, it affects the people around her and actually urges them to their own growth rather than the other way around. Our growth doesn't wither other people around us, it incites others to do the same. It inspires. I found that the more I expanded, the more I grew, the better it was for my environment. The effect of this would be always positive and would always be setting others on fire.

Women forget that, and they think that perhaps whatever they achieve is at the expense of their personal world and will somehow destroy their personal world. They never thought that whatever they became was in turn poured back into the personal world and enriched it, that they were enriching their children, they were enriching their husband, they were enriching their neighbors. We stopped really believing that the enrichment of the individual is actually what enriches our collective life. We forgot that. And for woman it was worse because she was not expected to produce in the first place. She was not expected to create. Culture didn't demand it of her; it didn't demand of her to become the best doctor or the best lawyer or the best painter or the best writer; it didn't demand anything of her except the fulfillment of her personal duties. So this was not an incentive for woman to develop whatever gift she had.

But where did woman get this lack of confidence in whatever ability she has? Is it because she chooses models without exceptional gifts that she cannot imitate? When I was young and I was reading, I chose materials that I could not possibly become. I wanted to be George Sand; I wanted to be a member of the French Academy; I wanted all kinds of impossible things, but as I grew mature I suddenly realized there were some things possible to me that had nothing to do with exceptional gifts.

Now the women's movement has been caught between the concept of self-development and growth and trying to find the obstacles that stand in the way of this growth and this self-development. We found some of the external factors; some of them were legal, some of them historical, some religious, some cultural, but we find it awfully hard to say that some of them come from within us, that as a result of these elements, we had lost our self-confidence. We had lost our impetus toward creation.

Woman's helplessness has given her a great deal of anxiety. We have had statistics about women breaking down more than men. That's a well-known statistic. My feeling was that they broke down because they had a surplus of anxieties because of helplessness. I mean the dependency on the man, the vicarious living through the man which I described in the novel *Ladders to Fire*, I described Lillian and I said she *breathed* through Jay. She experienced everything through him; when he wasn't there she wasn't enjoying life. In other words she received the whole dynamism of life from him. This is a very bad thing for *the man* on whom the woman is dependent. Every kind of vicarious living is really victimizing the person that you use for that purpose. And woman tended to do that.

Now we were not helped in our culture as women because first of all we weren't taught rivalry, and man was taught the fear of rivalry to such an extent that he considered the growth of woman to be also a threat to himself, which is very tragic. And this really comes out in the whole culture too. Rivalry takes prominence.

Not too long ago I was in Morocco, a totally different culture where rivalry does not exist. I was doing an article for a magazine and I had two guides who were always vying for getting the job to take me through the town. When I took one I would say: "Aren't the other one's feelings hurt?" And he would say: "Not at all, we are all brothers."

This concept of mutual benefit is something we haven't considered enough in connection with women's development. Man never thought woman's growth could be really an enhancing of his own life, a liberation of his own burdens. Two people to carry the load, the burdens of life, instead of one. We never thought of that, we never thought how greatly unity and closeness could really lighten his burden.

Man is driven to competition and to win. Woman has been driven the other way—not to compete and not to win because winning would mean that she was stronger than her children or stronger than her brothers. And often she doesn't want to overshadow or outdistance her husband—or she doesn't want to overshadow her boss.

There is always that feeling which keeps her from growing. The feeling that if she grows she is going to impede someone else's growth and that her concern should be not to take too much space and not to expand. . . . So woman carries many, many burdens. One is this going backward instead of forward into self-expansion and also erroneously considering this self-expansion to be aggressiveness. This word has always been used to discourage and disparage women who had a thrust toward growing.

I often myself used to confuse what I called my active self with aggressiveness until a semanticist pointed out to me that there is a difference between activity and aggressiveness. Aggressiveness is moving against someone: activity is simply the dynamic creative will that I want to awaken in you.

Another thing we must sort out is the way we have labeled things. We have said: "This is masculine, and man must behave this way, and this is feminine." Now we know very well that is not true, that all of us are composed of masculine and feminine qualities, and I hope one day we shall say instead: there are some women who are courageous and there are some men who are tender; and there are some men who are intuitive and there are some women who are scientific-minded. These ideas about roles are limiting to both men and women. That is why I believe woman has to work at liberation with men, because we can't do it by ourselves. We have to do it really all together. All races. All men. All women. It has to be everybody.

And it has to be simultaneous. Because when you feel free and the other person isn't, it's not an achievement. You're still bound, you're related, you're in some way still dependent. If one feels free and the other doesn't, the relationship doesn't work. So it's very important that we work *with* our differences—whether sexual or racial—whatever they might be. We have used everything with almost satanic genius, we used everything to make separatism. We've used religion to separate us, to divide us; we've used race to divide us; we have used everything that we pick up. Now we use the feminist movement to divide us from men. And that's what I don't want.

Then there is another thing which plagues women, which comes also from the culture, it comes from religion, it comes from the family. That is, the things that the culture encourages men to do, it discourages women from doing. It is made very clear to woman that her first and primary duty is to her personal life—whether it be to the husband, or children, or family, or parents. That is the primary thing. This is supposed to be her role in life. Now if a woman has really accepted that, then if she transgresses she has more guilt than the man. Our culture tells the man that he has to go beyond the personal because he has to achieve. He is excused for not being a particularly good father, or a particularly good son, or whatever it is that he doesn't fulfill in the personal life.

Yet woman *gains* something from this great emphasis on the personal life. She gains a very great humanism, which is a consideration of human beings as persons. Man, in his progress toward ideologies, toward science, toward philosophy, toward all the objective forms of thinking, separated himself from the personal. He rationalized in ideological terms in such a way that he became removed from any concept at all that his personal life was really at the root of his profession and his occupations and what he was interested in. Woman never lost sight of that personal life, and now something which started as a handicap, today I consider a *quality* which woman can then carry into her wider interests. But she has to retain this sense of the personal, because from that comes her sense of humanity. So she becomes a lawyer, she becomes a philosopher, she becomes a priest—it doesn't matter. What I hope she doesn't do is simply to annihilate all that she has learned through the centuries, which is the value of the individual.

Certainly there are some negative things which were inculcated in us very early. They are cultural, they are racial, they are part of the family life. But despite that I see women beginning to take a pride in themselves and also to realize that they are capable of skills. Whenever we were told that we couldn't do something, we accepted it. I was told for years that I couldn't think clearly about politics. And I believed it. Why did I believe it? I suddenly discovered that I wasn't incapable; I could balance my checkbook and I could do all sorts of little things that I was told I could not do.

Printing, for example. Everyone laughed when I brought the press and they said: "Of course you're not very good at technology or mechanics." But I learned to print and I learned to love it, thought it *was* very difficult. A woman printer was, you know, an unusual thing, and they would say that the tray would be too heavy and that typesetting was too complicated. These are notions that it's going to take some time to overcome.

Chapter Eleven from
The Life of Poetry

MURIEL RUKEYSER

Exchange is creation.

In poetry, the exchange is one of energy. Human energy is transferred, and from the poem it reaches the reader. Human energy, which is consciousness, the capacity to produce change in existing conditions.

But the manner of exchange, the gift that is offered and received—these must be seen according to their own nature.

Fenollosa, writing of the Chinese written character as a medium for poetry, says this: "All truth is the transference of power. The type of sentence in nature is a flash of lightning. It passes between two terms, a cloud and the earth."

This is the threshold, now the symbols are themselves in motion. Now we have the charge, flaming along the path from its reservoir to the receptive target. Even that is not enough to describe the movement of reaching a work of art.

One of our difficulties is that, accepting a science that was static and seeing the world about us according to the vision it afforded, we have tried to freeze everything, including living functions, and the motions of the imaginative arts.

We have used the term "mind" and allowed ourselves to be trapped into believing there was such a *thing*, such a *place*, such a locus of forces. We have used the word "poem" and now the people who live by division quarrel about "the poem as object." They pull it away from their own lives, from the life of the poet, and they attempt to pull it away from its meaning, from itself; finally, in a trance of shattering, they deny qualities and forms and all significance. Then, cut off from its life, they see the dead Beauty: they know what remorse is, they begin to look for some single cause of their self-hatred and contempt. There is, of course, no single cause. We are not so mechanical as that. But there was a symptom: these specialists in dying, they were prepared to believe there was such a thing as Still Life. For all things change in time; some are made of change itself, and the poem is of these. It is not an object; the poem is a process.

Charles Peirce takes Fenollosa's lightning flash, sets it away from the giving. Peirce writes: "All dynamical action, of action of brute force, physical or psychical, either takes place between two subjects . . . or at any rate is a resultant of such actions between pairs." It is important here to understand what Peirce means by *semiosis.*" . . . By semiosis I mean, on the contrary, an action, or influence, which is, or involves, a coöperation of *three* subjects, such as a sign, its object, and its interpretant; this tri-relative influence not being in any way resolvable into actions between pairs. . . . "

The giving and taking of a poem is, then, a triadic relation. It can never be reduced to a pair: we are always confronted by the poet, the poem, and the audience.

The poet, at the moment of his life at which he finished the poem.

The poem, as it is available, heard once, or in a book always at hand.

The audience, the individual reader or listener, with all his life, and whatever capacity he has to summon up his life appropriately to receive more life. At this point, I should like to use another word: "audience" or "reader" or "listener" seems inadequate. I suggest the old word "witness," which includes the act of seeing or knowing by personal experience, as well as the act of giving evidence. The overtone of responsibility in this word is not present in the others; and the tension of the law makes a climate here which is that climate of excitement and revelation giving air to the work of art, announcing with the poem that we are about to change, that work is being done on the self.

These three terms of relationship—poet, poem, and witness—are none of them static. We are changing, living beings, experiencing the inner change of poetry.

The relationships are the meanings, and we have very few of the words for them. Even our tests, the personality tests of which we presently are so proud, present the static forms of Rorschach blotches.

Any change must be seen as specifically in the examinee. Tests are to be made for the perception of change. We need tests in time, moving images on film, moving sounds and syllables on records; or both on sound film. Then we could begin to see how changing beings react to changing signs—how the witness receives the poem.

In a test of recognition, hardly a person knew his own hands, or his face in profile, or his body from behind. It was only when the group was shown films in which they could see themselves walking—face blanked out—that empathy arrived, and with it, recognition.

We know our rhythms. Our rhythms are more recognizably our selves than any of our forms. Sometimes in nature, form and rhythm are very close: the shape of a tree, for example, is the diagram of its relation to every force which has acted on it and in it; the "shape" of our consciousness—but you see to what folly use of models may lead.

The laws of exchange of consciousness are only suspected. Einstein says, "Now I believe that events in nature are controlled by a much stricter and more closely binding law than we recognize today, when we speak of one event being the *cause* of another. We are like a child who judges a poem by the rhymes and knows nothing of the rhythmic pattern. Or we are like a juvenile learner at the piano, *just* relating one note to that which immediately precedes or follows. To an extent this may be very well when one is dealing with very simple and primitive compositions; but it will not do for an interpretation of a Bach fugue."

I believe that one suggestion of such law is to be found in the process of poetry.

It is the process and the arrangement that gives us our clues. Here the links between the scientist and the poet are strong and apparent.

The links between poetry and science are a different matter. For, in recent poetry, there is to be seen a repetition of old fallacies. The by-products, the half-understood findings of science have been taken over, with the results of tragedy.

You may see these results in fashionable poetry: in the poetry of the sense of annihilation, of the smallness of things, aversion, guilt, and the compulsion toward forgiveness. This is strong magic here: if they want smallness, they will have their smallness; if they want it, they will at last have their forgiveness. But these artists go blaming, blaming. Let us look at what has happened. With the exploration of time and the newer notions of the universe, we have a generation who half-read the findings as they are popularized, and who emerge with little but self-pity. A characteristic title is The World Has Shrunk in the Wash.

What has really happened? What does this "smallness" mean to us? It means that in ourselves we go on from the world of primitive man, a "small" world surrounded by the unknown—whether that unknown be the jungle or curved infinity. Again, the "large" things are human capacities and the beliefs they live among. Our relation to each other and to ourselves are the only thing with survival value, once again. We can go on from a source in ourselves which we had almost lost. We can go on with almost forgotten strengths which are—according to your bias—profoundly religious, profoundly human. We can understand the primitive—not as clumsy, groping naif of a corrupted definition, or even the unskilled "unsophisticate" of modern aesthetic usage—for what he was and what we have to be: the newborn of an age, the pioneer, Adam who dares.

The century has only half-prepared us to be primitives. The time requires our full consciousness, humble, audacious, clear; but we have nightmares of contradiction. For all its symptoms of liberation, its revolutionary stirrings in persons and peoples, the Victorian period was also one of swollen dreams. Behind us overhang the projections of giantism, the inflated powers over all things, according to which nature became some colony of imperial and scientific man, and Fact and Logic his throne and scepter. He forgot that that scepter and that throne were signs. Fact is a symbol, Logic is a symbol: they are symbols of the real.

And reality may be seen as the completion of experience.

Experience itself cannot be seen as a point of time, a fact. The experience with which we deal, in speaking of art and human growth, is not only the event, but the event *and the entire past of the individual.* There is a series in any event, and the definition of the event is the last unit of the series. You read the poem: the poem you now have, the poem that exists in your imagination, is the poem and all the past to which you refer it.

The poet, by the same token, is the man (is the woman) with all the poet's past life, at the moment the poem is finished; that is, at the moment of reaching a conclusion, of understanding further what it means to feel these relationships.

In reading poems with groups of people, doing what is called "teaching poetry," I have found that I can best proceed if I can offer an experience first. You may know the startling and loosening effect of being shown a blank piece of paper, with its properties and possibilities, and then of seeing it suddenly crumpled in the outstretched hand, to become something else, with its present properties and possibilities.

In a sheet of paper is contained the Infinite, wrote Lu Chi, in his *Essay on Literature* (300 A.D.—translated by Shih-Hsiang Chen)—and from Lu Chi to I.A. Richards, the power of space waiting to be filled is demonstrated. I have seen it in a classroom of people widely disparate in background and intention—ranging from shipyard workers and machinists to college and high school students; newspaper people, from the Hearst paper, and the left-wing paper; several housewives; a social worker, a poetry teacher, a Jungian analyst; a few office workers, a German avant-garde writer now working as an upholsterer; the tormented editor of a shipyard paper, another teacher, a draftsman, a dancer. There was a moment of challenge and shock, then some embarrassed blankness. Then they began, as any group begins, in response to this, to write: direct, subjective writing. When they read their pages to each other, they are well introduced. But this is prologue.

In workshops, it is possible to deal with the poems submitted at each meeting: the therapy of the poetry class which emphasizes personality does not apply. There is a power for health in the art workshop, but it functions best when there is writing being done as freely and as continually as possible, and when definite actions of reference are offered to the group.

The action which is closest to the nature of a poem is that which will dramatize the process of reaching a conclusion. I have called for a volunteer in workshop, and asked the intrepid one whether he could make a poem—quality set aside for the moment—on the spot. After his moment of blankness, we could see his face change, and soon he said he had something. I asked him whether he could remember it; and he said Yes, he could. Then I asked him to leave the room, to wait in the hall and after a while, to write the poem down; I would come out for him a little later.

When he left the room, there was a stir. I asked the group whether there was a poem; with a few dissenters at first, they agreed that there was. Where did the poem exist? There was some discussion here; one angry person said the poem did not exist until it was on paper; the rest said it existed in the poet's mind, in the poet's imagination.

What was the poem made of, what was its material? I listed the answers on the blackboard. Sensations, impressions, ideals, response to immediate stimuli, memory, rhythm, rhyme, divine light, inspiration—what was it made of?—words, images, sound. A few people hazarded guesses based on their assumptions of the bias of the volunteer—his poem would mean this, it would have that social content, its structure might be such—

I went out into the hall, where the volunteer waited with a slip of paper in his hand. Briefly, I told him what had happened in the room since he left.

He came back to his place, and read his poem. Yes, it was exactly as he had composed it, while we watched. Well, perhaps one word was different.

Would he tear up the slip of paper? He tore it into small bits, a little random heap on the table before him.

Now where was the poem?

At this point the discussion takes a new direction and impetus. The poem exists in the imagination of the poet and the group; but are there as many poems as there are witnesses? What is the role of the words on the paper? Even, as a professor at the University of California asked, what would have happened if the volunteer had died in the hall—would there have been a poem?

We are on the way to answers. The nature of this reality has been established. We have all *gone through* an experience to which the questions and answers may now refer. We have seen the difference between art,—which is not destroyed when the paper is torn, because its material is not print on paper, but the imagination of the artist and the witnesses—and craft, whose material is otherwise. We have seen something come into existence, and be diffused—and, incidentally, we have seen how mistaken were the prejudices of the group concerning the prejudices of the poet. More has been acted out about point of view than a dozen lectures could describe—the difficult matter of the individual attitude, an "original relation to the universe," so elusive to the emotionally insecure, elusive to the point that one sometimes longs for the omission of the grammatical subject, as in classical Chinese writing—so that Shih-Hsiang Chen, in his comments on translation, says that he has translated the subject as "the poet," in an attempt to offer an expression "more connotative of a universal, objective viewpoint than 'I' or 'he.'" More has been acted out, in this workshop experiment, about the creative process, than any exposition could declare.

The process of writing a poem represents work done on the self of the poet, in order to make form. That this form has to do with the relationships of sounds, rhythms, imaginative beliefs does not isolate the process from any other creation. A total imaginative response is involved, and the first gestures of offering—even if the offering is never completed, and indeed even if the poem falls short. If it does, it has fallen in the conception, for the conception and the execution are identified here—whatever is conceived is made, is written.

Essentials are here, as in mathematical or musical creation—we need no longer distinguish, for we are speaking of the process itself, except for our illustrations. Only the essential is true; Joseph Conrad, in a letter of advice, drives this home by recommending deletions, explaining that these words are "not essential and therefore not true to the fact."

The process has very much unconscious work in it. The conscious process varies: my own experience is that the work on a poem "surfaces" several times, with new submergence after each rising. The "idea" for the poem, which may come as an image thrown against memory, as a sound of words that sets off a travelling of sound and meaning, as a curve of emotion (a form) plotted by certain crises of events or images or sound, or as a title which evokes a sense of inner relations; this is the first "surfacing" of the poem. Then a period of stillness may follow. The second surfacing may find the poem filled in, its voices distinct, its identity apparent, and another deep dive to its own depth of sleep and waiting. A last surfacing may find you ready to write. You may have jotted down a course of images, or a first line, or a whole verse, by now. This last conscious period finds you with all the work on yourself done—at least this is typical of the way I write a fairly sustained poem—and ready for the last step of all, the writing of a poem. Then the experience is followed, you reach its conclusion with the last word of your poem. One role is accomplished. At this point, you change into the witness. You remember what may be done, and much or little critical work—re-writing—may be done.

I know most clearly the process of writing a recent, fairly extended poem, *Orpheus*. The beginnings go far back, to childhood and a wish for identity, as rebirth, as co-ordination, as form. My interests here are double: a desire for form, and perhaps a stronger desire to understand the wish for form. The figure of Orpheus stands for loss and triumph over loss, among other things: the godhead of music and poetry, yes, in a mythology I was always familiar with at a distance at which it could be better dealt with than the mythology, say, of the Old Testament. In a poem written when I was nineteen, after a long hospitalization for typhoid fever contracted in an Alabama stationhouse during the second Scottsboro trial—a poem called *In Hades*,

Orpheus, I focussed on Eurydice, the ill woman who yearns backward from the burning green of the world to the paleness and rest—and death—of the hospital. Then the interest in Orpheus himself took precedence: I was at the brilliant performance of Gluck's opera *Orpheus* which Tchelitchew designed for the Metropolitan Opera, and was moved by that play of loss and the dragging loves and the music and thorny volcanic Hell; so moved and disturbed that, years later, I wished to go on from there, not to revisit those scenes of Hell.

On Forty-Second Street, late one night, I saw the nightwalkers go past the fifth-run movie houses, the Marine Barn, the Flea Circus, not as whole people, but as a leg, part of a shoulder, an eye askew. Pieces of people. This went into notes for a poem that never was written. They say, "MARINE BAR, portraits of an eye and the mouth, blue leg and half a face." This was eight years before the poem was written. Then there was a period of writing other poems and prose, of being away from New York and returning, and then a time of great scattering, a year later, when I wrote what became the beginning of *The Antagonists*:

> *Pieces of animals, pieces of all my friends*
> *prepare assassinations while I sleep. . . .*

This was a poem that began with the tearing of the "I" and moved on to a reconciliation in love and intensity. Near the phrases, in my notebook, I wrote "bringing the dead back to life."

Four years later, reading Thomson and Geddes' *Life*, I became interested again in morphology and specifically in the fact that no part of the body lives or dies to itself. I read what I could about the memory and lack of memory of fragments, of amputees, and of dislocated nerve centers. And at the same time I was writing, as part of another poem,

> *Orpheus in hell remembered rivers*
> *and a music rose*
> *full of human voices;*
> *all words you wish are in that living sound.*
> *and even torn to pieces*
> *one piece sang*
> *Come all ye torn and wounded here*
> *together*
> *and sang to its brother*
> *remembering.*

There, in Carmel, the course of the poem suddenly became clear. It did not concern Eurydice—not directly—it was of a later time. The murder of Orpheus began it; that early unsolved murder. Why did the women kill him? Reinach has written a paper about the murder. Was it because he loved Eurydice and would not approach them? Was it because he was homosexual, and they were losing their lovers to him? Was it because he had seen their orgies without taking part? All these theories had been advanced. But my poem started a moment later. I had it now! *Pieces of Orpheus*, I wrote that would be the title. The scene is the mountaintop, just after the murder. The hacked pieces lie in their blood, the women are running down the slope, there is only the mountain, the moon, the river, the cloud. He was able to make all things sing. Now they begin: "the voice of the Cloud to the killers of Orpheus," I wrote. I knew what would follow. The pieces of the body would begin to talk, each according to its own nature, but they would be lost, they would be nothing, being no longer together. Like those in love, apart, I thought. No, not like anything. Like pieces of the body, knowing there had been pain, but not able to remember what pain—knowing they had loved, but not remembering whom. They know there must be some surpassing effort, some risk. The hand moves, finds the lyre, and throws it upward with a fierce gesture. The lyre flies upward in night, whistling through the black air to become the constellation; as it goes up, hard, the four strings sing *Eurydice*. And *then* the pieces begin to remember; they begin to come together; he turns into the god. He is music and poetry; he is Orpheus.

I was not able to write the poem. I went back to Chicago and to New York that winter, and, among a hundred crucial pressures, looked up some of the Orphic hymns in the New York Public Library, I wrote "The mountaintop, in silence, after the murder" and "lions and towers of the sky" and "The pieces of the body begin to remember" and "He has died the death of the god." Now there begin to be notes. This is the middle of the winter, six years after the night on Forty-Second Street.

Again in California, in a year of intense physical crisis, threat, renewal, loss, and beginning. Now the notes begin to be very full. He did not look at Eurydice. He looked past her, at Hell. Now the wounds are the chorus: Touch me! Love me! Speak to me! This goes back to the yearning and self-pity of early love-poems, and a way must be found to end the self-pity.

Months later, the phrases begin to appear in fuller relationship. "The body as a circus, these freaks of Orpheus." Body Sonnets is one rejected notion. "Air-tree, nerve-tree, blood-maze"; Pindar said of him "Father of Songs."

"Sing in me, days and voices," I write; and a form takes shape. I will solve a problem that has been moving toward solution. My longer poems, like the *Elegies* and *The Soul and Body of John Brown*, contained songs. This poem will move toward its song: its own song and Orpheus' song. A poem leads to a song! The pieces that come together, become a self, and sing.

Now I was ready to write. There were pages of notes and false starts, but there was no poem. There were whole lines, bits of drawing, telephone messages in the margin. Now something was ready; the poem began, and the first section was written.

It was slower to come to the second and third sections; as they were finished, the song too was ready; but now I turned into reader. The resurrection itself needed sharpening. These symbols must not be finished; the witness himself wants to finish. But this friend is right, the women must be part of his song, the god must include his murderers if murder is part of his life. And this correspondent is right, pain is not *forgotten*. All of this re-writing is conscious throughout as distinct from the writing of the poem, in which suggestions, relations, images, phrases, sailed in from everywhere. For days of reminder and revery, everything became Orpheus. Until it was time to go back to the title. The working title was *Pieces of Orpheus*. But that was for myself. No longer the pieces, but the rebirth, stands clear. The name alone should head the poem. So: two words are crossed out: it is ready.

The role of memory is not explored. We know the memory of the unfinished act, or story, or joke, is stronger than that of the finished. These symbols are never finished; they continue to grow; perhaps that is their power. We know that the poetic strategy, if one may call it that, consists in leading the memory of an unknown witness, by means of rhythm and meaning and image and coursing sound and always-unfinished symbol, until in a blaze of discovery and love, the poem is taken. This is the music of the images of relationship, its memory, and its information.

Functions of information and memory have been related in Norbert Wiener's book of many sides and many excitements, *Cybernetics*. Here, among a hundred suggestions, we hear the "philosophical echoes" of "the transition from a Newtonian, reversible time to a Gibbsian, irreversible time." We are shown the necessity to be dynamically-minded, and the line of one philosopher is traced, from Leibniz's continuum of monads to the post-Gibbsian dynamic interpretations. We meet again that hero of our century, Maxwell's demon, and confronted as he is with his problems of entropy and equilibrium, we see something about the information which the sorting demon may receive from particles approaching the gate he guards in his container. We see that information here represents negative entropy.

Now a poem, like anything separable and existing in time, may be considered as a system, and the changes taking place in the system may be investigated. The notion of feedback, as it is used in calculating machines and such linked structures as the locks of the Panama Canal, is set forth. The relations of information and feedback in computing machines and the nervous system, as stated here, raise other problems. What are imaginative information and imaginative feedback in poetry? What are the emotional equivalents for these relationships? How far do these truths of control and communication apply to art?

The questions are raised, even with the older questions, like Proust's madeleine, still setting challenges to the sciences.

We know that the relationships in poetry are clearer when we think in terms of a dynamic system, whose tendencies toward equilibrium, and even toward entropy, are the same as other systems'. (Even Orpheus approached maximum entropy before he became a god.)

We know that poetry is not isolated here, any more than any phenomena can be isolated. Now again we see that all is unbegun.

The only danger is in not going far enough. The usable truth here deals with change. But we are speaking of the human spirit. If we go deep enough, we reach the common life, the shared experience of man, the world of possibility.

If we do not go deep, if we live and write half-way, there are obscurity, vulgarity, the slang of fashion, and several kinds of death.

All we can be sure of is that our art has life in time, it serves human meaning, it blazes on the night of the spirit; all we can be sure of is that at our most subjective we are universal; all we can be sure of is the profound flow of our living tides of meaning, the river meeting the sea in eternal relationship, in a dance of power, in a dance of love.

For this is the world of light and change: the real world; and the reality of the artist is the reality of the witnesses.

The Fisherwoman's Daughter

URSULA K. LE GUIN

I read the first version of this paper at Brown University and at Miami University in Ohio, and revised it heavily to read at Wesleyan College in Georgia. Then I wrote it all over again to read at Portland State University. I have a feeling I read it somewhere else, but can't reconstruct where. When I went to Tulane to be a Mellon fellow—to be precise, a quarter of a Mellon—I wrote it again, and that version, which I pretended was definitive, appeared in Tulane's series of Mellon papers, under the title "A Woman Writing." Asked to give the talk in a benefit series in San Francisco, I decided to include more about my mother, whose writing life was lived in the Bay Area; and that led to another full revision.

In preparing the manuscript of this book, I came to the immense folder containing the five—in places identical, in places widely differing—typescripts of the talk; and thought, "If I have to rewrite that thing once more I will die." So I merely included the latest version, without rereading it. My ruthless editor would have none of that. "Pusillanimous woman," she said, "what about all the bits that you left out?" "What about them?" I snarled. "I think if we just put them together it will work," said she. "Show me," said I, craftily. So she did. I hope it does.

What pleases me most about the piece, after so much work on it, is that I can look on it at last as a collaboration. The responses from the various audiences I read it to, both questions in the lecture hall and letters afterward, guided and clarified my thinking and saved me from many follies and omissions. The present re-collation and editing has given me back the whole thing—not shapely and elegant, but a big crazy quilt. And that was my working title for it when I first began gathering material: "Crazy Quilt." That name hints again at collaboration, which is what I saw myself as doing as I pieced together the works and words of so many other writers—ancestors, strangers, friends.

" 'So of course,' wrote Betty Flanders, pressing her heels rather deeper in the sand, 'there was nothing for it but to leave.'"

That is the first sentence of Virginia Woolf's *Jacob's Room.*[1] It is a woman writing. Sitting on the sand by sea, writing. It's only Betty Flanders, and she's only writing a letter. But first sentences are doors to worlds. This world of Jacob's room, so strangely empty at the end of the book when the mother stands in it holding out a pair of her son's old shoes, and saying, "What am I to do with these?"—this is a world in which the first thing one sees is a woman, a mother of children, writing.

On the shore, by the sea, outdoors, is that where women write? Not at a desk, in a writing room? Where does a woman write, what does she look like writing, what is my image, your image, of a woman writing? I asked my friends: "A woman writing: what do you see?" There would be a pause, then the eyes would light up, seeing. Some sent me to paintings, Fragonard, Cassatt, but mostly these turned out to be paintings of a woman reading or with a letter, not actually writing or reading the letter but never looking up from it with unfocused eyes: Will he never never return? Did I remember to turn off the pot roast?. . . . Another friend responded crisply, "A woman writing is taking dictation." And another said, "She's sitting at the kitchen table, and the kids are yelling."

And that last is the image I shall pursue. But first let me tell you my own first answer to my question: Jo March. From the immediacy, the authority, with which Frank Merrill's familiar illustrations of *Little Women*[2] came to my mind as soon as I asked myself what a woman writing looks like, I know that Jo March must have had real influence upon me when I was a young scribbler. I am sure she has influenced many girls, for she is not, like most "real" authors, either dead or inaccessibly famous; not, like so many artists in books, is she set apart by sensitivity or suffering or general superlativity; nor is she, like most authors in novels, male. She is close as a sister and common as grass. As a model, what does she tell scribbling girls? I think it worthwhile to follow the biography of Jo March the Writer until we come to that person of whom, as a child and until quite recently, I knew almost nothing: Louisa May Alcott.

We first meet Jo as a writer when sister Amy vengefully burns her manuscript, "the loving work of several years. It seemed a small loss to others, but to Jo it was a dreadful calamity." How could a book, several years' work, be "a small loss" to anyone? That horrified me. How could they ask Jo to forgive Amy? At least she nearly drowns her in a frozen lake before forgiving her. At any rate, some chapters later Jo is

> very busy in the garret . . . seated on the old sofa, writing busily, with her papers spread out on a trunk before her. . . . Jo's desk up here was an old tin kitchen. . . .

—the *Oxford English Dictionary* says, "New England: a roasting pan." So Jo's room of her own at this stage is a garret furnished with a sofa, a roasting pan, and a rat. To any twelve-year-old, heaven.

> Jo scribbled away till the last page was filled, when she signed her name with a flourish. . . . Lying back on the sofa she read the manuscript carefully through, making dashes here and there, and putting in many exclamation points, which looked like little balloons; then she tied it up with a smart red ribbon and sat a minute looking at it with a sober, wistful expression, which plainly showed how earnest her work had been.

I am interested here by the counterplay of a deflating irony—the scribbling, the dashes, the balloons, the ribbon—and that wistful earnestness.

Jo sends her story to a paper, it is printed, and she reads it aloud to her sisters, who cry at the right places. Beth asks, "Who wrote it?"

> The reader suddenly sat up, cast away the paper, displaying a flushed countenance, and with a funny mixture of solemnity and excitement, replied, in a loud voice, "Your sister."

The March family makes a great fuss, "for these foolish, affectionate people made a jubilee of every little household joy"—and there again is deflation, a writer's first publication reduced to a "little household joy." Does it not debase art? And yet does it not also, by refusing the heroic tone, refuse to inflate art into something beyond the reach of any "mere girl"?

So Jo goes on writing; here she is some years later, and I quote at length, for this is the central image.

> Every few weeks she would shut herself up in her room, put on her scribbling suit, and "fall into a vortex," as she expressed it, writing away at her novel with all her heart and soul, for till that was finished she could find no peace. Her "scribbling suit" consisted of a black woollen pinafore on which she could wipe her pen at will, and a cap of the same material, adorned with a cheerful red bow. . . . This cap was a beacon to the inquiring eyes of her family, who during these periods kept their distance, merely popping in their heads semi-occasionally to ask, with interest, "Does genius burn, Jo?" They did not always venture even to ask this question, but took an observation of the cap, and judged accordingly. If this expressive article of dress was drawn low upon the forehead, it was a sign that hard work was going on; in exciting moments it was pushed rakishly askew; and when despair seized the author it was plucked wholly off and cast upon the floor. At such times the intruder silently withdrew; and not until the red bow was seen gayly erect upon the gifted brow, did anyone dare address Jo.
>
> She did not think herself a genius by any means; but when the writing fit came on, she gave herself up to it with entire abandon, and led a blissful life, unconscious of want, care, or bad weather, while she sat safe and happy in an imaginary world, full of friends almost as real and dear to her as any in the flesh. Sleep forsook her eyes, meals stood untasted, day and night were all too short to enjoy the happiness which blessed her only at such times, and made these hours worth living, even if they bore no other fruit. The divine afflatus usually lasted a week or two, and then she emerged from her vortex, hungry, sleepy, cross, or despondent.

This is a good description of the condition in which the work of art is done. This is the real thing—domesticated. The cap and bow, the facetious turns and the disclaimers, deflate without degrading, and allow Alcott to make a rather extraordinary statement: that Jo is doing something very important and doing it entirely seriously and that there is nothing unusual about a young woman's doing it. This passion of work and this happiness which blessed her in doing it are fitted without fuss into a girl's commonplace life at home. It may not seem much; but I don't know where else I or many other girls like me, in my generation or my mother's or my daughter's, were to find this model, this validation.

Jo writes romantic thrillers and they sell; her father shakes his head and says, "Aim at the highest and never mind the money," but Amy remarks, "The money is the best part of it." Working in Boston as a governess-seamstress, Jo sees that "money conferred power: money and power, therefore, she resolved to have; not to be used for herself alone," our author's author hastily adds, "but for those whom she loved more than self. . . . She took to writing sensation stories." Her first visit to the editorial office of the *Weekly Volcano* is handled lightly, but the three men treat her as a woman who has come to sell herself— true Lévi-Straussians, to whom what a woman does is entirely subsumed in woman as commodity. Refusing shame, Jo writes on, and makes money by her writing: admitting shame, she does not "tell them at home."

> Jo soon found that her innocent experience had given her but few glimpses of the tragic world which underlies society; so, regarding it in a business light, she set about supplying her deficiencies with characteristic energy. . . . She searched newspapers for accidents, incidents, and crimes; she excited the suspicions of public librarians by asking for works on poisons; she studied faces in the street, and characters good, bad, and indifferent all about her. . . . Much describing of other people's passions and feelings set her to studying and speculating about her own—a morbid amusement, in which healthy young minds do not voluntarily indulge—

but which one might think appropriate, even needful, to the young novelist? However, "wrongdoing always brings its own punishment, and when Jo most needed hers, she got it."

Her punishment is administered by the Angel in the House, in the form of Professor Bhaer. Knowing that she is soiling her pure soul, he attacks the papers she writes for: "I do not like to think that good young girls should see such things." Jo weakly defends them, but when he leaves she rereads her stories, three months' work, and burns them. Amy doesn't have to do it for her any more; she can destroy herself. Then she sits and wonders: "I almost wish I hadn't any conscience, it's so convenient!" A cry from the heart of Bronson Alcott's daughter. She tries a pious tale and a children's story, which don't sell, and gives up: she "corked up her inkstand."

Beth dies, and trying to replace her, Jo tries "to live for others"— finally driving her mother to say, "Why don't you write? That always used to make you happy." So she does, and she writes both well and successfully—until Professor Bhaer returns and marries her, evidently the only way to make her stop writing. She has his two boys to bring up, and then her two boys, and then all those Little Men in the next volume; at the end of *Little Women*, in the chapter called "Harvest Time," she says, "I haven't given up the hope that I may write a good book yet, but I can wait."

The harvest seems indefinitely deferred. But, in Rachel Blau Du Plessis' phrase,[3] Jo writes beyond the ending. In the third volume, *Jo's Boys*, she has gone back in middle age to writing, and is rich and famous. There is realism, toughness, and comedy in the descriptions of her managing the household, mothering the teenagers, writing her chapters, and trying to avoid the celebrity hunters. In fact this, like the whole story of Jo the Writer, is quite close to Louisa Alcott's own story, with one large difference. Jo marries and has children. Lu did not.

And yet she undertook the responsibility for a family, some of whom were as improvident and self-centered as any baby. There is a heartbreaking note in her journal[4] for April 1869, when she was suffering a "bad spell" of mercury poisoning (the calomel given her to cure fever when she was a nurse in the Civil War made her sick the rest of her life):

> Very poorly. Feel quite used up. Don't care much for myself, as rest is heavenly, even with pain; but the family seems so panic-stricken and helpless when I break down, that I try to keep the mill going. Two short tales for L., 50 dollars; two for Ford, 20 dollars; and did my editorial work, though two months are unpaid for. Roberts wants a new book, but am afraid to get into a vortex lest I fall ill.

Alcott used the same word Jo used for her passions of writing; here are a couple of journal passages comparable to the "vortex" passage in *Little Women.*

> August 1860—"Moods" [a novel]. Genius burned so fiercely that for four weeks I wrote all day and planned nearly all night, being quite possessed by my work. I was perfectly happy, and seemed to have no wants.

> February 1861—Another turn at "Moods," which I remodelled. From the 2d to the 25th I sat writing, with a run at dusk; could not sleep, and for three days was so full of it I could not stop to get up. Mother made me a green silk cap with a red bow, to match the old green and red party wrap, which I wore as a "glory cloak." Thus arrayed sat in a grove of manuscripts, "living for immortality" as May said. Mother wandered in and out with cordial cups of tea, worried because I couldn't eat. Father thought it fine, and brought his reddest apples and hardest cider for my Pegasus to feed upon. . . . It was very pleasant and queer while it lasted. . . .

And it is pleasant to see how the family whose debts she slaved to pay off, and which she strove so to protect and keep in comfort, tried to protect and help her in return.

Like so many women of her century, then, Lu Alcott had a family, though she did not marry. "Liberty is a better husband than love to many of us," she wrote, but in fact she had very little liberty, in the sense of freedom from immediate, personal responsibilities. She even had a baby—her sister May's. Dying from complications of childbirth, May asked the beloved older sister, then forty-eight, to bring up little Lu; which she did until her death eight years later.

All this is complex, more complex, I think, than one tends to imagine; for the Victorian script calls for a clear choice—either books or babies for a woman, not both. And Jo *seems* to make that choice. I was annoyed at myself when I realized that I had forgotten Jo's survival as a writer—that my memory, except for one nagging scrap that led me to look up *Jo's Boys* at last, had followed that script. That, of course, is the power of the script: you play the part without knowing it.

Here is a classic—a scriptural—description of a writing woman, the mother of children, one of whom is just now in the process of falling down the stairs.

> Mrs Jellyby was a pretty, very diminutive, plump woman, of from forty to fifty, with handsome eyes, though they had a curious habit of seeming to look a long way off. . . . [She] had very good hair, but was too much occupied with her African duties to brush it. . . . We could not help noticing that her dress didn't nearly meet up the back, and that the open space was railed across with a latticework of stay-laces— like a summer-house.
>
> The room, which was strewn with papers and nearly filled by a great writing-table covered with similar litter, was, I must say, not only very untidy, but very dirty. We were obliged to take notice of that with our sense of sight, even while, with our sense of hearing, we followed the poor child who had tumbled downstairs: I think into the back kitchen, where somebody seemed to stifle him. But what principally struck us was a jade and unhealthy-looking, though by no means plain girl, at the writing-table, who sat biting the feather of her pen, and staring at us. I suppose nobody ever was in such a state of ink.[5]

I will, with difficulty, restrain myself from reading you the rest of *Bleak House*. I love Dickens and will defend his Mrs. Jellyby and her correspondence with Borrioboola-Gha as an aeternal send-up of those who meddle with foreign morals while remaining oblivious to the misery under their nose. But I observe also that he uses a woman to make this point, probably because it was, and is, safe: few readers would question the assumption that a woman should put family before public responsibility, or that if she does work outside the "private sphere" she will be neglectful of her house, indifferent to the necks of her children, and incompetent to fasten her clothing. Mrs. Jellyby's daughter is saved from her enforced "state of ink" by marriage, but Mrs. Jellyby will get no help from her husband, a man so inert that their marriage is described as the union of mind and matter. Mrs. Jellyby is a joy to me, she is drawn with so much humor and good nature; and yet she troubles me, because behind her lurks the double standard. Nowhere among Dickens' many responsible, intelligent women is there one who does real artistic or intellectual work, to balance Mrs. Jellyby and reassure us that it isn't what she does but how she does it that is deplorable. And yet the passage just quoted is supposed to have been written by a woman—the character Esther Summerson. Esther herself is a problem. How does she write half Dickens' novel for him while managing Bleak House and getting smallpox and everything else? We never catch her at it. As a woman writing, Esther is invisible. She is not in the script.

There may be a sympathetic portrait of a woman writer with children in a novel written by a man. I have read versions of this paper in Rhode Island, Ohio, Georgia, Louisiana, Oregon, and California, and asked each audience please to tell me if they knew of any such. I wait in hope. Indeed, the only sympathetic picture of a woman novelist in a man's novel that I know is the protagonist of *Diana at the Crossways*. Meredith shows her writing novels for her living, doing it brilliantly, and finding her freedom in her professionalism. But, self-alienated by a disastrous infatuation, she begins to force her talent and can't work— the script apparently being that love is incidental for a man, everything for a woman. At the end, well-off and happily married, she is expecting a baby, but not, it appears, a book. All the same, Diana still stands, nearly a century later, quite alone at her crossways.

Invisibility as a writer is a condition that affects not only characters but authors, and even the children of authors. Take Elizabeth Barrett Browning, whom we have consistently put to bed with a spaniel, ignoring the fact that when she wrote *Aurora Leigh* she was the healthy mother of a four-year-old—ignoring, in fact, the fact that she wrote *Aurora Leigh*, a book about being a woman writer, and how difficult one's own true love can make it for one.

Here is a woman who had several children and was a successful novelist, writing a letter to her husband about a hundred and fifty years ago, or maybe last night:

> If I *am* to write, I must have a room to myself, which shall be *my* room. All last winter I felt the need of some place where I could go and be quiet. I could not [write in the dining room] for there was all the setting of table and clearing up of tables and dressing and washing of children, and everything else going on, and . . . I never felt comfortable there, though I tried hard. Then if I came into the parlor where you were,

I felt as if I were interrupting you, and you know you sometimes thought so too.[6]

What do you mean? Not at all! Silly notion! Just like a woman!

Fourteen years and several more children later, that woman wrote
Uncle Tom's Cabin—most of it at the kitchen table.

A room of one's own—yes. One may ask why Mr. Harriet Beecher
Stowe got a room to himself to write in, while the woman who wrote
the most morally effective American novel of the 19th century got the
kitchen table. But then one may also ask why she accepted the kitchen
table. Any self-respecting man would have sat there for five minutes
and then stalked out shouting, "Nobody can work in this madhouse,
call me when dinner's ready!" But Harriet, a self-respecting woman,
went on getting dinner with the kids all underfoot *and* writing her
novels. The first question, to be asked with *awe*, is surely, How? But
then, Why? *Why* are women such patsies?

The quick-feminist-fix answer is that they are victims of and/or ac-
complices with the patriarchy, which is true but doesn't really get us
anywhere new. Let us go to another woman novelist for help. I stole
the Stowe quotation (and others) from Tillie Olsen's *Silences*, a book
to which this paper stands in the relation of a loving but undutiful
daughter—Hey Ma, that's a neat quotation, can I wear it? This next
one I found for myself, in the *Autobiography* of Margaret Oliphant, a
fascinating book, from the generation just after Stowe. Oliphant was
a successful writer very young, married, had three kids, went on writing, was left a widow with heavy debts and the three kids plus her
brother's three kids to bring up, did so, went on writing. . . . When
her second book came out, she was still, like Jo March, a girl at home.

> I had a great pleasure in writing, but the success and the three
> editions had no particular effect upon my mind. . . . I had
> nobody to praise me except my mother and [brother] Frank,
> and their applause—well, it was delightful, it was everything
> in the world—it was life—but it did not count. They were
> part of me, and I of them, and we were all in it.[7]

I find that extraordinary. I cannot imagine any male author saying
anything like that at all. There is a key here—something real that has
been neglected, been hidden, been denied.

> . . . The writing ran through everything. But then it was also
> subordinate to everything, to be pushed aside for any little

necessity. I had no table even to myself, much less a room to work in, but sat at the corner of the family table with my writing-book, with everything going on as if I had been making a shirt instead of writing a book. . . . My mother sat always at needlework of some kind, and talked to whoever might be present, and I took my share in the conversations, going on all the same with my story, the little groups of imaginary persons, these other talks evolving themselves quite undisturbed.

How's that for an image, the group of imaginary people talking in the imaginary room in the real room among the real people talking, and all of it going on perfectly quiet and unconfused. . . . But it's shocking. She can't be a real writer. Real writers writhe on solitary sofas in cork-lined rooms, agonizing after *le mot juste*—don't they?

My study, all the study I have ever attained to, is the little second drawing-room where all the life of the house goes on. . . .

—you recall that she was bringing up six children?—

. . . and I don't think I have ever had two hours undisturbed (except at night when everybody is in bed) during my whole literary life. Miss Austen, I believe, wrote in the same way, and very much for the same reason; but at her period the natural flow of life took another form. The family were half ashamed to have it known that she was not just a young lady like the others, doing her embroidery. Mine were quite pleased to magnify me and to be proud of my work, but always with a hidden sense that it was an admirable joke. . . .

—perhaps artists cast off their families and go to the South Sea Islands because they want to be perceived as heroes and their families think they are funny?—

. . . a hidden sense that it was an admirable joke, and no idea that any special facilities or retirement was necessary. My mother would have felt her pride much checked, almost humiliated, if she had conceived that I stood in need of any artificial aids of that description. That would at once have made the work unnatural to her eyes, and also to mine.

Oliphant was a proud Scotswoman, proud of her work and her strength; yet she wrote nonfiction potboilers rather than fight her male editors and publishers for better pay for her novels. So, as she says bitterly, "Trollope's worst book was better paid than my best." Her best is said to be *Miss Marjoribanks*, but I have never yet been able to get a copy of it; it has disappeared, along with all her other books. Thanks to publishers such as Virago we can now get Oliphant's *Hester*, a stunning novel, and *Kirsten* and a few others, but they are still taught, so far as I know, only in women's studies courses; they are not part of the Canon of English Literature, though Trollope's potboilers are. No book by a woman who had children has ever been included in that august list.

I think Oliphant gives us a glimpse of why a novelist might not merely endure writing in the kitchen or the parlor amid the children and the housework, but might endure it willingly. She seems to feel that she profited, that her writing profited, from the difficult, obscure, chancy connection between the artwork and the emotional/manual/managerial complex of skills and tasks called "housework" and that to sever that connection would put the writing itself at risk, would make it, in her word, unnatural.

The received wisdom of course is just the opposite: that any attempt to combine artwork with housework and family responsibility is impossible, unnatural. And the punishment for unnatural acts, among the critics and the Canoneers, is death.

What is the ethical basis of this judgment and sentence upon the housewife-artist? It is a very noble and austere one, with religion at its foundation: it is the idea that the artist must sacrifice himself to art. (I use the pronoun advisedly.) His responsibility is to his work alone. It is a motivating idea of the Romantics, it guides the careers of poets from Rimbaud to Dylan Thomas to Richard Hugo, it has given us hundreds of hero figures, typical of whom is James Joyce himself and his Stephen Dedalus. Stephen sacrifices all "lesser" obligations and affections to a "higher" cause, embracing the moral irresponsibility of the soldier or the saint. This heroic stance, the Gauguin Pose, has been taken as the norm—as natural to the artist—and artists, both men and women, who do not assume it have tended to feel a little shabby and second-rate.

Not, however, Virginia Woolf. She observed factually that the artist needs a small income and a room to work in, but did not speak of heroism. Indeed, she said, "I doubt that a writer can be a hero. I doubt that a hero can be a writer." And when I see a writer assume the full heroic posture, I incline to agree. Here, for example, is Joseph Conrad:

> For twenty months wrestled with the Lord for my creation . . . mind and will and conscience engaged to the full, hour after hour, day after day . . . a lonely struggle in a great isolation from the world. I suppose I slept and ate the food put before me and talked connectedly on suitable occasions, but I was never aware of the even flow of daily life, made easy and noiseless for me by a client, watchful, tireless affection.[8]

A woman who boasted that her conscience had been engaged to the full in such a wrestling match would be called to account by both women and men; and women are now calling men to account. What "put food" before him? What made daily life so noiseless? What in fact was this "tireless affection," which sounds to me like an old Ford in a junkyard but is apparently intended as a delicate gesture toward a woman whose conscience was engaged to the full, hour after hour, day after day, for twenty months, in seeing to it that Joseph Conrad could wrestle with the Lord in a very relatively great isolation, well housed, clothed, bathed, and fed?

Conrad's "struggle" and Jo March/Lu Alcott's "vortex" are descriptions of the same kind of all-out artistic work; and in both cases the artist is looked after by the family. But I feel an important difference in their perceptions. When Alcott receives a gift, Conrad asserts a right; where she is taken into the vortex, the creative whirlwind, becoming part of it, he wrestles, struggles, seeking mastery. She is a participant; he is a hero. And her family remain individuals, with cups of tea and timid inquiries, while his is depersonalized to "an affection."

Looking for a woman writer who might have imitated this heroic infantilism, I thought of Gertrude Stein, under the impression that she used Alice Toklas as a "wife" in this utilitarian sense; but that, as I should have guessed, is an anti-lesbian canard. Stein certainly took hero-artist poses and indulged an enormous ego, but she played fair; and the difference between her domestic partnership and that of Joyce or Conrad is illuminating. And indeed, lesbianism has given many artists the network of support they need—for there *is* a heroic aspect to the practice of art; it is lonely, risky, merciless work, and every artist needs some kind of moral support or sense of solidarity and validation.

The artist with the least access to social or aesthetic solidarity or approbation has been the artist-housewife. A person who undertakes responsibility both to her art and to her dependent children, with no "tireless affection" or even tired affection to call on, has undertaken a full-time double job that can be simply, practically, destroyingly impossible. But that isn't how the problem is posed—as a recognition of immense practical difficulty. If it were, practical solutions would be proposed, beginning with childcare. Instead the issue is stated, even now, as a moral one, a matter of ought and ought not. The poet Alicia Ostriker puts it neatly: "That women should have babies rather then books is the considered opinion of Western civilization. That women should have books rather than babies is a variation of that theme."[9]

Freud's contribution to this doctrine was to invest it with such a weight of theory and mythology as to make it appear a primordial, unquestionable fact. It was of course Freud who, after telling his fiancée what it is a woman wants, said that what we shall never know is what a woman wants. Lacan is perfectly consistent in following him, if I as a person without discourse may venture to say so. A culture or psychology predicated upon man as human and woman as other cannot accept a woman as artist. An artist is an autonomous, choice-making self: to be such a self a woman must unwoman herself. Barren, she must imitate the man—imperfectly, it goes without saying.[10]

Hence the approbation accorded to Austen, the Brontës, Dickinson, and Plath, who though she made the mistake of having two children compensated for it by killing herself. The misogynist Canon of Literature can include these women because they can be perceived as incomplete women, as female men.

Still, I have to grit my teeth to criticize the either-books-or-babies doctrine, because it has given real, true comfort to women who could not choose or chose not to marry and have children, and saw themselves as "having" books instead. But though the comfort may be real, I think the doctrine false. And I hear that falseness when a Dorothy Richardson tells us that other women can have children but nobody else can write *her* books. As if "other women" could have had *her* children—as if books came from the uterus! That's just the flip side of the theory that books come from the scrotum. This final reduction of the notion of sublimation is endorsed by our chief macho dodo writer, who has announced that "the one thing a writer needs to have is balls." But he doesn't carry the theory of penile authorship to the extent of saying that if you "get" a kid you can't "get" a book and so fathers can't write. The analogy collapsed into identity, the you-can't-create-if-you-procreate myth, is applied to women only.

I've found I have to stop now and say clearly what I'm not saying. I'm not saying a writer ought to have children, I'm not saying a parent ought to be a writer. I'm not saying any woman *ought* to write books *or* have kids. Being a mother is one of the things a woman can do— like being a writer. It's a privilege. It's not an obligation, or a destiny. I'm talking about mothers who write because it is almost a taboo topic—because women have been told that they *ought not* to try to be both a mother and a writer because both the kids and the books will *pay*—because it can't be done—because it is unnatural.

This refusal to allow both creation and procreation to women is cruelly wasteful: not only has it impoverished our literature by banning the housewives, but it has caused unbearable personal pain and self-mutilation: Woolf obeying the wise doctors who said she must not bear a child; Plath who put glasses of milk by her kids' beds and then put her head in the oven.

A sacrifice, not of somebody else but of oneself, is demanded of women artists (while the Gauguin Pose demands of men artists only that they sacrifice others). I am proposing that this ban on a woman artist's full sexuality is harmful not only to the woman but to the art.

There is less censure now, and more support, for a woman who wants both to bring up a family and work as an artist. But it's a small degree of improvement. The difficulty of trying to be responsible, hour after hour day after day for maybe twenty *years*, for the well-being of children and the excellence of books, is immense: it involves an endless expense of energy and an impossible weighing of competing priorities. And we don't know much about the process, because writers who are mothers haven't talked much about their motherhood— for fear of boasting? for fear of being trapped in the Mom trap, discounted?—nor have they talked much about their writing as in any way connected with their parenting, since the heroic myth demands that the two jobs be considered utterly opposed and mutually destructive.

But we heard a hint of something else from Oliphant; and here (thanks, Tillie) is the painter Käthe Kollwitz:

> I am gradually approaching the period in my life when work comes first. When both the boys were away for Easter, I

hardly did anything but work. Worked, slept, ate, and went for short walks. But above all I worked.

And yet I wonder whether the "blessing" isn't missing from such work. No longer diverted by other emotions, I work the way a cow grazes.

That is marvelous—"I work the way a cow grazes." That is the best description of the "professional" at work I know.

Perhaps in reality I accomplish a little more. The hands work and work, and the head imagines it's producing God knows what, and yet, formerly, when my working time was so wretchedly limited, I was more productive, because I was more sensual; I lived as a human being must live, passionately interested in everything. . . . Potency, potency is diminishing.[11]

This *potency* felt by a woman is a potency from which the Hero-Artist has (and I choose my words carefully) cut himself off, in an egoism that is ultimately sterile. But it is a potency that has been denied by women as well as men, and not just women eager to collude with misogyny.

Back in the seventies Nina Auerbach wrote that Jane Austen was able to write because she had created around her "a child-free space." Germ-free I knew, order-free I knew, but child-free? And Austen? who wrote in the parlor, and was a central figure to a lot of nieces and nephews? But I tried to accept what Auerbach said, because although my experience didn't fit it, I was, like many women, used to feeling that my experience was faulty, not right—that it was *wrong*. So I was probably wrong to keep on writing in what was then a fully child-filled space. However, feminist thinking evolved rapidly to a far more complex and realistic position, and I, stumbling along behind, have been enabled by it to think a little for myself.

The greatest enabler for me was always, is always, Virginia Woolf. And I quote now from the first draft of her paper "Professions for Women,"[12] where she gives her great image of a woman writing.

I figure her really in an attitude of contemplation, like a fisherwoman, sitting on the bank of a lake with her fishing rod held over its water. Yes that is how I see her. She was not thinking; she was not reasoning; she was not constructing a plot; she was letting her imagination down into the depths of her consciousness while she sat above holding on by a thin but quite necessary thread of reason.

Now I interrupt to ask you to add one small element to this scene. Let us imagine that a bit farther up the bank of the lake sits a child, the fisherwoman's daughter. She's about five, and she's making people out of sticks and mud and telling stories with them. She's been told to be very quiet please while Mama fishes, and she really is very quiet except when she forgets and sings or asks questions; and she watches in fascinated silence when the following dramatic events take place. There sits our woman writing, our fisherwoman, when—

. . . suddenly there is a violent jerk; she feels the line race through her fingers.

The imagination has rushed away; it has taken to the depths; it has sunk heaven knows where—into the dark pool of extraordinary experience. The reason has to cry "Stop!" the novelist has to pull on the line and haul the imagination to the surface. The imagination comes to the top in a state of fury.

Good heavens she cries—how dare you interfere with me—how dare you pull me out with your wretched little fishing line? And I—that is, the reason—have to reply, "My dear you were going altogether too far. Men would be shocked." Calm yourself I say, as she sits panting on the bank—panting with rage and disappointment. We have only got to wait fifty years or so. In fifty years I shall be able to use all this very queer knowledge that you are ready to bring me. But not now. You see I go on, trying to calm her, I cannot make use of what you tell me—about women's bodies for instance—then passions—and so on, because the conventions are still very strong. If I were to overcome the conventions I should need the courage of a hero, and I am not a hero.

I doubt that a writer can be a hero. I doubt that a hero can be a writer.

. . . Very well, says the imagination, dressing herself up again in her petticoat and skirts, we will wait. We will wait another fifty years. But it seems to me a pity.

It seems to me a pity. It seems to me a pity that more than fifty years have passed and the conventions, though utterly different, still exist to protect men from being shocked, still admit only male experience of women's bodies, passions, and existence. It seems to me a pity that so many women, including myself, have accepted this denial of their own experience and narrowed their perception to fit it, writing as if their sexuality were limited to copulation, as if they knew nothing about pregnancy, birth, nursing, mothering, puberty, menstruation, menopause, except what men are willing to hear, nothing except what men are willing to hear about housework, childwork, lifework, war, peace, living, and dying as experienced in the female body and mind and imagination. "Writing the body," as Woolf asked and Hélène Cixous asks, is only the beginning. We have to rewrite the world.

White writing, Cixous calls it, writing in milk, in mother's milk. I like that image, because even among feminists, the woman writer has been more often considered in her sexuality as a lover than in her sexuality as pregnant-bearing-nursing-childcaring. Mother still tends to get disappeared. And in losing the artist-mother we lose where there's a lot to gain. Alicia Ostriker thinks so. "The advantage of motherhood for a woman artist," she says—have you ever heard anybody say that before? the *advantage* of motherhood for an artist?—

> The advantage of motherhood for a woman artist is that it puts her in immediate and inescapable contact with the sources of life, death, beauty, growth, corruption. . . . If the woman artist has been trained to believe that the activities of motherhood are trivial, tangential to the main issues of life, irrelevant to the great themes of literature, she should untrain herself. The training is misogynist, it protects and perpetuates systems of thought and feeling which prefer violence and death to love and birth, and it is a lie.
>
> . . . "We think back through our mothers, if we are women," declares Woolf, but through whom can those who are themselves mothers . . . do their thinking? . . . we all need data, we need information, . . . the sort provided by poets, novelists, artists, from within. As our knowledge begins to accumulate, we can imagine what it would signify to all women, and men, to live in a culture where childbirth and mothering have occupied in literature and art for the last

five hundred years, or . . . that warfare has occupied since
literature began.[13]

My book *Always Coming Home* was a rash attempt to imagine such
a world, where the Hero and the Warrior are a stage adolescents go
through on their way to becoming responsible human beings, where
the parent-child relationship is not forever viewed through her child's
eyes but includes the reality of the mother's experience. The imagining
was difficult, and rewarding.

Here is a passage from a novel where what Woolf, Cixous, and
Ostriker ask for is happening, however casually and unpretentiously.
In Margaret Drabble's *The Millstone*,[14] Rosamund, a young scholar
and freelance writer, has a baby about eight months old, Octavia. They
share a flat with a friend, Lydia, who's writing a novel. Rosamund is
working away on a book review:

> I had just written and counted my first hundred words when
> I remembered Octavia; I could hear her making small
> happy noises. . . .
>   I was rather dismayed when I realized she was in Lydia's
> room and that I must have left the door open, for Lydia's
> room was always full of nasty objects like aspirins, safety
> razors and bottles of ink; I rushed along to rescue her and the
> sight that met my eyes when I opened the door was enough to
> make anyone quake. She had her back to the door and was
> sitting in the middle of the floor surrounded by a sea of torn,
> strewed, chewed paper. I stood there transfixed, watching the
> neat small back of her head and her thin stalk-like neck and
> flowery curls: suddenly she gave a great screech of delight
> and ripped another sheet of paper. "Octavia," I said in hor-
> ror, and she started guiltily, and looked round at me with a
> charming deprecating smile: her mouth, I could see, was
> wedged full of wads of Lydia's new novel.
>   I picked her up and fished the bits out and laid them care-
> fully on the bedside table with what was left of the typescript;
> pages 70 to 123 seemed to have survived. The rest was in
> varying stages of dissolution: some pages were entire but
> badly crumpled, some were in large pieces, some in small
> pieces, and some, as I have said, were chewed up. The damage
> was not, in fact, as great as it appeared at first sight to be,

for babies, though persistent, are not thorough: but at first sight it was frightful. . . . In a way it was clearly the most awful thing for which I had ever been responsible, but as I watched Octavia crawl around the sitting room looking for more work to do, I almost wanted to laugh. It seemed so absurd, to have this small living extension of myself, so dangerous, so vulnerable, for whose injuries and crimes, I alone had to suffer. . . . It really was a terrible thing . . . and yet in comparison with Octavia being so sweet and so alive it did not seem so very terrible. . . .

Confronted with the wreckage, Lydia was startled, but not deeply distressed:

> . . . and that was it, except for the fact that Lydia really did have to rewrite two whole chapters as well as doing a lot of boring sellotaping, and when it came out it got bad reviews anyway. This did not succeed in making Lydia angry.

I have seen Drabble's work dismissed with the usual patronizing adjectives reserved for women who write as women, not imitation men. Let us not let her be disappeared. Her work is deeper than its bright surface. What is she talking about in this funny passage? Why does the girl-baby eat not her mother's manuscript but another woman's manuscript? Couldn't she at least have eaten a manuscript by a man?—no, no, that's not the point. The point, or part of it, is that babies eat manuscripts. They really do. The poem not written because the baby cried, the novel put aside because of a pregnancy, and so on. Babies eat books. But they spit out wads of them that can be taped back together; and they are only babies for a couple of years, while writers live for decades; and it is terrible, but not very terrible. The manuscript that got eaten *was* terrible; if you know Lydia you know the reviewers were right. And that's part of the point too—that the supreme value of art depends on other equally supreme values. But that subverts the hierarchy of values; "men would be shocked. . . ."

In Drabble's comedy of morals the absence of the Hero-Artist is a strong ethical statement. Nobody lives in a great isolation, nobody sacrifices human claims, nobody even scolds the baby. Nobody is going to put their head, or anybody else's head, into an oven; not the mother, not the writer, not the daughter—these three and one who, being women, do not separate creation and destruction into *I create/ You are destroyed*, or vice versa. Who are responsible, take responsibility, for both the baby and the book.[15]

But I want now to turn from fiction to biography and from general to personal; I want to talk a bit about my mother, the writer.

Her maiden name was Theodora Kracaw; her first married name was Brown; her second married name, Kroeber, was the one she used on her books; her third married name was Quinn. This sort of many-namedness doesn't happen to men; it's inconvenient, and yet its very cumbersomeness reveals, perhaps, the being of a woman writer is not one simple thing—the author—but a multiple, complex process of being, with various responsibilities, one of which is her writing.

Theodora put her personal responsibilities first—chronologically. She brought up and married off her four children before she started to write. She took up the pen, as they used to say—she had the most amazing left-handed scrawl—in her mid-fifties. I asked her once, years later, "Did you want to write, and put it off intentionally, till you'd got rid of us?" And she laughed and said, "Oh, no, I just wasn't *ready.*" Not an evasion or a dishonest answer, but not, I think, the whole answer.

She was born in 1897 in a wild Colorado mining town, and her mother boasted of having been *born* with the vote—in Wyoming, which ratified woman suffrage along with statehood—and rode a stallion men couldn't ride; but still, the Angel in the House was very active in those days, the one whose message is that a woman's needs come after everybody else's. And my mother really came pretty close to incarnating that Angel, whom Woolf called "the woman men wish women to be." Men fell in love with her—all men. Doctors, garage mechanics, professors, roach exterminators. Butchers saved sweetbreads for her. She was also, to her daughter, a demanding, approving, nurturing, good-natured, loving, lively mother—a first-rate mother. And then, getting on to sixty, she became a first-rate writer.

She started out, as women often do, by writing some books for children—not competing with men, you know, staying in the "domestic sphere." One of these, *A Green Christmas*, is a lovely book that ought to be in every six-year-old's stocking. Then she wrote a charming and romantic autobiographical novel—still on safe, "womanly" ground. Next she ventured into Native American territory with *The Inland Whale*; and then she was asked to write the story of an Indian named Ishi, the only survivor of a people massacred by the North

American pioneers, a serious and risky subject requiring a great deal of research, moral sensitivity, and organizational and narrative skill.

So she wrote it, the first best seller, I believe, that the University of California Press ever published. *Ishi* is still in print in many languages, still used, I think, in California schools, still deservedly beloved. It is a book entirely worthy of its subject, a book of very great honesty and power.

So, if she could write that in her sixties, what might she have written in her thirties? Maybe she really "wasn't ready." But maybe she listened to the wrong angel, and we might have had many more books from her. Would my brothers and I have suffered, have been cheated of anything, if she had been writing them? I think my aunt Betsy and the household help we had back then would have kept things going just fine. As for my father, I don't see how her writing could have hurt him or how her success could have threatened him. But I don't know. All I do know is that once she started writing (and it was while my father was alive, and they collaborated on a couple of things), she never stopped; she had found the work she loved.

Once, not long after my father's death, when *Ishi* was bringing her the validation of praise and success she very much needed, and while I was still getting every story I sent out rejected with monotonous regularity, she burst into tears over my latest rejection slip and tried to console, saying that she wanted rewards and success for me, not for herself. And that was lovely, and I treasured her saying it then as I do now. That she didn't really mean it and I didn't really believe it made no difference. Of course she didn't want to sacrifice her achievement, her work, to me—why on earth should she? She shared what she could of it with me by sharing the pleasures and anguishes of writing, the intellectual excitement, the shoptalk—and that's all. No angelic altruism. When I began to publish, we shared that. And she wrote on; in her eighties she told me, without bitterness, "I wish I had started sooner. Now there isn't time." She was at work on a third novel when she died.

As for myself: I have flagrantly disobeyed the either-books-or-babies rule, having had three kids and written about twenty books, and thank God it wasn't the other way around. By the luck of race, class, money, and health, I could manage the double-tightrope trick—and especially by the support of my partner. He is not my wife; but he brought to marriage an assumption of mutual aid as its daily basis, and on that basis you can get a lot of work done. Our division of labor was fairly conventional; I was in charge of house, cooking, the kids, and novels, because I wanted to be, and he was in charge of being a professor, the car, the bills, and the garden, because he wanted to be. When the kids were babies I wrote at night; when they started school I wrote while they were at school; these days I write as a cow grazes. If I needed help he gave it without making it into a big favor, and—this is the central fact—he did not begrudge me the time I spent writing, or the blessing of my work.

That is the killer: the killing grudge, the envy, the jealousy, the spite that so often a man is allowed to hold, trained to hold, against anything a woman does that's not done in his service, for him, to feed his body, his comfort, his kids. A woman who tries to work against that grudge finds the blessing turned into a curse; she must rebel and go it alone, or fall silent in despair. Any artist must expect to work against daily, personal, vengeful resistance. And that's exactly what many women artists get from the people they love and live with.

I was spared all that. I was free—born free, lived free. And for years that personal freedom allowed me to ignore the degree to which my writing was controlled and constrained by judgments and assumptions which I thought were my own, but which were the internalized ideology of a male supremacist society. Even when subverting the conventions, I disguised my subversions from myself. It took me years to realize that I chose to work in such despised, marginal genres as science fiction, fantasy, young adult, precisely because they were excluded from critical, academic, canonical supervision, leaving the artist free; it took ten more years before I had the wits and guts to see and say that the exclusion of the genres from "literature" is unjustified, unjustifiable, and a matter not of quality but of politics. So too in my choice of subjects: until the mid-70s I wrote my fiction about heroic adventures, high-tech futures, men in the halls of power, men—men were central characters, the women were peripheral, secondary. Why don't you write about women? my mother asked me. I don't know how, I said. A stupid answer, but an honest one. I did not know how to write about women—very few of us did—because I thought that what men had written about women was the truth, was the true way to write about women. And I couldn't.

My mother could give me what I needed. When feminism began to reawaken, she hated it, called it "those women's libbers"; but it was she who had steered me years and years before to what I would and did need, to Virginia Woolf. "We think back through our mothers," and we have many mothers, those of the body and those of the soul. What I needed was what feminism, feminist literary theory and criticism and practice, had to give me. And I can hold it in my hands—not only *Three Guineas*, my treasure in the days of poverty, but now all the wealth of *The Norton Anthology of Literature by Women* and the reprint houses and the women's presses. Our mothers have been returned to us. This time, let's hang on to them.

And it is feminism that has empowered me to criticize not only my society and myself but—for the moment now—feminism itself. The books-as-babies myth is not only a misogynist hang-up, it can be a feminist one. Some of the women I respect most, writing for publications that I depend on for my sense of women's solidarity and hope, continue to declare that it is "virtually impossible for a heterosexual woman to be a feminist," as if heterosexuality were heterosexism; and that social marginality, such as that of lesbian, childless, black, or Native American women, "appears to be necessary" to form the feminist. Applying these judgments to myself, and believing that as a woman writing at this point I have to be a feminist to be worth beans, I find myself, once again, excluded—disappeared.

The rationale of the exclusionists, as I understand it, is that the material privilege and social approbation our society grants the heterosexual wife, and particularly the mother, prevent her solidarity with less privileged women and insulate her from the kind of anger and the kind of ideas that lead to feminist action. There is truth in this; maybe it's true for a lot of women; I can oppose it only with my experience, which is that feminism has been a life-saving *necessity* to women trapped in the wife/mother "role." What do the privilege and approbation accorded the housewife-mother by our society in fact consist of? Being the object of infinite advertising? Being charged by psychologists with total answerability for children's mental well-being, and by the government with total answerability for children's welfare, while being regularly equated with apple pie by sentimental warmongers? As a social "role," motherhood, for any woman I know, simply means that she does everything everybody else does plus bringing up her kids.

To push mothers back into "private life," a mythological space invented by the patriarchy, on the theory that their acceptance of the "role" of mother invalidates them for public, political, artistic responsibility, is to play Old Nobodaddy's game, by his rules, on his side.

In *Writing Beyond the Ending*, Du Plessis shows how women novelists write about the woman artist: they make her an ethical force, an activist trying "to change the life in which she is also immersed."[16] To have and bring up kids is to be about as immersed into life as one can be, but it does not always follow that one drowns. A lot of us can swim.

Again, whenever I give a version of this paper, somebody will pick up on this point and tell me that I'm supporting the Superwoman syndrome, saying that a woman *should* have kids write books be politically active and make perfect sushi. I am not saying that. We're all asked to be Superwoman; I'm not asking it, our society does that. All I can tell you is that I believe it is a lot easier to write books while bringing up kids than to bring up kids while working nine to five plus housekeeping. But that is what our society, while sentimentalizing over Mom and the Family, demands of most women—unless it refuses them any work at all and dumps them onto welfare and says, Bring up your kids on food stamps, Mom, we might want them for the army. Talk about superwomen, those are the superwomen. Those are the mothers up against the wall. Those are the marginal women, without either privacy or publicity; and it's because of them more than anyone else that the woman artist has a responsibility to "try to change the life in which she is also immersed."

And now I come back round to the bank of that lake, where the fisherwoman sits, our woman writer, who had to bring her imagination up short because it was getting too deeply immersed. . . . The imagination dries herself off, still swearing under her breath, and buttons up her blouse, and comes to sit beside the little girl, the fisherwoman's daughter. "Do you like books?" she says, and the child says, "Oh, yes. When I was a baby I used to eat them, but now I can read them. I can read all of Beatrix Potter by myself, and when I grow up I'm going to write books, like Mama."

"Are you going to wait till your children grow up, like Jo March and Theodora?"

"Oh, I don't think so," says the child. "I'll just go ahead and do it."

"Then will you do as Harriet and Margaret and so many Harriets and Margarets have done and are still doing, and hassle through the prime of your life trying to do two full-time jobs that are incompatible with each other in practice, however enriching their interplay may be both to the life and the art?"

"I don't know," says the little girl. "Do I have to?"

"Yes," says the imagination, "if you aren't rich and you want kids."

"I might want one or two," says reason's child. "But why do women have two jobs where men only have one? It isn't reasonable, is it?"

"Don't ask me!" snaps the imagination. "I could think up a dozen better arrangements before breakfast! But who listens to me?"

The child sighs and watches her mother fishing. The fisherwoman, having forgotten that her line is no longer baited with the imagination, isn't catching anything, but she's enjoying the peaceful hour; and when the child speaks again she speaks softly. "Tell me, Auntie. What is the one thing a writer has to have?"

"I'll tell you," says the imagination. "The one thing a writer has to have is not balls. Nor is it a child-free space. Nor is it even, speaking strictly on the evidence, a room of her own, though that is an amazing help, as is the goodwill and cooperation of the opposite sex, or at least the local, in-house representative of it. But she doesn't have to have that. The one thing a writer has to have is a pencil and some paper. That's enough, so long as she knows that she and she alone is in charge of that pencil, and responsible, she and she alone, for what it writes on the paper. In other words, that she's free. Not wholly free. Never wholly free. Maybe very partially. Maybe only in this one act, this sitting for a snatched moment being a woman writing, fishing the mind's lake. But in this, responsible; in this, autonomous; in this, free."

"Auntie," says the little girl, "can I go fishing with you now?"

NOTES

1. Virginia Woolf, *Jacob's Room* (Harcourt Brace Jovanovich, n.d.), 7.
2. The edition of *Little Women* I used was my mother's and is now my daughter's. It was published in Boston by Little, Brown, undated, around the turn of the century, and Merrill's fine drawings have also been reproduced in other editions.
3. Rachel Blau du Plessis, *Writing Beyond the Ending: Narrative Strategies of Twentieth-Century Women Writers* (Indiana University Press, 1985).
4. Louisa May Alcott, *Life, Letters, and Journals* (Roberts Brothers, 1890). The passages quoted are on 203, 122, and 125.
5. Charles Dickens, *Bleak House* (Thomas Y. Crowell, n.d.), 41.
6. Harriet Beecher Stowe, 1841, quoted in Tillie Olsen, *Silences* (Dell, 1983), 227.

7. This and the subsequent connected passages are from the *Autobiography and Letters of Mrs. Margaret Oliphant*, edited by Mrs. Harry Coghill (Leicester University Press, The Victorian Library, 1974), 23, 24.
8. Joseph Conrad, quoted in Olsen, *Silences*, 30.
9. Alicia Ostriker, *Writing Like a Woman*, Michigan Poets on Poetry Series (University of Michigan Press, 1983), 126.
10. A particularly exhilarating discussion of this issue is the essay "Writing and Motherhood" by Susan Rubin Suleiman, in *The (M)other Tongue: Essays in Feminist Psychoanalytic Interpretation*, edited by Garner, Kahane, and Springnether (Cornell University Press, 1985). Suleiman gives a short history of the 19th-century books-or-babies theory and its refinement in the 20th century by such psychologists as Helene Deutsch, remarking that "it took psychoanalysis to transform moral obligation into a psychological 'law,' equating the creative impulse with the procreative one and decreeing that she who has a child feels no need to write books." Suleiman presents a critique of the feminist reversal of this theory (she who has a book feels no need to have children) and analyzes current French feminist thinking on the relationship between writing and femininity/motherhood.
11. Käthe Kollwitz, *Diaries and Letters*, quoted in Olsen, *Silences*, 235, 236.
12. The talk, known in its revised form as "Professions for Women" and so titled in the Essays, was given on January 21, 1931, to the London National Society for Women's Service, and can be found complete with all deletions and alternate readings in Mitchell Leaska's editing of Woolf's *The Partigers* (Harcourt Brace Jovanovich, 1978).
13. Ostriker, *Writing Like a Woman*, 131.
14. Margaret Drabble, *The Millstone* (NAL Plume Books, 1984), 122–23. Also published under the title *Thank You All Very Much*.
15. My understanding of this issue has been much aided by Carol Gilligan's *In a Different Voice* (Harvard University Press, 1982), we well as by Jean Baker Miller's modestly revolutionary *Toward a New Psychology of Women* (Beacon Press, 1976). Gilligan's thesis, stated very roughly, is that our society brings up males to think and speak in terms of their rights, females in terms of their responsibilities, and that conventional psychologies have implicitly evaluated the "male" image of a hierarchy of rights as "superior" (hierarchically, of course) to the "female" image of a network of mutual responsibilities. Hence a man finds it (relatively) easy to assert his "right" to be free of relationships and dependents, à la Gauguin, while women are not granted and do not grant one another any such right, preferring to live as part of an intense and complex network in which freedom is arrived at, if at all, mutually. Coming at the matter from this angle, one can see why there are no or very few "Great Artists" among women, when the "Great Artist" is defined as inherently superior to and not responsible toward others.
16. Du Plessis, *Writing Beyond the Ending*, 101.

Books and Babies

ALICE MCDERMOTT

While in graduate school in the late 1970s, I took a course in contemporary fiction by women and read, at a time when it still seemed radical and ground-breaking, *The Women's Room* by Marilyn French. I recall that the book inspired a great deal of discussion but none quite so passionate as what ensued when one of the members of the class, a middle-aged woman who, like the novel's heroine, had reared her children and now returned to school, objected to French's depiction of motherhood as "an unending mound of dirty dishes" and an endless stream of urine in the eye. An outrageous distortion, the woman said. She claimed that the time she herself had spent at home with her young children was the most glorious time of her life.

We single twentysomethings in the class responded with pitying smiles. Clearly childbirth had addled the woman's brain. Of course you were meant to believe it was the most glorious time of your life, one of us explained, but look at it for what it really was: lost time, time you're trying to make up for now. Look at what even the fiercest motherly love becomes for each of the women in the novel: another pair of emotional shackles, golden handcuffs.

A decade later, those of us who had so rationally disabused our older friend of any romantic notions about reproduction were sending birth announcements and gushing letters to one another across the country. The letters read like book-jacket blurbs for some Vatican marriage manual: "Becoming a mother is the best thing I've ever done." "It's like floating in warm milk." "I could fill a stadium with babies."

Now the fiction we were reading and writing depicted motherhood as something more than a burden or a biological happenstance, now there were happy, loving mothers appearing as heroines in our novels and stories. And yet some sense of those emotional shackles lingered, for it seemed time and again that these happy mothers who loved their children did so at their own risk.

The novels we were now reading and recommending to one another (Sue Miller's *The Good Mother* comes to mind, Mary Gordon's *Men and Angels*, Toni Morrison's *Beloved*) all contained mothers who loved their children fiercely, who even celebrated that love, but who were nevertheless brought by it not to exalted and contented old age, but to the edge of the abyss, to some version of Sophie's choice.

The happy mother in fiction began to seem like the sweet-faced soldier in old war movies, the one who shows his young wife's photo or befriends a puppy in the first reel—the one most clearly marked for catastrophe.

As a writer I recognize that much of this can be accounted for by the demands of plot—no doubt all happy mothers are like happy families: alike. And as Tolstoy warned us, sustained joy doesn't make much of a story. But these days, as I lift myself out of the delighted fog that accompanied the birth of my third child and find myself once again in conversation with other mothers, trying to define what it is we feel as we progress through this whole experience of labor and delivery and watching our children grow—and grow away from us—I can't help but wonder if there is something else that keeps fiction writers, especially those of us who are mothers ourselves, from making the complexity, the challenge, the joy of our experience the full subject of our work.

I wonder if it's superstition: if we feel that to admit to such contentment in life would compromise our status as artists—perhaps recalling the poor actress in *The Portrait of Dorian Gray* who fell in love and lost her talent. Perhaps we fear alienating our male colleagues who would no doubt respond to such a work with the cry that fatherhood, too, is wonderful. (And we, the mothers of sons, would be obliged to tell them, soothingly. Of course, dear. Of course it is. Even better.)

More and more, I find myself recalling the story of Niobe, Queen of Thebes, who appeared before her people as they worshipped the goddess Leto and pointed out that she, Niobe, mother of seven sons and seven daughters, was far more worthy of their praise than Leto who was mother of only two. Her people, remarkably enough, saw the wisdom in this, put an end to their rituals, and went home.

I sometimes suspect that had her story ended there, with Niobe's triumph, the motherhood novel might now be a genre all to itself, as common as the coming-of-age novel, the war novel, the novel that begins or ends with, or turns on, murder, but Leto calls on her twins to avenge her and one by one Niobe's 14 children are slain. She is left bereft, weeping, and finally turned to silent stone.

I know plenty of women who understand Niobe's pride. I've read the essays they've written for women's magazines and baby books, I know of some poets who have captured it, but I've yet to hear her voice, undiminished by Leto's retribution, in fiction. It may simply be that such happiness doesn't make for much of a story. It may be that some of us see Leto as book critic and take Niobe's story as a cautionary tale to keep our mouths shut. It may be that there is some abiding sense that society and biology have indeed conspired to delude us and we only think that the days we spend with our children are the most glorious of our lives.

But at this stage in my own career as a mother, as I beam over my own brood, the writer in me begins to suspect something else: I begin to suspect that what we feel for our children is perhaps too satisfying, too marvelous to be carried fully into fiction. Fiction requires the attendant threat, the dramatic reversal, not only because these are the things that make for plot and tension and a sense of story, but because without them any depiction of our joy might appear overstated. We hesitate to include in our fiction what so often strikes us in life as something too good to be true.

Interviews with Annie Leibovitz

MELISSA HARRIS

There is some sort of crisis in my work, a shift in direction. Just a few years back I came to understand that the work couldn't always be about some assigned subject. It had to be about photography, and also about subjects that interested me. And this was a *big* thing. I knew it was going to be a huge commitment to try to change my work. It's hard to change, because no one really wants you to change; everyone wants bright colors, and they want people jumping up and down and smiling, laughing.

What is happening now is that I am finally doing pictures for myself. When I put together the "Performance Artists" series for *Vanity Fair*, I did it purely for myself; I was sure it was going to be put on the back burner and end up not being used. I was really surprised when Tina Brown said she wanted to run it right away. It was then that I realized that I am my own worst enemy. I'm the one, by doing what I think other people want from me, who has held myself back. I've been lucky with my work and I want to make the best use of this situation. I feel that I haven't let myself grow or listened enough to my own voice. It's so important to listen to your own voice. While I have done that, I've listened so much to everyone else as well. . . .

It's not as if anyone tells me how to go and take a picture, but I know what an editor needs, and I know what works. For example, a lot of my early work (not the *early* early work) was formed by photographing for *Rolling Stone*. The style—the overstrobed style—came from working with them. It created *my* style: the two went hand in hand, the way I saw and what the magazine wanted. It would be wrong to say either that *Rolling Stone* made me or that I made *Rolling Stone*. But if you're together, you influence each other . . . you can't help but be influenced by the particular problems of a magazine. And although I can't really *change* a magazine's sensibility, I can add to it. I can say other things. I can show them that other things work, things that aren't necessarily part of the formula.

The mystery of the set-up picture is still important to me. I am fascinated by the idea that the picture is set up and it is a session. At one time, I thought, "I wish my pictures could feel more spontaneous." I used to fight the studio, but now I am more and more attracted to the kind of beauty that can only be produced in the studio.

I'm surprised at how comfortable I am with things being formal, yet I will always wish things happened a little more . . . naturally. After you've learned to play with what you're looking at, it's really hard to stop doing that. You just want to make sure that if you're going to play with something, you're doing it for a good reason.

Now, it's so hard to say what work I do for myself and what I don't do for myself. I did the "Performance Artists" series for *Vanity Fair*, but I was doing it with a sensibility that was more personal, and as I said, I thought the pictures I was taking wouldn't be published. That was a great lesson. What made that series so compelling for me was, first of all, that I picked the subjects myself. Not that I haven't always loved doing the research on subjects that I'm assigned; that's the way that I claim them for myself. But it meant a lot to me to be able to pick the performance artists and to make the decision to select only women. I felt that the women had more to say than the men.

Right now, I'm working on a project on AIDS for *Vanity Fair*. It's been so moving to photograph people who are literally living with AIDS. They are still working and going about their lives, and they have all become even more extraordinary as people.

One of the subjects is the marvelous actor Ron Vawter. Ron operates on a whole other level. You end up going there with him, and you've got to stay close to the ceiling for a while! Then you leave him, and come back down. But you've been given a gift, because he's so generous with himself. He's really very special. While I was with him, he kept wanting me to see that he had AIDS, as if I had been walking right by it. He said, "You see my nails? Look at these bumps!" But all I could think was how beautiful he is.

After I left him, I thought maybe I wasn't addressing myself to the issue. Another subject was Tom Stoddard, the well-known lawyer and gay activist who teaches at New York University. Tom said he'd let me photograph him getting his chemotherapy. I wanted to show that this, too, is just a part of his life.

I also wanted the portfolio to include people living with AIDS who are not gay. And people who are not IV-drug users. I am trying to present a more rounded picture. But I've found that it is hard to persuade people to be photographed regardless of who they are, whether they are successful or not. Many people don't want to be involved because they're afraid of losing their jobs, which means they would lose their health coverage.

I had better luck in San Francisco, where I've been doing a campaign for the San Francisco AIDS Foundation, photographing both HIV-positive people and people with AIDS. These subjects are a great cross-section of the city, and include a heterosexual couple. The man is a captain in the Air Force and he wore his uniform for the shoot.

Most of the people I photographed from the San Francisco AIDS Foundation want to look beautiful, because they really are. I'm giving them what they want, and I enjoy doing that.

I like people to look good. I don't mean good as in glamorous. I was photographing my parents for their fiftieth wedding anniversary, and I thought. "Maybe I'm going to do an Avedon." I was thinking of the pictures he took of his father. Then I look at my parents and I *want* them to be beautiful. I mean, I want to love how they look.

My move from *Rolling Stone* to *Vanity Fair* was to try to discover and develop my own sense of what beauty is. But it goes beyond that; it's something I do naturally. I don't even know I'm doing it. People don't look like that; they aren't lit with a strobe. These days, I'm trying to get away from the "lit" look. I don't mind doing it on occasion, and there are times when it makes sense. But what I've been using lately is a combination of natural light with a strobe light only as a fill, or sometimes natural light alone.

In the advertising work I've done, no one has told me how to take the picture. I couldn't work any other way. Still, I don't want to underestimate how working for American Express or the Gap somehow does influence the picture—even though no one is telling me how to take it.

Sometimes my work for *Vanity Fair* can feel to me more like advertising than the advertising work does. The cover of the magazine is no longer, to me, a photograph. It's turned into a *cover*. It's one of the most frustrating things in the world for me when I go to shoot with very little time, and I end up spending the whole time shooting the *cover*, and never making a *photograph*. You know, there's a difference. The infamous Demi Moore cover is not a photograph to me. It has a kind of mental depth, but it doesn't have *photo* depth. It worked as a cover, though.

I started out as a photo-journalist, and quickly became what people call a portrait photographer. Maybe portraits will always be what interest me most, but I've always wanted to take pictures without people in them. I've started doing assignments for Condé Nast's *Traveler* magazine. I went to Monument Valley for them. I loved doing portraits of rocks. It was an opportunity to concentrate just on light and form.

When I take portraits of people, I can usually get them to relax—although I don't try to make them relax. In fact, I'm as interested in someone being uncomfortable as I am in their being comfortable. There is a myth that the portrait photographer is supposed to make the subject relax, and that's the real person. But I'm interested in *whatever* is going on. And I'm not that comfortable myself!

I use the Polaroid a great deal with the portraits. I really rely on it as I shoot. And the very first Polaroid image is often the one I end up redoing on film. I feel safe with the Polaroid, because it's not the real picture. I think what I'm doing is exploring the composition of the photograph—because the camera sees so differently from the way the eye sees. And sometimes the real magic happens quite quickly, at the beginning, when you're taking the Polaroid. Afterwards you're sort of . . . repeating it. And it's not quite the same thing.

I'm still fascinated by the surprise of images—that images can be so powerful. And I want them to be powerful *before* they're laid down in the magazine spread. There are a lot of photographs that work well for magazines, but don't work outside of them. But real photographs have to have a life outside of the magazine; I mean, outside that very powerful form of presentation a magazine provides. Each image has to stand on its own. But being shown in a magazine, like *Aperture*, or in the sequence of a book, like the recent big book of my work from the last twenty years, or on the walls of a museum or a gallery—these are also powerful forms of presentation. It's always interesting to me when the single photograph is put together with other photographs. That's when I see best what I'm doing. I realize how much I'm simplifying everything, to get at some essence of a person of an idea, and trying to say more with less.

The Transformation of Silence into Language and Action

AUDRE LORDE

I have come to believe over and over again that what is most important to me must be spoken, made verbal and shared, even at the risk of having it bruised or misunderstood. That the speaking profits me, beyond any other effect. I am standing here as a Black lesbian poet, and the meaning of all that waits upon the fact that I am still alive, and might not have been. Less than two months ago I was told by two doctors, one female and one male, that I would have to have breast surgery, and that there was a 60 to 80 percent chance that the tumor was malignant. Between that telling and the actual surgery, there was a three-week period of the agony of an involuntary reorganization of my entire life. The surgery was completed, and the growth was benign.

But within those three weeks, I was forced to look upon myself and my living with a harsh and urgent clarity that has left me still shaken but much stronger. This is a situation faced by many women, by some of you here today.[1] Some of what I experienced during that time has helped elucidate for me much of what I feel concerning the transformation of silence into language and action.

In becoming forcibly and essentially aware of my mortality, and of what I wished and wanted for my life, however short it might be, priorities and omissions became strongly etched in a merciless light, and what I most regretted were my silences. Of what had I *ever* been afraid? To question or to speak as I believed could have meant pain, or death. But we all hurt in so many different ways, all the time, and pain will either change or end. Death, on the other hand, is the final silence. And that might be coming quickly, now, without regard for whether I had ever spoken what needed to be said, or had only betrayed myself into small silences, while I planned someday to speak, or waited for someone else's words. And I began to recognize a source of power within myself that comes from the knowledge that while it is most desirable not to be afraid, learning to put fear into a perspective gave me great strength.

I was going to die, if not sooner then later, whether or not I had ever spoken myself. My silences had not protected me. Your silence will not protect you. But for every real word spoken, for every attempt I had ever made to speak those truths for which I am still seeking, I had made contact with other women while we examined the words to fit a world in which we all believed, bridging our differences. And it was the concern and caring of all those women which gave me strength and enabled me to scrutinize the essentials of my living.

The women who sustained me through that period were Black and white, old and young, lesbian, bisexual, and heterosexual, and we all shared a war against the tyrannies of silence. They all gave me strength and concern without which I could not have survived intact. Within those weeks of acute fear came the knowledge—within the war we are all waging with the forces of death, subtle and otherwise, conscious or not—I am not only a casualty, I am also a warrior.

What are the words you do not yet have? What do you need to say? What are the tyrannies you swallow day by day and attempt to make your own, until you will sicken and die of them, still in silence? Perhaps for some of you here today, I am the face of one of your fears. Because I am woman, because I am Black, because I am lesbian, because I am myself—a Black woman warrior poet doing my work—come to ask you, are you doing yours?

And of course I am afraid, because the transformation of silence into language and action is an act of self-revelation, and that always seems fraught with danger. But my daughter, when I told her of our topic and my difficulty with it, said, "Tell them about how you're never really a whole person if you remain silent, because there's always that one little piece inside you that wants to be spoken out, and if you keep ignoring it, it gets madder and madder and hotter and hotter, and if you don't speak it out one day it will just up and punch you in the mouth from the inside."

In the cause of silence, each of us draws the face of her own fear—fear of contempt, of censure, of some judgment, of recognition, of challenge, of annihilation. But most of all, I think, we fear the visibility without which we cannot truly live. Within this country where racial difference creates a constant, if unspoken, distortion of vision, Black women have on one hand always been highly visible, and so, on the other hand, have been rendered invisible through the depersonalization of racism. Even within the women's movement, we have had to fight, and still do, for that very visibility which also renders us most vulnerable, our Blackness. For to survive in the mouth of this dragon we call america, we have had to learn this first and most vital lesson—that we were never meant to survive. Not as human beings. And neither were most of you here today, Black or not. And that visibility which makes us most vulnerable is that which also is our greatest strength. Because the machine will try to grind you into dust anyway, whether or not we speak. We can sit in our corners mute forever while our sisters and our selves are wasted, while our children are distorted and destroyed, while our earth is poisoned; we can sit in our safe corners mute as bottles, and we will still be no less afraid.

In my house this year we are celebrating the feast of Kwanza, the African-american festival of harvest which begins the day after Christmas and lasts for seven days. There are seven principles of Kwanza, one for each day. The first principle is Umoja, which means unity, the decision to strive for and maintain unity in self and community. The principle for yesterday, the second day, was Kujichagulia—self-determination—the decision to define ourselves, name ourselves, and speak for ourselves, instead of being defined and spoken for by others. Today is the third day of Kwanza, and the principle for today is Ujima—collective work and responsibility—the decision to build and maintain ourselves and our communities together and to recognize and solve our problems together.

Each of us is here now because in one way or another we share a commitment to language and to the power of language, and to reclaiming of that language which has been made to work against us. In the transformation of silence into language and action, it is vitally necessary for each one of us to establish or examine her function in that transformation and to recognize her role as vital within that transformation.

For those of us who write, it is necessary to scrutinize not only the truth of what we speak, but the truth of that language by which we speak it. For others, it is to share and spread also those words that are meaningful to us. But primarily for us all, it is necessary to teach by living and speaking those truths which we believe and know beyond understanding. Because in this way alone we can survive, by taking part in a process of life that is creative and continuing, that is growth.

And it is never without fear—of visibility, of the harsh light of scrutiny and perhaps judgment, of pain, of death. But we have lived through all those already, in silence, except death. And I remind myself all the time now that if I were to have been born mute, or had maintained an oath of silence my whole life long for safety, I would still have suffered, and I would still die. It is very good for establishing perspective.

And where the words of women are crying to be heard, we must each of us recognize our responsibility to seek those words out, to read them and share them and examine them in their pertinence to our lives. That we not hide behind the mockeries of separations that have been imposed upon us and which so often we accept as our own. For instance, "I can't possibly teach Black women's writing—their experience is so different from mine." Yet how many years have you spent teaching Plato and Shakespeare and Proust? Or another, "She's a white woman and what could she possibly have to say to me?" Or, "She's a lesbian, what would my husband say. or my chairman?" Or again, "This woman writes of her sons and I have no children." And all the other endless ways in which we rob ourselves of ourselves and each other.

We can learn to work and speak when we are afraid in the same way we have learned to work and speak when we are tired. For we have been socialized to respect fear more than our own needs for language and definition, and while we wait in silence for that final luxury of fearlessness, the weight of that silence will choke us.

The fact that we are here and that I speak these works is an attempt to break that silence and bridge some of those differences between us, for it is not difference which immobilizes us, but silence. And there are so many silences to be broken.

NOTES

1. This essay was originally presented at the "Lesbian and Literature Panel" for the Modern Language Association on December 28, 1977.

Special Topic Bibliographies

These special topic bibliographies have been prepared as introductions to the various approaches to the interdisciplinary study of women and creativity. None of these listings is comprehensive or complete. The materials selected for inclusion have been chosen for their availability and intelligibility for the educated general reader as well as the specialist.

On the Creative Process

Amsler, Marc. *Creativity and the Imagination: Case Studies from the Classical Age to the Twentieth Century.* University of Delaware Press, 1987.

Arieti, Silvano. *Creativity: The Magic Synthesis.* Basic Books, 1976.

Barron, Frank. *Creativity and Personal Freedom.* D. Van Nostrand Co., 1968.

———. *Creative Person and Creative Process.* Holt, Rinehart and Winston, 1969.

Becker, George. *The Mad Genius Controversy: A Study in the Sociology of Deviance.* Sage, 1978.

Berdiaev, Nikolai. *The Meaning of the Creative Act.* Gollancz, 1955.

Boden, M. *The Creative Mind.* Basic Books, 1990.

Briggs, John. *Fire in the Crucible: The Alchemy of Creative Genius.* St. Martin's Press, 1988.

Cahn, Walter. *Masterpieces: Chapters on the History of an Idea.* Princeton University Press, 1979.

Clark, Kenneth. *What Is a Masterpiece?* Thames and Hudson, 1981 (1979).

Coleridge, Samuel Taylor. *Biographia Literaria.* Dent Dutton, 1975 (1906).

Duff, William. *An Essay on Original Genius: And Its Various Modes of Exertion in Philosophy and the Fine Arts, Particularly in Poetry.* Scholars' Facsimiles, 1964 (1767).

Engell, James. *The Creative Imagination: Enlightenment to Romanticism.* Harvard University Press, 1981.

Feldman, David Henry. *Nature's Gambit: Child Prodigies and the Development of Human Potential.* Teachers College Press, 1991.

Foucault, Michel. "What Is An Author?," in *The Foucault Reader*, ed. Paul Rabinow. Peregrine, 1986.

Freeman, James. *Creativity: A Selective Review of Research*. Society for Research into Higher Education Ltd., 1971.

Gardner, Howard. *Art, Mind, and Brain: A Cognitive Approach to Creativity.* Basic Books, 1982.

———. *Creating Minds*. Basic Books, 1993.

Ghiselin, Brewster, ed. *The Creative Process*. Mentor, 1952.

Grudin, Robert. *The Grace of Great Things: Creativity and Innovation*. Ticknor and Fields, 1990.

Havelka, Jaroslav. *The Nature of the Creative Process in Art*. Martinus Nijhoff, 1968.

Jung, Carl Gustav. *The Spirit in Man, Art and Literature*. Princeton University Press, 1972 (1966).

Koestler, Arthur. *The Act of Creation*. Macmillan, 1964.

Kosinski, Leonard V. *Readings on Creativity and Imagination in Literature*. National Council of Teachers, n.d.

Madigan, Carol Ostag. *Brainstorms and Thunderbolts: How Creative Genius Works*. Macmillan, 1983.

Mahlendorf, Ursula R. *The Wellsprings of Literary Creation: An Analysis of Male and Female "Artist Stories" from the German Romantics to American Writers of the Present*. Camden House, 1985.

Maritain, Jacques. *Creative Intuition in Art and Poetry.* Princeton University Press, 1978.

Martindale, Colin. *The Clockwork Muse: The Predictability of Artistic Change*. Basic Books, 1990.

May, Rollo. *The Courage to Create*. Norton, 1975.

Mitias, Michael H., ed. *Creativity in Art, Religion, and Culture*. Königshausen & Neumann, 1985.

Nelson, B., ed. *Freud on Creativity and the Unconscious*. Harper and Row, 1958.

Neumann, Erich. *Art and the Creative Unconscious: Four Essays*. Princeton University Press, 1969 (1959).

———. *Creative Man: Five Essays*. Princeton University Press, 1979.

Perkins, D. N. *The Mind's Best Work*. Harvard University Press, 1981.

Rank, Otto. *Art and Artist: Creative Urge and Personality Development*. Norton, 1989 (1932).

Rothenberg, Albert. *Emerging Goddess: The Creative Process in Art and Science*. University of Chicago Press, 1979.

——— and Carl R. Hausman, eds. *The Creativity Question*. Duke University Press, 1976.

Schopenhauer, Arthur. "On Genius," in *The Essential Schopenhauer*. Allen and Unwin, 1962.

Simonton, D. K. *Genius, Creativity, and Leadership*. Harvard University Press, 1984.

———. *Scientific Genius*. Cambridge University Press, 1989.

Sternberg, R. J. *The Nature of Creativity.* Cambridge University Press, 1988.
Storr, Anthony. *The Dynamics of Creation.* Secker and Warburg, 1972.
Taylor, Irving A., and J. W. Getzels, eds. *The Dynamics of Creation.* Aldine Publishing, 1975.
Torrance, E. P. *Guiding Creative Talent.* Prentice-Hall, 1962.
Vernon, P., ed. *Creativity.* Penguin, 1970.
Wallace, D., and H. E. Gruber, eds. *Creative People at Work.* Oxford University Press, 1990.
Wallach, M. *The Intelligence-Creativity Distinction.* General Learning Corporation, 1971.
Weisberg, R. *Creativity, Genius, and Other Myths.* Freeman, 1986.
West, Thomas G. *In the Mind's Eye: Visual Thinkers, Gifted People with Learning Difficulties, Computer Images, and the Ironies of Creativity.* Prometheus Books, 1991.

On Women and Creativity

Alaya, Flavia. "Victorian Science and the 'Genius' of Woman," *Journal of the History of Ideas* 38 (1977), 261–80.
Auerbach, Nina. "Artists and Mothers: A False Alliance," *Women and Literature* 6 (1978), 9–14.
———. *Romantic Imprisonment: Women and Other Glorified Outcasts.* Columbia University Press, 1986.
Battersby, Christine. *Gender and Genius: Towards a Feminist Aesthetic.* Indiana University Press, 1989.
Beauvoir, Simone de. *The Second Sex.* Penguin, 1972 (1949).
———. "Women and Creativity," *French Feminist Thought*, ed. Toril Moi. Blackwell, 1987.
DeShazer, Mary K. *Inspiring Women: Reimagining the Muse.* Pergamon, 1986.
Deutsch, Helene. *The Psychology of Women: A Psychoanalytic Interpretation.* Bantam, 1973 (1945).
Duff, William. *Letters on the Intellectual and Moral Character of Women.* Garland, 1974 (1807).
Ecker, Giselda, ed. *Feminist Aesthetics.* The Women's Press, 1985.
Erikson, Erik H. "Womanhood and the Inner Space" in his *Identity: Youth and Crisis.* Norton, 1968.
———. "Once More the Inner Space," in his *Life History and the Historical Moment.* Norton, 1975.
Estés, Clarissa Pinkola. *Women Who Run with Wolves.* Random House, 1992.
Freud, Sigmund. "Femininity," in *New Introductory Lectures on Psychoanalysis*, Vol. 22 of *The Standard Edition of the Complete Psychological Works*, ed. James Strachey. Hogarth Press, 1953–73.
Fuller, Margaret. *Woman in the Nineteenth Century.* Norton, 1970 (1855).

Garner, Shirley Nelson, Claire Kahane, and Madelon Sprengnether, eds. *The Mother Tongue: Essays in Feminist Psychoanalytic Interpretation*. Cornell University Press, 1985.

Gelfand, Elissa D., and Virginia T. Hules, eds. *French Feminist Criticism: Women, Language and Literature: An Annotated Bibliography*. Garland, 1985.

Gilligan, Carol. *In a Different Voice: Psychological Theory and Women's Development*. Harvard University Press, 1982.

Griffin, Susan. *Woman and Nature: The Roaring Inside Her*. The Women's Press, 1984 (1978).

Harding, M. Esther. *The Way of All Women*. Harper and Row, 1970.

———. *Woman's Mysteries*. Harper and Row, 1971.

Heilbrun, Carolyn. *Writing a Woman's Life*. Ballantine Books, 1988.

Helsinger, Elizabeth K., with R. L. Sheets and W. Veeder, eds. *The Woman Question: Literacy Issues*, Vol. III of *The Woman Question: Society and Literature in Britain and America, 1837–83*. Manchester University Press, 1983.

Helson, Ravenna. "Women and Creativity," in *The Creativity Question*, ed. Albert Rothenburg and Carl R. Hausman. Duke University Press, 1976.

Horney, Karen. *Feminine Psychology*. Norton, 1967.

Jones, Ann Rosalind, "Writing the Body: Toward an Understanding of *L'Ecriture féminine*" in *The New Feminist Criticism: Essays on Women, Literature and Theory*, ed. Elaine Showalter. Virago, 1986.

Kofman, Sarah. *The Enigma of Woman: Woman in Freud's Writing*. Cornell University Press, 1985 (1980).

Kristeva, Julia. *Powers of Horror: An Essay on Abjection*. Columbia University Press, 1982.

Lerner, Gerda. *The Creation of Feminist Consciousness*. Oxford University Press, 1993.

Miller, Jean Baker. *Toward a New Psychology of Women*. Beacon Press, 1976.

Neumann, Erich. *The Great Mother*. Princeton University Press, 1955.

———. *Amor and Psyche*. Princeton University Press, 1956.

Ortner, Sherry B. "Is Female to Male as Nature Is to Culture?" in *Woman, Culture, and Society*, eds. Michelle Z. Rosaldo and Louise Lamphere. Stanford University Press, 1974.

Ozick, Cynthia. "Women and Creativity: The Demise of the Dancing Dog," in *Women in Sexist Society*, ed. Vivian Gornick and Barbara K. Moran. Basic Books 1971.

Paglia, Camille. *Sexual Personae: Art and Decadence From Nefertiti to Emily Dickinson*. Yale University Press, 1990.

———. *Vamps and Tramps: New Essays*. Vintage, 1994.

Porter, Katherine Anne. "Notes on Writing," in *The Creative Process*, ed. Brewster Ghiselin. Mentor, 1952.

Rich, Adrienne. *Of Woman Born: Motherhood as Experience and Institution*. Bantam, 1977.

———. *On Lies, Secrets, and Silence*. Norton, 1979.

Schopenhauer, Arthur. "On Women," in *The Essential Schopenhauer*. Allen and Unwin, 1962.

Snyder-Ott, Joelynn. *Women and Creativity*. Les Femmes Publishing, 1978.

Spacks, Patricia Meyer. "Selves in Hiding," in *Women's Autobiography: Essays in Criticism*, ed. Estelle C. Jeliner. Indiana University Press, 1980.

Women and Creativity, from *Creativity with Bill Moyers*. PBS Video, 1982.

Woolf, Virginia. *A Room of One's Own*. Harcourt Brace, 1929.

On Women in the Arts

Barry, Joseph, ed. and trans. *George Sand in her Own Words*. Anchor, 1979.

Brink, J. R., ed. *Female Scholars: A Tradition of Learned Women Before 1800*. Eden Press, 1980.

Broe, Mary Lynn, and Angela Ingram, eds. *Women's Writing in Exile*. University of North Carolina Press, 1989.

Broude, Norma, and Mary Garrard, eds. *Feminism and Art History: Questioning the Litany*. Harper and Row, 1982.

———. *The Expanding Discourse: Feminism and Art History*. HarperCollins, 1992.

Cahill, Susan, ed. *Writing Women's Lives: An Anthology of Autobiographical Narratives by Twentieth-Century American Women Writers*. HarperCollins, 1994.

Chadwick, Whitney. *Women Artists and the Surrealist Movement*. Little, Brown, 1985.

———. *Women, Art, and Society*. Thames and Hudson, 1990.

Clifton, Lucille. *Generations*. Curtis Brown Ltd., 1976.

Cully, Margo, ed. *American Women's Autobiography: Fea(s)ts of Memory*. University of Wisconsin Press, 1992.

De Mille, Agnes. *And Promenade Home*. Little, Brown and Company, 1958.

Dotterer, Ronald, and Susan Bowers, eds. *Sexuality, the Female Gaze, and the Arts: Women, the Arts, and Society*. Susquehanna University Press, 1992.

———. *Gender, Culture, and the Arts: Women, the Arts, and Society*. Associated University Presses, 1993.

Duncan, Isadora. *The Art of the Dance*. Theatre Arts Books, 1969 (1928).

Erdrich, Louise. "A Woman's Work: Too Many Demands, and Not Enough Selves," *Harper's* 286.1716 (May 1993), 35–46.

Fine, Elsa Honig. *Women and Art*. Allenheld and Schram, 1978.

Garrard, Mary. *Artemisia Gentileschi: The Image of the Female Hero in Baroque Art*. Princeton University Press, 1989.

Gilbert, Sandra M., and Susan Grubar. *The Madwoman in the Attic: The Woman Writer and the Nineteenth-Century Literary Imagination*. Yale University Press, 1979.

Gordon, Mary. *Good Boys and Dead Girls, and Other Essays*. Viking, 1991.

Goulianos, Joan, ed. *By a Woman Writ: Literature from Six Centuries by and about Women*. New English Library, 1974.

Graham, Martha. *The Notebooks of Martha Graham*. Harcourt Brace, 1973.

———. *Blood Memory: An Autobiography*. Doubleday, 1991.

Greer, Germaine. *The Obstacle Race*. Farrar, Straus and Giroux, 1979.

Gutwirth, Madelyn. *Madame de Staël, Novelist: The Emergence of the Artist as Woman*. University of Illinois Press, 1978.

Harris, Ann Sutherland, and Linda Nochlin. *Women Artists 1550–1950*. Los Angeles County Museum of Art and Alfred A. Knopf, 1976.

Jamison, Judith. *Dancing Spirit: An Autobiography*. Doubleday, 1993.

Lessing, Doris. *The Golden Notebook*. Ballantine, 1971.

MacCannell, Juliet Flower. *The Other Perspective in Gender and Culture: Rewriting Women and the Symbolic*. Columbia University Press, 1990.

Moers, Ellen. *Literary Women*. The Women's Press, 1978.

Moi, Toril. *Sexual/Textual Politics: Feminist Literary Theory*. Metheun, 1985.

Munro, Eleanor. *Originals: American Women Artists*. Simon and Schuster, 1982 (1979).

Neuls-Bates, Carol, ed. *Women in Music: An Anthology of Source Readings from the Middle Ages to the Present*. Harper and Row, 1982.

Nevelson, Louise. *Dawns and Dusks: Conversations with Diana MacKowan*. Scribners, 1976.

Newman, Barbara. *Sister of Wisdom: St. Hildegaard's Theology of the Feminine*. University of California Press, 1987.

Nin, Anaïs. *The Journals of Anaïs Nin*, ed. Gunther Stuhlmann, 6 volumes. Peter Owen, 1966-76.

Nochlin, Linda. *The Politics of Vision: Essays on Nineteenth Century Art and Society*. Harper and Row, 1989.

———. *Women, Art, and Power; and Other Essays*. Harper and Row, 1988.

Oates, Joyce Carol. *(Woman) Writer: Occasions and Opportunities*. E. P. Dutton, 1988.

O'Keeffe, Georgia. *Georgia O'Keeffe*. Viking Press, 1976.

Olsen, Tillie. *Silences*. Doubleday, 1979.

Parker, Rozsika. *Framing Feminism: Art and the Women's Movement 1970–85*. Pandora, 1987.

———and Griselda Pollock. *Old Mistresses: Women, Art, and Ideology*. Routledge, 1981.

Perkins, Charlotte Gilman. *The Yellow Wallpaper*. Feminist Press, 1973.

Pizan, Christine de. *The Book of the City of Ladies*. Picador, 1983 (1405).

Pollock, Griselda. *Mary Cassatt*. Jupiter Books, 1980.

———. *Vision and Difference: Feminism, Femininity, and the History of Art*. Routledge, 1988.

Poovey, Mary. *The Proper Lady and the Woman Writer: Ideology as Style in the Works of Mary Wollstonecraft, Mary Shelley, and Jane Austen*. University of Chicago Press, 1985 (1984).

Reich, Nancy B. *Clara Schumann: The Artist and the Woman*. Gollancz, 1985.

Russ, Joanna. *How to Suppress Women's Writings*. The Women's Press, 1984 (1983).

Showalter, Elaine. *A Literature of Their Own: British Women Novelists from Brontë to Lessing*. Princeton University Press, 1977.

———. *The Female Malady: Women, Madness and English Culture, 1830–1980*. VikingPenguin, 1987.

Spacks, Patricia Meyer. *The Female Imagination*. Alfred A. Knopf, 1975 (1972).

Sternburg, Janet, ed. *The Writer on Her Work*. Norton, 1980–81.

Tanning, Dorothea. *Birthday*. The Lapis Press, 1986.

Todd, Janet. *Feminist Literary History: A Defence*. Polity Press, 1988.

Tomalin, Claire. *The Life and Death of Mary Wollstonecraft*. Penguin, 1985 (1974).

Walker, Alice. *In Search of Our Mothers' Gardens*. Harcourt Brace Jovanovich, 1983.

Warhol, Robyn R., and Diane Price Herndl, eds. *Feminisms: An Anthology of Literary Theory and Criticisms*. Rutgers University Press, 1991.

Washington, Mary Helen, ed. *Invented Lives: Narratives of Black Women from 1860 to 1960*. Doubleday, 1987.

Webber, Jeannette L., and Joan Grumman. *Woman as Writer*. Houghton Mifflin, 1978.

Welty, Eudora. *One Writer's Beginnings*. Harvard University Press, 1984 (1983).

West, Cornel, and bell hooks, eds. *Breaking Bread: Insurgent Black Intellectual Life*. South End Press, 1991.

Woolf, Virginia. *The Death of the Mother and Other Essays*. Harcourt Brace, 1942.

———. *Women and Writing*. The Women's Press, 1979.

Notes on Contributors

DIANE APOSTOLOS-CAPPADONA is Professorial Lecturer in Religion and Art, Liberal Studies Program, Georgetown University. She is the author of *Dictionary of Christian Art; The Spirit and the Vision: The Influence of Christian Romanticism on the Development of 19th-Century American Art;* and the forthcoming *Dictionary of Women in Religious Art.*

CHRISTINE BATTERSBY is a Lecturer in Philosophy at the University of Warwick, United Kingdom. She has published articles on ethics, eighteenth-century thought, and the philosophy of women. Her most recent book is *Gender and Genius: Towards a New Feminist Aesthetics.*

IRIS BÜNSCH received her Ph.D. from the University of Kiel, Germany. She teaches English at the Universities of Giessen and Kiel. Her most recent book is *Three Female Myths of the 20th Century: Garbo—Callas—Navratilova.*

LUCINDA EBERSOLE is a writer, editor, and filmmaker specializing in popular culture. She recently co-edited *Mondo Marilyn*, a collection of stories and poems about Marilyn Monroe.

MARTHA GRAHAM was a dancer and choreographer who broke with traditional concepts of dance to create a new language of movement and changed cultural perceptions of dance. She has been identified as the most significant 20th-century American artist. She was the author of *Blood Memory: An Autobiography* and *The Notebooks of Martha Graham.*

MELISSA HARRIS is a writer and journalist in New York City.

bell hooks is Distinguished Professor of English, The City College of New York. Her most recent books are *Teaching to Transgress: Education as the Practice of Freedom* and *Outlaw Culture: Resisting Representations.*

URSULA K. LE GUIN is one of America's finest writers, as acknowledged by her receipt of the Hugo, Nebula, Gandalf, Kafka, and National Book Awards. Her most recent book is *Blue Moon over Thurman Street.*

ANNIE LEIBOVITZ is an internationally acclaimed photojournalist. She began taking pictures for *Rolling Stone* in 1970 and became its chief photographer in 1973. She is a featured photographer for *Vanity Fair* magazine.

AUDRE LORDE was born and raised in New York City by Grenadian parents. An accomplished and influential poet, her last book of poetry, *The Marvelous Arithmetics of Distance,* was published posthumously.

ALICE MCDERMOTT is a well-known novelist whose works include *A Bigamist's Daughter, That Night,* and *At Weddings and Wakes.*

JEAN BAKER MILLER is a noted psychologist and writer. She is the author of the ground-breaking book *Toward a New Psychology of Women.*

LOUISE NEVELSON was one of the leading American sculptors in the 20th-century. A recipient of several distinguished awards, including the National Medal for the Arts, Nevelson carved a new path for women in the arts. She was the author of *Dawns and Dusks: Conversations with Diana MacKowan.*

ANAÏS NIN was an internationally acclaimed writer. Her diaries, which she kept from childhood until her death, have been required reading for a generation of women.

LINDA NOCHLIN is Lila Acheson Wallace Professor of Modern Art, Institute of Fine Arts, New York University. A renowned art historian, she is one of the leading commentators on women artists. Her most recent book is *The Politics of Vision: Essays on Nineteenth Century Art and Society.*

GEORGIA O'KEEFFE was one of the leading American painters of the 20th century. Her paintings, using the stark images of the nation's Southwest, made her one of America's most distinctive painters. She was the author of *Georgia O'Keeffe.*

MURIEL RUKEYSER was a poet and essayist who produced four volumes of translation, one of fiction, one of criticism, two biographies, and eighteen volumes of poetry. A new collection of her writings, *The Muriel Rukeyser Reader,* has recently been published.

JOELYNN SNYDER-OTT is an artist and writer. Her most recent book is *Women and Creativity.*

PATRICIA MEYER SPACKS is Edgar F. Shannon Professor of English and Chair, Department of English, at the University of Virginia, and the 1994 President of the Modern Language Association. Her most recent book is *Boredom: The Literary History of a State of Mind.*

MICHELE WALLACE is Associate Professor of English and Women's Studies at The City College of New York and The Graduate Center, CUNY. She has been a regular contributor to *Zeta*, the *Village Voice*, and *Art Forum.*

MONIQUE WITTIG is Professor of French and Italian at the University of Arizona. She is the author of several books, including *Les Guerrillères* and *The Lesbian Body.*

Copyright Acknowledgments

INDEX

Index

Of related interest from Continuum

Diane Apostolos-Cappadona, editor

Art, Creativity, and the Sacred
An Anthology in Religion and Art
New Revised Edition

This book is divided into five parts: *Artists—The Spiritual Dimension;*
Art Historians—The Religious in Art; Historians of Religion—Art in
Religious Traditions; Philosophers and Theologians—Reflections on Art;
and *Religion and Art-Interdisciplinary Vision.* Contributors include:
Doug Adams, David and Linda Altshuler, John W. Cook, Ananda K.
Coomaraswamy, Ceclia Davis Cunningham, Stephen De Staebler, Jane
Daggett Dillenberger, John Dillenberger, John W. Dixon, Mircea Eli-
ade, Lois Ibsen Gilkey, Wassily Kandinsky, Karen Laub-Novak, Rich-
ard B. Pilgrim, Thomas Franklin O'Meara, Charles Scribner III, Leo
Steinberg, Joshua Taylor, Paul Tillich, David Tracy, Nicholas Wolter-
storff, Roger Wedell, and Melinda Wortz.

"A Seminal work . . . widely adopted."—Religious Studies Review

352 pages 0-8264-0829-X $19.95

Diane Apostolos-Cappadona

Dictionary of Christian Art

The aim of the *Dictionary of Christian Art* is to give the reader access
to the pictorial tradition that was once the common visual vocabulary
of Christians. In more than 1,000 entries, from *Aaron* to *Zucchetto,*
the *Dictionary* identifies and explains the major signs, symbols, figures,
and topics that have emerged in the 2,000 years of Christian art from

its earliest beginnings to today. The *Dictionary of Christian Art* is also profusely illustrated with more than 160 reproductions.

"An indispensable reference to Christian motifs, subject matter, iconography, and theology in visual art."—**Publishers Weekly**

"Its combination of appeal to a wide variety of readers, engaging subject, and lack of up-to-date competitors makes it an essential purchase of academic, public, and seminary libraries."—**Booklist**

Selected by the Book-of-The Month Club and Newbridge Book Clubs

384 pages 160 illustrations 0-8264-0779-X $39.50

Mircea Eliade

Symbolism, the Sacred, and the Arts
Edited by Diane Apostolos-Cappadona

This book, in four parts *(Theories of Symbolism, Art and the Sacred, Sites of the Sacred, and Literature and the Sacred)* includes the following essays: "Cultural Fashions and the History of Religion," "Divinities: Art and the Divine," "The Sacred and the Modern Artist," "A Dialogue with Marc Chagall," "Sacred Architecture and Symbolism," "Eugène Ionesco and 'The Nostalgia for Paradise,'" "Literary Imagination and Religious Structure," and more.

"Fertile, provocative, and stimulating. . . . This collection of Eliade's essays and lectures is an excellent initiation into his thought."—**America**

"Sheds light on Eliade's conception of literature, religion, philosophy, and aesthetics, as well as on his methodology."—**The Journal of Religion**

208 pages 0-8264-0618-1 $14.95

At your bookstore, or to order call toll free: 1-800-937-5557. The Continuum Publishing Company, 370 Lexington Avenue, New York, NY 10017